The Foundations of US Air Doctrine
The Problem of Friction in War

by

BARRY D. WATTS
Lieutenant Colonel, USAF

AIR UNIVERSITY (AU)
AIR UNIVERSITY PRESS
MAXWELL AIR FORCE BASE, ALABAMA

December 1984

DISCLAIMER

This study represents the views of the author and does not necessarily reflect the official opinion of the Air University Center for Aerospace Doctrine, Research, and Education (CADRE) or the Department of the Air Force. This manuscript has been reviewed and cleared for public release by security and policy review authorities.

Library of Congress Cataloging-in-Publication Data

Watts, Barry D.
    The Foundations of US Air Doctrine.

    "December 1984."
    Bibliography: p.
    Includes index.
    1. United States. Air Force. 2. Aeronautics, Military—United States. 3. Air warfare. I. Title.
II. Title: Foundations of US air doctrine. III. Title: Friction in war.
UG633.W34   1984   358.4'00973   84-72550
    355'.0215— dc 19

ISBN 1-58566-007-8

First Printing December 1984
Second Printing September 1991
Third Printing July 1993
Fourth Printing May 1996
Fifth Printing January 1997
Sixth Printing June 1998
Seventh Printing July 2000
Eighth Printing June 2001
Ninth Printing September 2001

THE AUTHOR

Lieutenant Colonel Barry D. Watts (MA philosophy, University of Pittsburgh; BA mathematics, US Air Force Academy) has been teaching and writing about military theory since he joined the Air Force Academy faculty in 1974. During the Vietnam War he saw combat with the 8th Tactical Fighter Wing at Ubon, Thailand, completing 100 missions over North Vietnam in June 1968. Subsequently, Lieutenant Colonel Watts flew F-4s from Yokota AB, Japan, and Kadena AB, Okinawa. More recently, he has served as a military assistant to the Director of Net Assessment, Office of the Secretary of Defense, and with the Air Staff's Project CHECKMATE.

*To Those Who Will Fly and
Fight in Years to Come*

CONTENTS

Page

DISCLAIMER	iii
BIOGRAPHICAL SKETCH	v
LIST OF ILLUSTRATIONS	xi
ACKNOWLEDGEMENTS	xiii
AUTHOR'S FOREWORD	xv
Notes	xvii

Chapter

1	INTRODUCTION	1
	Notes	3
2	DOUHET AND MITCHELL	5
	Douhet's Image of War: Unrestrained Offense	6
	Mitchell's "Aerial Knights"	7
	Notes	13
3	THE FIRST US STRATEGIC AIR WAR PLAN	17
	Daylight, High Altitude, Precision Bombardment Doctrine	18
	AWPD–1	18
	The Image of War in AWPD–1	22
	Notes	25
4	THE POLICY AND STRATEGY OF DETERRENCE	27
	Brodie's Assumptions	28
	Brodie's Image of All-Out War in the Missile Age	33
	A Paradox of Deterrence Theory	36
	Notes	39
5	A CLAUSEWITZIAN CRITIQUE	43
	The Core Beliefs of Mainstream US Air Doctrine	43
	Some Ramifications	45
	Friction	47
	Collective Risk	53
	Notes	55

Chapter		Page
6	FRICTION IN 20TH CENTURY WARFARE	59
	Part 1: Friction in the Combined Bomber Offensive, World War II	60
	Weather	61
	October 1943: Information, Doctrinal Rigidity, Enemy Countermeasures	62
	Big Week and the Problem of Industrial Impact Assessments	71
	March and April 1944: Friction as a Weapon	75
	Epilogue in Korea: Railway Interdiction, August 1951–May 1952	85
	Part 2: Friction in the Missile Age	87
	The Not-So-Delicate Balance of Terror	88
	The Emergence of Friction in Brodie's Thought	91
	The Cuban Missile Crisis	92
	Notes	95
7	TOWARD A LESS MECHANISTIC IMAGE OF WAR	105
	US Air Doctrine and Laplacian Determinism	106
	Cartesian Hypotheses, Uncertainty, Undecidability	108
	The Human Cost of War	110
	Combat Psychology as Context	111
	Some Consequences of Embracing a More Organic Image of War	116
	Learning from History	116
	Nurturing Military Genius	117
	Exemplars for Future Wars: Friction as a Weapon and Entropy	119
	Summing Up	121
	Notes	123
APPENDIX	General Eaker's Presentation of the Combined Bomber Offensive Plan to the Joint Chiefs of Staff	133
SELECTED BIBLIOGRAPHY		151
INDEX		159

LIST OF ILLUSTRATIONS

Page

Figure 1: August 1941 Army Air Corps Plan for an Air Offensive Against Germany 20

Figure 2: Mission to Schweinfurt, 14 October 1943 64

Photographs

Brigadier General William M. "Billy" Mitchell	8
Major General Haywood S. Hansell, Jr.	21
General Hansell in August 1943	21
"Little Boy" Atomic Bomb	30
Prestrike Target Photograph of Hiroshima, Japan	30
Atomic Burst at Hiroshima, 6 August 1945	31
Atomic Bomb Damage at Hiroshima	32
Friction in War: Weather, Weariness	49
Friction in War: The Unexpected	50-51
Friction in War: German Flak Over Vienna, Austria	52
Schweinfurt, 14 October 1943: First Wave	65
Schweinfurt, 14 October 1943: Third Wave	66
Schweinfurt, 14 October 1943: Heading Home	67
Schweinfurt: Post-Strike	68
Boeing B–17 Going Down South of Dunkirk, France	69
B–17 Hit by Nazi Air-to-Air Rocket	69
B–24 Liberator Downed by German Flak	70
On Fire But Still Deadly	73
B–17 Releasing a String of Bombs	74
P–51 Mustangs in Close Formation	77
The Long Reach	78
Strategic Air Power, Winter 1944–45	79
Lieutenant General James H. Doolittle	82
Major General William E. Kepner	83
In the Air	84
On the Ground	84

ACKNOWLEDGEMENTS

During the roughly two and a half years of spare time research and writing that it took me to complete this study, numerous individuals lent invaluable assistance. I might well have not persevered through a first draft—which took a good year—without the encouragement and guidance of Professor David MacIsaac, John Boyd, and Lieutenant Colonels Don Baucom, Joe Guilmartin, and Lance Lord.

The more arduous part of the journey, however, was getting from the initial draft to the last. Besides those who encouraged me from the outset, many others (thankfully) took the time to struggle through one or more drafts and provide the substantive comments I needed to correct outright mistakes, fill gaping holes, and pull together the loose threads in my arguments. Of significant help in this regard were Colonel Ken Alnwick and John Schenk at Air University, Professor Joe Sitterson of George Washington University, Colonel David Andre of OSD Net Assessment, Professor Williamson Murray of Ohio State University's Mershon Center, Major Jim Hale and Colonel Bill Hogan of Project CHECKMATE, Colonel Fred Shiner, Professor Thomas Fabyanic whose notion of collective risk so materially aided Chapter 5, George Kuhn, Major Don Fawkes, Jeff Ethell, Pierre Sprey, and Chuck Spinney.

Of the others who were kind enough to read versions of the draft, there are two I want to mention separately because they so strongly disagreed with what I had to say: Dr. Ken Werrell and Major General Haywood S. Hansell, Jr. In General Hansell's case especially, while his disagreement may not be surprising, he had the intellectual stature to help me nevertheless.

At the Air University Press, I want to extend my appreciation to the editors and the Document Processing Center. They introduced me to the mysteries of production and kept on top of the details long after I had grown weary.

Last, but certainly not least, I must thank my wife, Hope, and my daughters, Stacey and Becky. Without their love and understanding I would have never started, much less finished.

AUTHOR'S FOREWORD

But what kind of assumptions do we tend to make? How do these assumptions channel our thinking? What alternative perspectives are available?[1]

Graham Allison

Science is a very human form of knowledge. We are always at the brink of the known; we always feel forward for what is to be hoped. Every judgment in science stands on the edge of error and is personal. Science is a tribute to what we can know although we are fallible. In the end, the words were said by Oliver Cromwell: "I beseech you, in the bowels of Christ, think it possible you may be mistaken."[2]

Jacob Bronowski

This study revolves around friction, meaning the ubiquitous uncertainties and inescapable difficulties that form the atmosphere of real war. More specifically, it attempts to utilize the Clausewitzian concept of general friction as a basis for assessing—and, if necessary, reshaping—the foundations of US air doctrine.

This critical application of friction gives rise to four primary conclusions:

(1) The key assumptions underlying mainstream US doctrine for conventional air warfare have not evolved appreciably since Air Corps Tactical School (ACTS) theorists elaborated their theory of precision, industrial bombardment during the 1930s.

(2) Judged by their essential premises and logic, post-Hiroshima theories of deterrence are little more than an updating for the nuclear age of ACTS bombardment doctrine.

(3) Both ACTS bombardment doctrine and deterrence theory appear fundamentally flawed insofar as they omit the frictional considerations that distinguish real war from war on paper.

(4) Reflection upon the extent to which friction pervades the elemental processes of actual combat suggests that the range of situations in which greater numbers or superior weapons *guarantee* victory is relatively limited; even in the age of thermonuclear weapons, the outcomes of battles still turn, more often than not, on the character and intelligence of a few brave individuals.

The first step in giving substance to these claims is to explain what the central beliefs of US airmen traditionally have been. The reader should be warned, however, that I have approached the writings on war of airmen like Major General Haywood S. Hansell, Jr., and nuclear strategists like Bernard Brodie—as well as those of Carl von Clausewitz himself—from the perspective of two interrelated questions. What overriding assumptions about war did these individuals embrace? And what image of war as a total phenomenon is bound up in their assumptions? In large part, answering these questions is a matter of historical inquiry and, to be candid, I have been far less concerned with writing history for its own sake than with using the past to illuminate the problems of the present. I, therefore, leave it to the reader to judge whether I have managed to do so without injuring the historical record.

The other word of forewarning I would offer the reader stems from the controversial character of the synthesis I have endeavored to construct. Few American airmen would be eager to categorize their more deeply held beliefs about aerial warfare as *fundamentally flawed*. Consequently, the demands on this study for evidence—both explanatory and documentary—are unusually high. One way I have sought to satisfy these demands has been by the inclusion of extensive notes at the end of each chapter. Although I tried to make the text stand on its own as much as possible, there are places, especially in the final chapter, where the text's full import may not be clear without reference to the accompanying notes. This arrangement will, I know, be disconcerting to some and distracting to others. But I have not been able to find a better way of including the necessary evidence without overly encumbering the text. And in any event, this expedient has the further merit of providing a faint taste of what friction is all about: for the careful reader's problem of following more than one line of development simultaneously is remarkably parallel to the kinds of rude, seemingly impossible demands that friction imposes upon men in war.

NOTES

FOREWORD

1. Graham T. Allison, *Essence of Decision: Explaining the Cuban Missile Crisis* (Boston: Little, Brown and Company, 1971), p. v.

2. Jacob Bronowski, *The Ascent of Man* (Boston and Toronto: Little, Brown and Company, 1973), p. 374. Oliver Cromwell's crushing defeat of Royalist forces under the exiled King Charles II at Worcester on September 3rd, 1651, ended the second English civil war. During the seven years that passed from the "Crowning of Mercy" of Worcester to Cromwell's death from malaria on 3 September 1658, he ruled England, first in effect and later officially, as a military dictator (Lynn Montross, *War Through the Ages* (New York: Harper and Brothers, 3d ed., 1960), p. 308). Bronowski's choice of Cromwell's words in the cited quotation is specially appropriate in light of the influence that the lord protector has subsequently had on military affairs in the United States. "Twelve generations have lived and died since Worcester, yet the shadow of the lord protector, sword in hand, still falls heavily upon the warfare of Britain and the United States. Never since that time has a British or American government been prepared at the outbreak of hostilities for the tests to come. For the English-speaking peoples have made it plain that they would rather risk defeat than dictatorship; and the dread of a second Cromwell has influenced the campaigns of Marlborough and Wellington, of Washington, Grant and Lee" (Montross, p. 310).

CHAPTER 1

INTRODUCTION

Friction is the only concept that more or less corresponds to the factors that distinguish real war from war on paper.[1]

Carl von Clausewitz, 1832

War is never a technical problem only, and if in pursuing technical solutions you neglect the psychological and the political, then the best technical solutions will be worthless.[2]

Hermann Balck, 1979

    The fundamental thinking of US aviators about the air weapon, be it airplane or nuclear missile, has long been beset by certain shortcomings. First and foremost, as professional soldiers we have failed to nurture a comprehensive understanding of war as a total phenomenon. A century and a half after his death, Clausewitz remains virtually unique in having tried to construct an overarching theory of war based on evidence, and few American soldiers have studied Clausewitz deeply enough to appreciate the motivation for this endeavor, much less the premises from which it proceeded. Second, as professional airmen we continue to rely upon air power ideas that were conceived in circumstances vastly different from those we face today. Not only were our basic ideas about the air weapon developed during an era in which air power and the quest for autonomy from the US Army had become crusades, but they have gone virtually unchanged right down to the present day.

    These shortcomings raise legitimate doubts, I believe, as to the capacity of the US Air Force to do the one thing that successful military organizations have always done: *adapt to changing conditions better than the adversary.* Unless we, as professional airmen, develop a more adequate understanding of war as a totality, and unless we manage to attain some measure of objectivity, of informed historical perspective regarding our more deeply held beliefs about the air weapon, I would question our ability to adapt successfully to the demands of American security in the late 20th century.

Of course, we need not fail to adapt. Toward this end, my thoughts in recent years have increasingly come to dwell upon two aspects of traditional American theories of air power. How well have they been able to cope with the accelerating pace and unprecedented scale of technological change in the means of war that have so marked conflict in this century? How well have they been validated by harsh realities of actual combat?

Clearly these questions overlap. They also elicit intense emotions, if not entrenched opinions, from soldiers as well as scholars, and are difficult to tackle head on. I have chosen, therefore, to broach them via a less familiar question which, hopefully, will prove more fruitful. To what extent has mainstream US air doctrine preeminently envisaged aerial warfare as a vast engineering project whose details could, in every important respect, be calculated as precisely as the stress loadings on a dam or the tensile strength requirements for a bridge?

My response to this question has four parts. First, in Chapters 2, 3, and 4, I identify and articulate those premises about the nature of war upon which the US daylight bomber offensive against Germany during World War II was based and, later, post-Hiroshima theories of deterrence. Next, in Chapter 5, I evaluate the basic beliefs underlying this doctrinal heritage to see if they adequately take into account the *cumulative* effects of those *frictional difficulties* which, in Clausewitz's view, form the inescapable atmosphere of violent conflict: namely, physical danger, extraordinary demands for exertion, chance, uncertainty in information, and the enemy's unpredictability. Third, because this Clausewitzian critique indicates that American thinking about air power has systematically neglected the various factors that "distinguish real war from war on paper," I consider in Chapter 6 whether friction remains as central in contemporary military operations as it was on the Napoleonic battlefields of Clausewitz's experience.[3] Finally, in Chapter 7, I explore some of the conceptual changes that will have to be made in US air power doctrine if friction is to be given its proper due and the gap between pure theory and the actual practice of war bridged.

NOTES

CHAPTER 1

1. Carl von Clausewitz, *On War*, ed. and trans. Michael Howard and Peter Paret (Princeton, New Jersey: Princeton University Press, 1976), p. 119. *On War* first appeared in 1832, the year after Clausewitz's death.

2. Pierre Sprey, *Translation of Taped Conversation with General Hermann Balck, 12 January 1979, and Brief Biographical Sketch* (Columbus, Ohio: Battelle, 1979), p. 22. From 1914 to 1918, Balck fought on the Western, Eastern, Italian, and Balkan fronts; during this period he was wounded seven times and won the Iron Cross First Class while still an ensign (p. 2). Over the course of World War II, Balck's combat assignments included command of a motorized infantry regiment under Heinz Guderian in May 1940; command of a *Panzer* regiment during the *Wehrmacht*'s Greek campaign of April 1941; command of 11th *Panzer* Division at the battles of Voronezh, the Chir River, Tatsinskaya and Manichskaya in Russia (May 1942–January 1943); command of 48th *Panzer* Corps under Erich von Manstein at the battles of Kiev, Radomyshl, and Tarnopol; and command of Army Group G opposite George C. Patton's Third Army from 21 September through late December 1944 (pp. 2–4).

3. Clausewitz first broached the problem of spanning the gap between the pure concept of war and the concrete shape that war generally assumes in Chapters 4 through 8 of Book One of *On War*. Yet so important did Clausewitz deem this subject that, even after extensive development in the first two books, he felt compelled to return to it in the eighth and final book of *On War* (pp. 577–81).

CHAPTER 2

DOUHET AND MITCHELL

In war, the will is directed at an animate object that *reacts*.[1]

Carl von Clausewitz

An Independent Air Force must therefore be completely free of any preoccupation with the actions of the enemy force. Its sole concern should be to do the enemy the greatest possible amount of surface damage in the shortest possible time, which depends upon the available air forces and the choice of enemy targets.[2]

Giulio Douhet, 1921

Starting with Douhet, this chapter will begin to explore the images of war that have formed the core of traditional American precision bombardment doctrine. My reasons for starting with the Italian theorist are, in part, the usual ones; it is customary to start with Douhet, and his basic work, *Il Domino dell'Aria (The Command of the Air)*, constitutes the first comprehensive theory of air power in history. But I also have some other, less conventional reasons for revisiting Douhet. To US Army aviators between the world wars, bombardment became both a means and an end. It was a means in that the airplane's potential to devastate the industrial heartland of an enemy nation—the centerpiece of Douhet's theory—seemed to offer the best means of justifying and obtaining autonomy from the US Army; it was an end insofar as the conviction that precision bombardment constituted the primary military purpose of aviation came to be accepted as the dominant view within the Army Air Corps.[3] Furthermore, after the atomic bombings at Hiroshima and Nagasaki, bombardment became, if anything, even more firmly entrenched in American thinking about the air weapon. As I will argue in Chapters 4 and 5, the framework of deterrence elaborated by Bernard Brodie after World War II turns out to be little more than an explicit updating of Douhet for the "missile age," and the notion of directly attacking the enemy's vital centers with bombing persisted as the ideal application of air power in the minds of senior Air Force leaders at least through the end of the Vietnam War. For these reasons, *Il Domino dell'Aria* offers a legitimate exemplar of the logical underpinnings of US air doctrine.

Douhet's Image of War: Unrestrained Offense

What basic image of war is presumed in Douhet's *Command of the Air?* The book's thrust on this fundamental issue is hardly mysterious. Early in the opening chapter, "The New Form of War," Douhet declares:

> The form of any war—and it is the form which is of primary interest to men of war—depends upon the technical means of war available. It is well known, for instance, that the introduction of firearms was a powerful influence in changing the forms of war in the past.[4]

Literally interpreted, this passage suggests that technical means constitute the most important feature of war, and, as *The Command of the Air* unfolds, this interpretation is confirmed repeatedly. To cite one of Douhet's starkest formulations:

> War is no longer fought in a series of scattered individual encounters, no matter how brave or skillful the individuals may be. War today is fought by masses of men and machines . . . . What determines victory in aerial warfare is fire power.[5]

The context of this second passage is especially revealing. Douhet's immediate objective here was to establish that there could be no meaningful role in future wars for the sort of individualized fighter-versus-fighter combat that had become so widespread on the Western Front during World War I. In his eyes, the "knight-errantry" of highly skilled aces like Manfred von Richthofen and Billy Bishop had become an anachronism that no nation genuinely concerned with commanding the air could henceforth afford.[6] True to form, this thesis was grounded on a technical point: namely, that the slower bombardment aircraft, if more heavily armed, could "always get the best of the faster pursuit plane."[7]

The full extent of Douhet's commitment to a view of war that gave preeminence to technical means, however, is perhaps most readily seen in his definition of aerial strategy. A judicious piecing together of his core idea, submerged in two related but slightly separated discussions, yields the assertion that the *choice of enemy targets* (meaning the selection of objectives, the grouping of zones, and determination of the order in which they should be destroyed) "may be defined as aerial strategy."[8]

It was but a short step from this definition to the conclusion that the only reliable means of gaining control of the air and imposing your will on the enemy was the accumulation of physical damage to ground targets.[9] Douhet's justification for taking this step seems to have rested mainly on the contention that air forces are inherently more offensive than armies or navies—a claim which he tried to support with quasi-mathematical arguments. For example, early in *The Command of the Air* Douhet argued that if you have, say, 20 installations within range of an enemy air force, then to defend you would need "a minimum aerial force twenty times as large."[10] And later in the book he went on to assert that when 10 planes carrying an aggregate payload of 20 tons of bombs strike a target with a circular surface area 500 meters in diameter, "we have mathematical certainty that the target will be destroyed."[11]

While neither of these arguments is very convincing,[12] the main thing to notice is the unflinching consistency with which Douhet followed his thesis about the uniquely offensive character of air power to its logical conclusion:

> Viewed in its true light, aerial warfare admits of no defense, only offense. *We must, therefore, resign ourselves to the offensives the enemy inflicts upon us, while striving to put all our resources to work to inflict even heavier ones upon him.* This is the basic principle which must govern the development of aerial warfare.[13]

As illuminated by this passage, there is little, if any, room in Douhet's thinking for the enemy as an active agent whose plans or actions should be taken into account. Instead, Douhet's vision of aerial warfare was, irredeemably, attrition warfare of the most mechanical sort. What drove his thinking in this direction? Above all else, I would suggest that, like Fredrick Lanchester before him,[14] it was an infatuation with the theoretical aspects of changes in the technical means of combat—with, if you will, a desire to give aerial warfare the rigor of an engineering science—that led Douhet to so mechanistic an outlook.

Mitchell's "Aerial Knights"

Compared to such unremitting doctrinarism, Billy Mitchell's ideas on air power—at least around the time of his court-martial in 1925—seem almost a model of practicality. For instance, Douhet's pointed denigration of the exceptional men and machines demanded by World War I dogfighting contrasts sharply with Mitchell's belief that pursuit aviation would not only retain a role in future air forces comparable to the infantry's in the army, but would also require the "greatest qualities of individual daring, resourcefulness, coolness, and physical ability."[15] Similarly, whereas Douhet stressed the destructive potential of bombardment above all else,[16] Mitchell chose to emphasize the interdependence between pursuit and bomber aviation.

> The Bombardment and friendly Pursuit must work together.... Each must understand the methods, powers and limitations of the other.... Pursuit should realize that while a Bombardment formation is a formidable defense unit and can give a good account of itself when attacked by enemy pursuit, it is certain to suffer heavy casualties if subjected to incessant attack by a greatly superior pursuit force. Bombardment on the other hand, should know that Pursuit is needed to protect Attack and Observation aviation and to carry out missions against enemy pursuit. To afford Bombardment close pursuit protection is unnecessary and a waste of Pursuit aviation.[17]

Still, disagreement on specifics like the long-term utility of pursuit aviation does not mean that Mitchell's underlying conception of war differed dramatically from Douhet's. In point of fact, Billy Mitchell's thinking sprang from the same

FOUNDATIONS OF US AIR DOCTRINE

BRIGADIER GENERAL WILLIAM M. "BILLY" MITCHELL
In the crusade for American air power, Billy Mitchell did not hesitate to lay his military career on the line. (US Air Force Photo)

conundrum that animated Douhet over how the airplane might eventually affect the face of battle, and Mitchell's solution was shaped by technical considerations every bit as much as that given in *Command of the Air*.

Consider the initial focus of Mitchell's *Winged Defense*. The first substantive point made in the opening chapter, "The Aeronautical Era," concerned the aircraft's potential to transcend geographic barriers such as oceans. Because, Mitchell wrote,

> the air covers the whole world, aircraft are able to go anywhere on the planet. They are not dependent on the water as a means of sustentation, nor on the land, to keep them up. Mountains, deserts, oceans, rivers, and forests offer no obstacles.[18]

Hence, even for the United States, the "whole country now becomes the frontier and, in the case of war, one place is just as exposed to attack as another place."[19]

The next major point raised in *Winged Defense* was the airplane's seemingly unprecedented destructive power.

> Aircraft possess the most powerful weapons ever devised by man. They carry not only guns and cannon but heavy missiles that utilize the force of gravity for their propulsion and which can cause more damage than any other weapon.[20]

As of 1925, the most impressive support for this second claim probably lay in the widely publicized bombing tests of June–July 1921, which saw Martin bombers from Mitchell's First Provisional Air Brigade sink such "unsinkables" as the German battleship *Ostfriesland*.[21] So it is not surprising that Mitchell went on to bolster his broad claim about the destructive potential of aerial weapons by noting that one large gravity bomb "hitting a battleship will completely destroy it."[22]

However, the most convincing evidence of Mitchell's commitment to what I would describe as an engineering-science approach to war is not the content of these initial points, but the conclusions he was willing to draw from them. For without much further ado, Mitchell vaulted to the judgment that the airplane offered an entirely new method of subduing industrial centers vital to the enemy's war effort.

> Heretofore, to reach the heart of a country and gain victory in war, the land armies had to be defeated in the field and a long process of successive military advances made against it. Broken railroad lines, blown up bridges, and destroyed roads necessitated months of hardships, the loss of thousands of lives, and untold wealth to accomplish. Now an attack from an air force using explosive bombs and gas may cause the complete evacuation of and cessation of industry in these places. This would deprive armies, air forces, and navies even, of their means of maintenance.[23]

This inference was a heady one.[24] Yet Mitchell did not hesitate to go further, insisting in the very next paragraph that the airplane's advent meant that a new set of rules for the conduct of war would have to be devised and a whole new set of ideas about strategy learned. This particular innovation in weaponry not only doomed the battleship but very greatly changed the missions of armies and navies.[25]

Mitchell's motivation for so decisive a break with the past seems clear enough. From the visionary standpoint of foreseeing the future face of war, his hope was to find an effective form of offensive action that would avert the drawn out slaughter of World War I trench warfare. The airplane, particularly its capacity for bombardment of the industrial heartland of the enemy's nation, appeared to offer a ready-made solution. As Mitchell stated in the preface to *Winged Defense:*

> No longer will the tedious and expensive process of wearing down the enemy's land forces by continuous attacks be resorted to. The air forces will strike immediately at the enemy's manufacturing and food centers, railways, bridges, canals, and harbors. The saving of lives, manpower, and expenditures will be tremendous for the winning side.[26]

In light of the bomber's great theoretical promise, Mitchell went on to paint an enticing picture of what warfare based on air power might be like.

> It is probable that future wars again will be conducted by a special class, the air force, as it was by the armored knights in the Middle Ages. Again the whole population will not have to be called in the event of national emergency, but only enough of it to man the machines that are the most potent in national defense.[27]

I would point out, though, that at the less grandiose level of operational employment by Mitchell's special class of "aerial knights," his vision of future warfare was, at best, somewhat murky. In one of his more explicit descriptions of future air operations, Mitchell wrote:

> The air force rises into the air in great masses of airplanes. Future contests will see hundreds of them in one formation.... Every air attack on other aircraft is based on the theory of surrounding the enemy in the middle of a sphere with all our own airplanes around the whole periphery shooting at it. If we attack a city or locality, we send airplanes over it at various altitudes from two or three hundred feet up to thirty thousand all attacking at once so that if any means of defense were devised which could hit airplanes or cause them to be destroyed from the ground, the efforts would be completely nullified, because they [the enemy] could neither see, hear, nor feel all of them. No missile-throwing weapons or any other devices have yet been created or thought of which can actually stop an air attack, so that the only defense against aircraft are other aircraft which will contest the supremacy of the air by air battles.[28]

On the one hand, these words of Mitchell's can be read as emphasizing the notion of using swarms of aircraft, attacking from all directions, to achieve swift, decisive victory. His central idea, on this interpretation, would be to deny the enemy both the time and opportunity to adapt. But this passage can also be construed as endorsing the more mechanistic thought that an aerial attack, if mounted with sufficient mass, is virtually unstoppable. Granted, a defender of Mitchell could justifiably object that this second reading follows only if we further assume that aerial supremacy has first been obtained. Nonetheless, if pushed, this very caveat unravels Mitchell's vision of the airplane as a solution to the failed land offensives of 1915–17.

To achieve air supremacy, so Mitchell reasoned, the enemy air fleet had to be forced into the air to do battle. How? Mitchell's answer in *Winged Defense* was to go after "a location of such importance to the enemy that he must defend it against a bombardment attack by airplanes."[29] This answer, however, brings us full circle. Should mastery of the air not be speedily obtained by provoking head-on air battles pitting mass against mass, then almost surely the outcome will be just the sort of prolonged, grueling struggle of attrition that Mitchell hoped to avert.

As we will see in Chapter 6, this result turns out to be precisely the fate which began to overtake the American bomber campaign against Hitler's Third *Reich* by the late summer of 1943.[30] Far from achieving the swift, cheap defeat of the enemy envisaged by air power theorists like Douhet and Mitchell, the Combined Bomber Offensive literally turned the airspace over Western Europe into "a battleground with fortresses and trenches."[31] Even for the winners, the "terrible reality was that war in the air was even deadlier for those who flew from 1939 to 1945 than war in the trenches" had been.[32] And to voice what consequently becomes the obvious question: Why was the gap between air power's grand promise and its actual application so great?[33]

NOTES

CHAPTER 2

1. von Clausewitz, p. 149.
2. Giulio Douhet, *The Command of the Air,* trans. Dino Ferrari (New York: Coward-McCann, 1942), p. 59. *Command of the Air* was originally published by the Italian Air Ministry in 1921.
3. Perry McCoy Smith, *The Air Force Plans for Peace: 1943–1945* (Baltimore and London: Johns Hopkins, 1970), p. 19.
4. Douhet, p. 6.
5. Douhet, pp. 43–44. For Douhet, the bloody and ponderous nature of trench warfare on the Western Front showed that war as a whole had become "a direct, brutal clash between opposite forces" (p. 16).
6. To cite Douhet's text at length: "In spite of its claim to offensive characteristics, the pursuit plane was used [during World War I] exclusively as a defensive means . . . and aerial combat became merely a series of duels in which the skill and courage of individual aces were displayed in all their brilliance. Pursuit squadrons were a loose agglomeration of knights-errant of the air . . . . We can see now that such a situation has something false in it, something that does not ring true; for war is no longer fought in a series of scattered individual encounters, no matter how brave or skillful the participants may be. War today is fought by masses of men and machines. So this aerial knight-errantry ought to be supplanted by a real cavalry of the air . . . and we must, therefore, change our present conception of aerial warfare—or go under" (Douhet, pp. 43–44).
7. Douhet, p. 44.
8. Douhet, pp. 50 and 59.
9. Operationally, Douhet's guiding principle was: *"Inflict the greatest damage in the shortest possible time"* (Douhet, p. 51).
10. Douhet, p. 17.
11. Douhet, p. 36. As evidenced by pages 12 through 19 of Lieutenant (later Brigadier General) Kenneth N. Walker's *Thesis on the Attack of New York City From the Air* (Langley Field, Virginia: Air Corps Tactical School, 7 May 1929; file 248.241-28A, Albert F. Simpson Historical Research Center, Maxwell AFB, Alabama). Douhet's quasi-mathematical approach to calculating bombing effects and aerial force requirements later took root in the US Army Air Corps.
12. The problem with Douhet's first argument—that a defender needs many times the force size of the attacker—is that it can be applied with equal force to armored units or aircraft carriers. As for Douhet's claim about the certainty of bombing results, it was so decisively refuted by World War II bombing experience that Brodie later described Douhet's estimates of what his 20-ton "bombing units" could accomplish in terms of "recurring fantasies" (Bernard Brodie, *Strategy in the Missile Age* (Princeton, New Jersey: Princeton University Press, 1959), p. 89).
13. Douhet, p. 55.
14. Fredrick Lanchester is known today for a pair of differential equations which purport to describe small unit attrition. One of these equations, Lanchester's so-called "linear law," is supposed to depict engagements between opposing units equipped with "ancient" weapons such as swords or battleaxes; the other, his "square law," allegedly applies to opposing units equipped with "modern long-range weapons—fire-arms, in brief" (F. W. Lanchester, *Aircraft in Warfare: The Dawn of the Fourth Arm* (London: Constable, 1916), p. 40). But as Lanchester himself made clear, his theorizing concentrated exclusively on the "material" aspects of combat (predominantly on the numbers of weapons, their

ranges, and individual efficiencies) in order to elicit those elementary principles that could be "based upon facts of a purely scientific character" (p. 39). Thus, the often decisive effects of surprise and maneuver, as well as differences between the skill and motivation of individual combatants, their organizations, tactics, and objectives, were all conveniently assumed away by Lanchester for the sake of facilitating mathematical treatment.

15. William Mitchell, *Winged Defense* (New York and London: G. P.Putman's Sons, 1925), p. 164. While *Winged Defense* was by no means Mitchell's only pre-court-martial work on air power, it was the one from which he chose to read whole chapters during his testimony before the Morrow Board (Alfred P. Hurley, *Billy Mitchell: Crusader for Air Power* (Bloomington and London: Indiana University Press, 1975), p. 103). The Morrow Board convened on 21 September 1925, over a month before Mitchell's court-martial began.

16. The half-buried premise behind Douhet's dismissal of World War I pursuit aviation was the conviction that any aerial activity that did not contribute directly to the build-up of surface damage on enemy targets was a waste of effort and resources (Douhet, p. 44).

17. W. M. Mitchell, *Notes on the Multi-Motored Bombardment Group Day and Night*, pp. 104–105 (a copy of which can be found in the Mitchell papers, container number 35, at the Library of Congress). Mitchell printed this manual out of his own pocket and, sometime in 1923, it was made available to the Air Service Tactical School (DeWitt S. Copp, *A Few Great Captains* (Garden City, New York: Doubleday, 1980), p. 319). The Air Service Tactical School at Langley Field, Virginia, became the Air Corps Tactical School with the passage by Congress of the 1926 Air Corps Act; in 1931 the school moved to Maxwell Field outside Montgomery, Alabama (I. B. Holley, Jr., *An Enduring Challenge: The Problem of Air Force Doctrine* (Colorado: US Air Force Academy, 1974), 16th Harmon Memorial Lecture in Military History, p. 3).

18. Mitchell, *Winged Defense*, p. 4.
19. Mitchell, *Winged Defense*, p. 4.
20. Mitchell, *Winged Defense*, p. 4.
21. Mitchell described these bombing tests at length in the first two chapters of *Winged Defense*. For the political and bureaucratic context in which they transpired, see Hurley, *Billy Mitchell: Crusader for Air Power*, pp. 64–76.

22. Mitchell, *Winged Defense*, p. 4. While the assertion that a single unguided bomb containing chemical explosives can completely destroy a battleship would generally be considered an exaggeration even today, Mitchell appears to have been earnest in this claim. As evidence, consider his recurring insistence that aircraft are more efficient than seacraft because an average of 2 to 4,000 airplanes can be built for the price of one battleship (p. 110; also Mitchell, *Notes on the Multi-Motored Bombardment Group Day and Night*, pp. 72–73). Of course, the premise that implicitly supports this conclusion is the contention that a single, well-aimed bomb dropped from an airplane can, in theory, sink any ship. Only if this point is granted does it make sense to compare the bomber's cost directly to the battleship's. But even today we could legitimately question Mitchell's reasoning on the grounds that, in combat, the bomber crew would encounter operational frictions (variable winds, antiaircraft fire from the ship, etc.) likely to render such devastating destruction nearly impossible to achieve with regularity using a single, free-fall, non-nuclear bomb.

23. Mitchell, *Winged Defense*, pp. 5–6. In fairness to bombardment enthusiasts like Mitchell and Douhet, it should be noted that they assumed, contrary to what later transpired during World War II, that poison gas would be used freely along with high explosives in conducting offensive bombardment campaigns. At the same time, the visionary notion that the airplane provided a new, more direct method of waging war was the inspiration of both American and British bombardment enthusiasts throughout the 1920s and 1930s. In the words of the foremost British proponent of bombardment between the world wars, Sir Hugh Trenchard, "It is not ... necessary for an air force, in order to defeat the enemy nation, to defeat its armed forces first. Air power can dispense with that intermediate step, can pass over enemy navies and armies, and penetrate air defenses and attack direct the centres of production, transportation, and communications from which the enemy war effort is maintained" (Max Hastings, *Bomber Command* (New York: Dial Press/James Wade, 1979), p. 40).

24. In the end, the inference that the airplane offered a new method of waging war was also well nigh the main conclusion drawn in *Winged Defense*. "Air power," Mitchell proclaimed, "holds out the hope to the nations that, in the future, air battles taking place miles away from the frontiers will be so decisive and of such far-reaching effect that the nation losing them will be willing to capitulate without resorting to a further contest on land or water on account of the degree of destruction which would be sustained by the country subjected to unrestricted air attack" (Mitchell, *Winged Defense*, p. 122).

25. Mitchell, *Winged Defense*, pp. xv and xvi.

26. Mitchell, *Winged Defense*, pp. xv–xvi.

27. Mitchell, *Winged Defense*, p. 19.

28. Mitchell, *Winged Defense*, pp. 8–9.

29. Mitchell, *Winged Defense*, p. 9.

30. By the end of August 1943, the struggle between Germany's fighter defenses and the Allied heavy bomber effort had become "a massive battle of attrition over the *Reich* . . . with each side inflicting serious damage on the other" (Williamson Murray, *Strategy for Defeat: The Luftwaffe, 1933–1945* (Maxwell Air Force Base, Alabama: Air University Press, 1983), p. 182).

31. Johannes Steinhoff, "The German Fighter Battle Against the American Bombers," *Command and Commanders in Modern Military History: The Proceedings of the Second Military Symposium, US Air Force Academy, 2–3 May 1968* (Washington, DC: US Government Printing Office, 2d ed., 1971), p. 319.

32. Murray, *Strategy for Defeat: The Luftwaffe, 1933–1945*, p. 302. For example, during the period 20 February through 30 April 1944, which marked the height of the American effort to defeat the German fighter force in western Europe, Eighth Air Force lost an average of more than 100 heavy bomber crewmen a day (Roger A. Freeman with Alan Crouchman and Vic Maslen, *Mighty Eighth War Diary* (London: Jane's, 1981), pp. 183–234); similarly, from 1940 through 1945, 51 percent of the British Bomber Command's aircrews died on operations, and the attrition of *Luftwaffe* pilots over the course of the war was probably well into the 90th percentile (Murray, *Strategy for Defeat: The Luftwaffe, 1933–1945*, p. 303).

33. As Murray has written more recently, "One of the great ironies in military history may lie in the claim of post-World War I air power theorists that aircraft would provide an escape for the horror of the last conflict's trenches" (Williamson Murray, "Attrition and the Luftwaffe," *Air University Review*, March–April 1983, p. 66).

CHAPTER 3

THE FIRST US STRATEGIC AIR WAR PLAN

Everything in war is simple, but the simplest thing is difficult. The difficulties accumulate and end by producing a kind of friction that is inconceivable unless one has experienced war.[1]

Carl von Clausewitz

A well-planned and well-conducted bombardment attack, once launched, cannot be stopped.[2]

Kenneth N. Walker

The theory of industrial (or strategic) bombardment that, by the eve of World War II, had emerged as the dominant view on aerial employment at the Air Corps Tactical School (ACTS) was the culmination of a line of development spanning nearly two decades and involving a large cast of characters. Indeed, so difficult to unravel is the tangled skein of sources and influences out of which Air Corps bombardment doctrine coalesced that the Tactical School's conclusions on war strategy "cannot be attributed to any one person or even any one group of persons, nor to any one nation or any single decade."[3]

Nevertheless, since we are principally concerned with the foundations of mainstream US theory for strategic air warfare, there is no need to become enmeshed in questions of who deserves credit for the origination of particular air power ideas. Our interest is in the shared assumptions and paradigms of Army Air Corps bomber enthusiasts—in illuminating the basic images of conflict presumed in their mature views on aerial strategy. It will, therefore, suffice to concentrate upon four men: Harold L. George, Kenneth N. Walker, Haywood S. Hansell, Jr., and Laurence S. Kuter. These individuals were all prominent at the Tactical School in developing and advocating the doctrine of precision industrial bombardment that American airmen took with them into World War II;[4] they constituted the Air Staff planning team that, in August 1941, drafted AWPD-1 (Air War Plans Division I),[5] which became "the basic blueprint for the creation of the Army Air Forces and the conduct of the air war" against Nazi Germany;[6] and later, they were all promoted to general for their contributions to the cause of air power.

Daylight, High Altitude, Precision Bombardment Doctrine

Before proceeding, I want to provide a concise statement of the theory of industrial bombardment that ACTS bomber enthusiasts had derived by 1939. In brief, the prevailing air power doctrine at the Tactical School just prior to World War II can be formulated as follows:

> The most efficient way to defeat an enemy is to destroy, by means of bombardment from the air, his war-making capacity; the means to this end is to identify by scientific analysis those particular elements of his war potential the elimination of which will cripple either his war machine or his will to continue the conflict; these elements having been identified, they should be attacked by large masses of bombardment aircraft flying in formation, at high altitude, in daylight, and equipped with precision bombsights that will make possible the positive identification and destruction of "pinpoint" targets; finally, such bombing missions having been carried out, the enemy, regardless of his strength in armies and navies, will lack the means to support continued military action.[7]

At the heart of this theory lay three interlocking principles. There was, to begin with, the idea that the machinery of a modern industrial state would swiftly cease to function if certain vital elements within its more important economic systems could be destroyed. This proposition, the so-called industrial web concept, originated with Donald Wilson[8] and was elaborated by Muir S. Fairchild.[9] Hand in glove with the industrial web concept went the idea that sufficient precision to destroy vital links in an enemy state's industrial web could be achieved with daylight bombardment from high altitude. Finally, there was Kenneth Walker's deeply held conviction that well-planned, well-flown bomber formations could always get through and, hence, that such formations could be self-defending.

AWPD–1

Turning to the image of war embedded in Air Corps precision bombardment theory, the basic paradigm is perhaps most starkly revealed in the original effort of men like Harold George to apply it. This pioneering application came about as follows. In early July 1941, President Franklin D. Roosevelt asked the Secretaries of War and the Navy for an estimate of the overall production requirements to defeat America's potential enemies.[10] Eventually, this request led to the formation of a four-man "task group" (George, Walker, Hansell, and Kuter) within the Air War Plans Division of General Henry H. "Hap" Arnold's infant Air Staff.

The group's initial problem was to define its task. After some discussion, (then Colonel) George, who was team leader and chief, formulated the task as that of planning a "strategic air offensive to debilitate the German war machine and topple the German state if possible, and to prepare for the support of an invasion."[11]

It was in the actual execution of this formidable planning task that the image of war inherent in Air Corps thinking asserted itself most unambiguously. According to General Hansell's subsequent accounts, the first step taken by the AWPD-1 planning team was to determine air power's relationship "to the achievement of the national purpose and to the other forces" under the strategic premise that initial priority would be given to the European theater.[12] While the theory of air power shared by these four airmen held that the most efficient way to defeat Germany would be to destroy her industrial capacity by aerial bombardment, they recognized that there was little hope of selling victory through air power alone to Army Chief of Staff General George C. Marshall and Secretary of War Henry L. Stimson.[13] Consequently, they settled on a statement for the overall objective of the air effort that "leaned heavily toward victory through air power, but which provided for air support of an invasion and subsequent combined operations on the continent *if the air offensive should not prove conclusive.*"[14]

Having finessed the volatile issue of air power's relationship to the army, navy, and US national purpose, Colonel George's planning team then turned to what Douhet had called the most difficult and delicate task in aerial strategy: targeting.[15] As General Hansell later described the difficulties encountered in this second stage of the analysis:

> Many factors formed vital links in Germany's industrial and military might. The overriding question was: Which were the most vital links? And among these, which were the most vulnerable to air attack? And from among that category, which would be most difficult to replace, or to "harden" by dispersal or by going underground? Each link in the chain had its own interconnecting links, and the search had to be for the one or more keys to the entire structure.[16]

In spite of the analytic challenges embodied by these questions, the AWPD-1 planning team ultimately settled on four basic target systems totaling 154 individual targets:

(1) Electric power (50 generating plants and switching stations).

(2) Transportation (47 marshaling yards, bridges, and locks).

(3) Synthetic petroleum production (27 plants).

(4) The *Luftwaffe*, especially its fighter arm (18 airplane assembly plants, 6 aluminum plants, and 6 magnesium plants).[17]

The last of these four systems, the German air force, was described as an "intermediate objective of overriding importance" on the grounds that German fighter defenses would have to be overcome for the strategic air offensive to be effective.[18] The other three systems—electric power, transportation, and synthetic oil—were designated "Primary Objectives," meaning that in the opinion of the team, they constituted those vital links whose destruction or neutralization would mean that Germany's entire economy would cease to function. To achieve this end, the planners assumed the full bomber force (over 3,800 mediums and heavies)

FOUNDATIONS OF US AIR DOCTRINE

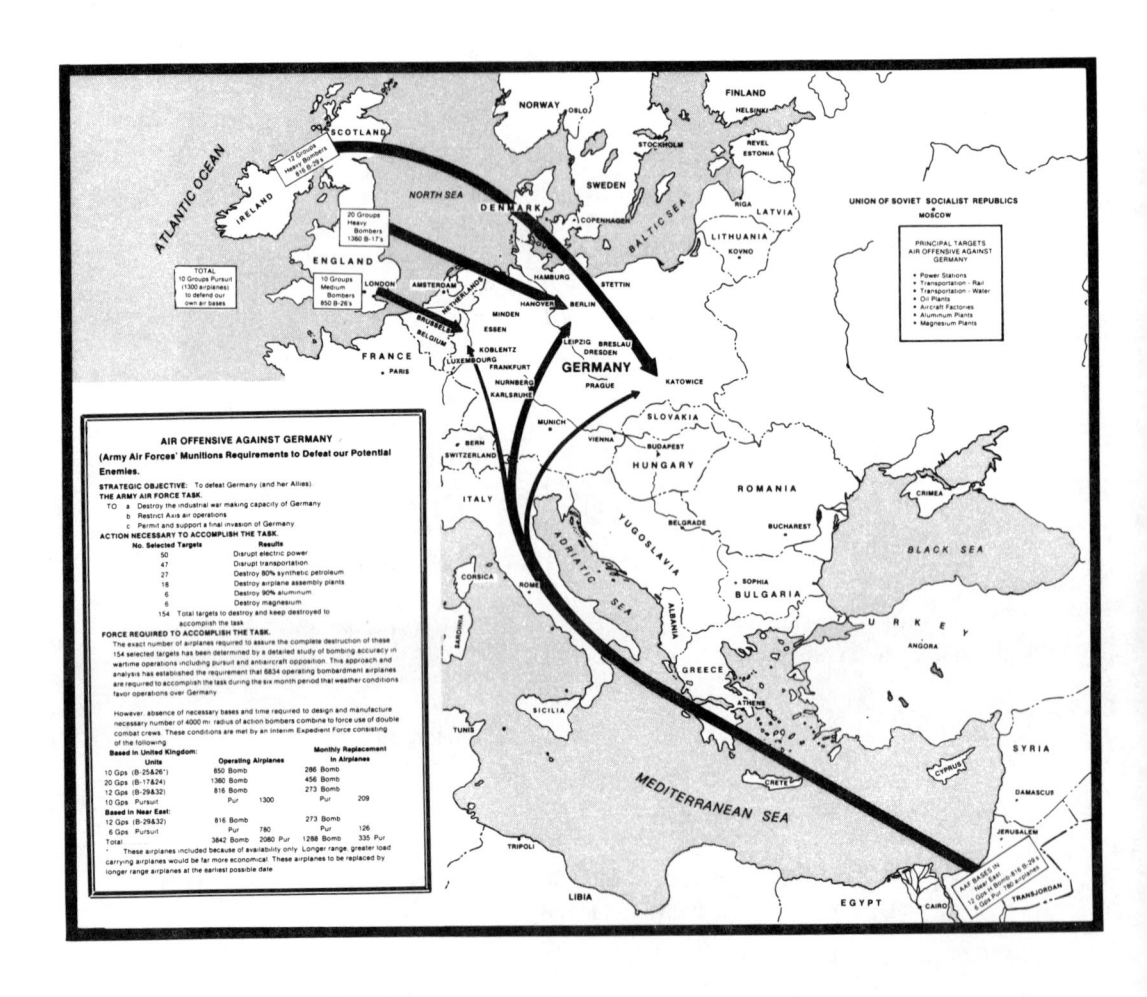

Figure 1. August 1941 Army Air Corps Plan for an Air Offensive Against Germany

MAJOR GENERAL HAYWOOD S. HANSELL, JR.
It is easy enough, nearly a half-century after the fact, to find things to criticize in the thinking of Air Corps Tactical School bombardment theorists like General Hansell. Nonetheless, the conceptual framework that he and his colleagues labored to construct not only remains the bedrock of Air Force ideas about war to this day, but constitutes a level of conceptual achievement and vision that few, if any, US airmen have since attained. (US Air Force Photo)

GENERAL HANSELL IN AUGUST 1943
(US Air Force Photo)

would be devoted exclusively to attacking the complete AWPD–1 target list for a period of six months.[19]

Finally, the AWPD–1 planners calculated the aerial forces required to execute such a bombing campaign. This last step started with further analysis of the 154 targets to ascertain the total number of bombardment operations necessary to destroy, disrupt, or neutralize each system for a period of six months or longer. This determination, in turn,

> was based on a fairly detailed analysis about the proper bomb to use against each particular structure, and the number of hits that would be required to cause the necessary damage. After that, we could determine the number of bombs required to achieve a high probability (90 percent) of obtaining that number of hits on each target, *using peacetime bombing range errors multiplied by a factor of 2.25*. This factor represented the estimated influence of enemy fighter attacks, antiaircraft artillery fire, and other combat conditions on bombing accuracy. We based this conclusion on British experience in their early days of daylight bombing, and accepted as a result a circular error probability of about 1,250 feet. Using probability tables for multiple attacks, the number of bombs which should be dropped to obtain 90 percent chance of securing at least the desired number of hits on each target was computed, taking into consideration the size of the target and the 1,250-foot probable error.[20]

The Image of War in AWPD–1

The broad vision that motivated Colonel George's planning team was, unquestionably, the belief and doctrine that precision bombardment offered a new, revolutionary means of warfare. Armies necessarily relied upon combined arms and had first to defeat opposing armies before they could begin to be decisive; navies, which required task groups, were in a similar situation; but among air forces, well-conceived bomber formations could operate independently and, ignoring all hostile forces, directly and decisively destroy both the means and will of the enemy nation to resist.[21] How? By taking a scientific approach to the problem of target selection (in Douhet's broad sense of which targets to hit, in what order, and so on). The mature Air Corps theory of precision bombardment that George, Walker, Hansell, Kuter, Donald Wilson, and others had helped to develop called for the identification, *by scientific analysis,* of those key links in the enemy's economy whose elimination would either cripple his capacity to wage war or else shatter his will to continue fighting. The efforts of the AWPD–1 planners followed this doctrinal thesis to the letter. From start to finish, their focus was on the analysis of targets—especially of industrial targets—and their main activity was that of devising a targeting scheme which they judged capable of tearing to shreds the fabric of Germany's economy. I would, therefore, argue that their thinking was mechanistic in character—more akin to that of artillery officers laying out a plan of fire against inanimate targets than to classical, Clausewitzian strategists.[22]

The tendency in ACTS thinking to view war as fundamentally an engineering science is so obvious, and so pronounced, as to require no further explication. Indeed, there is only one additional point that seems relevant: the context in which Colonel George and his fellow air enthusiasts perceived the planning effort that produced AWPD-1. Although the request that led to this air plan appears to have been intended simply to produce a basis for planning weapons production,[23] General Arnold and Colonel George were quick to seize upon the opportunity it presented for the Air Corps to plan its own future.[24] Thus, the total acceptance by the AWPD-1 planning team of the Douhetan notion of aerial strategy as targeting—and, along with it, of Douhet's mechanistic view of war itself—cannot be dismissed as mere expedient. The AWPD-1 planners knowingly sought, not without success, to set the tone and direction of Air Force thinking for decades to come.[25]

NOTES

CHAPTER 3

1. von Clausewitz, p. 119.
2. Haywood S. Hansell, Jr., *The Air Plan that Defeated Hitler* (Atlanta, Georgia: Higgins-McArthur/Longino and Porter, 1972), p. 15. Walker's students at the Air Corps Tactical School credited him with the origination of this idea (Robert F. Futrell, *Ideas, Concepts, Doctrine: A History of Basic Thinking in the United States Air Force 1907–1964* (Maxwell AFB, Alabama: Air University, 1971), p. 33). By the mid-1930s, had you come to Maxwell Field and picked up nearly any of the Air Corps Tactical School's textbooks, you would have found Walker's dictum about the bomber always getting through somewhere in it (Thomas A. Fabyanic, *The Development of Airpower Between the Wars*, author's transcript of the video tape of a lecture to the Air Command and Staff College, Maxwell AFB, Alabama, 3 February 1983, pp. 10–11).
3. David MacIsaac, *Strategic Bombing in World War Two: The Story of the United States Strategic Bombing Survey* (New York and London: Garland, 1976), p. 8. While American air power historians have generally credited Mitchell rather than Douhet with having exercised the greatest influence on the development of Air Service (later Air Corps) Tactical School doctrine in the twenties and thirties, there have been dissenting views. For a balanced exposition of the evidence and arguments on both sides of this issue, see Perry M. Smith, "Douhet and Mitchell: Some Reappraisals," *Air University Review*, September–October 1967, pp. 97–101.
4. George headed the bombardment section at the Air Corps Tactical School during the period 1931–34 and was director of the Department of Air Tactics and Strategy for 1934–35; Walker and Kuter served as instructors in bombardment during, respectively, the years 1929–33 and 1935–38; and Hansell was an instructor in air force for 1935–38 (Hansell, *The Air Plan that Defeated Hitler*, pp. 14, 24, 30, and 316). These four airmen were by no means the only important contributors to Air Corps bombardment doctrine during the period 1926–41. Nevertheless, I would personally concur with Fabyanic's judgment that General Hansell was "perhaps the guiding conceptual thinker" among those who made major contributions during these years (Fabyanic, *The Development of Airpower Between the Wars*, p. 14).
5. Hansell, *The Air Plan that Defeated Hitler*, pp. 68-69.
6. Haywood S. Hansell, Jr., "The Plan that Defeated Hitler," *Air Force Magazine*, July 1980, p. 110. Following the Japanese attack on Pearl Harbor, the Air Staff updated AWPD-1 into AWPD-42. Hansell headed this second planning effort, as well as a third, convened by General Ira C. Eaker in March 1943, which produced the plan for the Combined Bomber Offensive from the United Kingdom (Hansell, *The Air Plan that Defeated Hitler*, pp. 100 and 157).
7. MacIsaac, *Strategic Bombing in World War Two: The Story of the United States Strategic Bombing Survey*, p. 7.
8. Donald Wilson, "Origin of a Theory for Air Strategy," *Aerospace Historian*, March 1971, pp. 19–20 and 25. According to Wilson, the industrial web concept originated in the 1933–34 course at the ACTS for which Wilson was the principal instructor and lecturer. Wilson headed the Tactical School's air force section during the years 1931–34 and directed the Air Tactics and Strategy Department from 1936 to 1941 (Hansell, *The Air Plan that Defeated Hitler*, p. 44).
9. For example, during the 1935–36 course at the Air Corps Tactical School, Fairchild presented a lecture entitled "Air Power and the City" in which he argued, in light of the disruption caused to New York City by a power outage in 1935, that accurately placed bombs from just 18 aircraft would suffice to bring the entire city to a halt (Fabyanic, *The Development of Airpower Between the Wars*, p. 5.).

FOUNDATIONS OF US AIR DOCTRINE

10. Hansell, *The Air Plan that Defeated Hitler*, p. 61. President Roosevelt's 9 July 1941 letter was construed by the War Department general staff to refer to the production requirements for the United States and Britain to defeat Germany, Italy, and Japan (p. 62).

11. Hansell, *The Air Plan that Defeated Hitler*, pp. 75-76.

12. Hansell, "The Plan that Defeated Hitler," p. 107.

13. Hansell, *The Air Plan that Defeated Hitler*, pp. 72-73.

14. Hansell, "The Plan that Defeated Hitler," p. 108.

15. Douhet, p. 50.

16. Hansell, *The Air Plan that Defeated Hitler*, p. 79.

17. Air War Plans Division, Air Staff, *Graphic Presentation and a Brief: AWPD/1, Munitions Requirements of the Army Air Forces to Defeat Our Potential Enemies*, Part 1, August 1941, file 145.82, Albert F. Simpson Historical Research Center, Maxwell AFB, Alabama.

18. Hansell, "The Plan that Defeated Hitler," p. 108.

19. Hansell, *The Air Plan that Defeated Hitler*, p. 78.

20. Hansell, *The Air Plan that Defeated Hitler*, p. 86. Regarding the factor of 2.25 mentioned by General Hansell, the AWPD–1 planners wrote: "War time errors [are] assumed to be 2.25 times those of peace time. The force required in war time [to have a 90-percent probability of imposing the required level of damage on a given target complex] is thus 2.25 squared or 5 times that for peace time bombing." ("Tab No. 2b: Basis for Calculations of the Force Required to Destroy Targets," *AWPD/1, Munitions Requirements of the Army Air Forces to Defeat Our Potential Enemies*, August 1941, file 145.82–1, Simpson Historical Research Center, Maxwell AFB, Alabama, p. 3). As Fabyanic has pointed out, however, the handling of probabilities implicit in these force size calculations was flawed. In effect, the AWPD–1 planners assumed that "each individual bomb would be independently targeted, sighted, and released"—a luxury that German air defenses seldom, if ever, afforded American heavy bomber crews during World War II (Fabyanic, *The Development of Airpower Between the Wars*, p. 21).

21. Fabyanic, *The Development of Airpower Between the Wars*, pp. 17–18.

22. To clarify—at least in broad terms—what I mean by a classical (or Clausewitzian) strategist, I would refer the reader to von Manstein's account of how the 1940 German plan for the invasion of France came into being (see Erich von Manstein, *Lost Victories*, trans. Anthony G. Powell (Chicago: Henry Regnery, 1958), pp. 94–126). Of special note is von Manstein's genius for anticipating possible enemy countermoves in advance of events. Placement of the German *Schwerpunkt* (loosely, the German main effort) in the center, from the Ardennes region of France over the Meuse River toward the lower Somme River, suggests that the logical British-French response in May 1940 would have been a "large-scale offensive on both sides of the Meuse" against the flanks of Army Group A (p. 125). (*Schwerpunkt* is one of those metaphorical German expressions that tends to lose important implicit connotations when translated into English.) In the event, of course, the Allied high command was too paralyzed with shock to make the logical military response. Impressive, nonetheless, is the fact that von Manstein's plan included explicit countermoves designed to complete envelopment of the French forces even if the Allies had responded in a timely manner to the dire threat posed by Army Group A's drive out of the Ardennes.

23. MacIsaac, *Strategic Bombing in World War Two: The Story of the United States Strategic Bombing Survey*, p. 12.

24. Hansell, *The Air Plan that Defeated Hitler*, pp. 65–66.

25. Targeting analysis of the sort pioneered by the AWPD–1 team in August 1941 persists, remarkably unchanged, in Air Force planning and force structuring activities to this day. The most obvious example is probably the SIOP (Single Integrated Operational Plan). For a concise history of SIOP targeting since 1960, see Aaron L. Friedberg, "A History of the US Strategic 'Doctrine'—1945 to 1980," *Journal of Strategic Studies*, December 1980, pp. 40–44 and 46–48. Note in particular that since 1945, US "nuclear strategy," at least as explained by Friedberg, has largely centered around the issue of which *target system* (in Hansell's sense) to emphasize (p. 45). Equally illustrative of the success of George's planning team in shaping subsequent Air Force thinking, however, is the custom, now institutionalized in the Planning, Programming and Budgeting System, of using targeting analysis to develop an *objective* (or minimum-risk) Air Force force structure as a basic input to the budget process.

CHAPTER 4

THE POLICY AND STRATEGY OF DETERRENCE

Since time has rescued him [Giulio Douhet] from his first and gravest error—his gross overestimate of physical effects per ton of bomb dropped—by introducing the nuclear bomb, Douhet's thoughts are for any unlimited war more valid today than they were during his lifetime or during World War II.[1]

Bernard Brodie, 1951

Known ability to defend our retaliatory force constitutes the only unilaterally attainable situation that provides potentially a perfect defense of our home land.[2]

Bernard Brodie, 1956

From Douhet to Herman Kahn, via the Manhattan Project and Cape Canaveral, is a very short journey indeed.[3]

John Keegan, 1981

The theorists we have examined so far all came to see the airplane as the instrument and means of a new form of warfare with the potential to eclipse all others. They boldly predicted that the bomber's greater speed, freedom of action, and destructive power relative to traditional armies and naval forces would enable those nations possessing bomber fleets to leap over the trenches in which World War I land warfare had become so tragically enmeshed and swiftly defeat the enemy by directly attacking the industrial heart of his society.[4]

As we will see in this chapter, post-Hiroshima deterrence theorists reached very similar claims based on the breathtaking advances in speed and destructiveness made possible by nuclear weapons. The immediate objective of the discussion is to demonstrate that the fundamental assumptions and arguments about the changed nature of future war embraced by the architects of deterrence are basically indistinguishable in their logic from those Douhet, Mitchell, and Hansell based on the long-range bomber. Concurrently, this chapter also lays the foundation necessary for the argument I will mount in Chapter 6 concerning the continuing relevance of Clausewitzian friction—even in the age of thermonuclear-tipped missiles.

To epitomize post-Hiroshima theories of deterrence, I have selected Bernard Brodie's 1959 work *Strategy in the Missile Age*. There are at least three reasons for this choice. *Strategy in the Missile Age* continues to be virtually the only true classic on the gut issues of nuclear strategy (first-strike or retaliatory?), nuclear missile age force posture (which offensive and defensive capabilities should we buy?), and aggregate defense spending (how much is enough?).[5] Further, the book contains more than Brodie's ideas on deterrence alone. The second part of *Strategy in the Missile Age* summarizes what were, more or less, the prevailing views on deterrence and strategic issues among the leading civilian theorists who worked at the Rand Corporation[6] during the late fifties.[7] Lastly, *Strategy in the Missile Age* explicitly links post-Hiroshima thinking about atomic weapons with pre-World War II theories of strategic (or industrial) bombardment. Among other evidence, Brodie included "long-range missiles as well as aircraft" in his definition of 'air power,'[8] continued as late as 1958 to describe the intent of the project that produced *Strategy in the Missile Age* as that of developing "the general theory of air strategy in a nuclear era,"[9] and expressly endorsed the framework of strategic thought created by Douhet as being "peculiarly pertinent to any general war in the nuclear age."[10] *Strategy in the Missile Age*, therefore, seems uniquely qualified to bridge the historical distance between the theory of industrial bombardment worked out at the Air Corps Tactical School and the ideas about general nuclear war that sprang up in the United States following the atomic bombings at Hiroshima and Nagasaki.

Brodie's Assumptions

As we saw in Chapter 2, Mitchell's theorizing about aerial strategy, like Douhet's, took as its starting point those special characteristics of the airplane that seemed to distinguish air power from older forms of warfare.[11] *Strategy in the Missile Age* exhibits this same conceptual point of departure. To be sure, discussion of the special characteristics of airplanes has been replaced by an examination of the destructive effects of nuclear weapons. But the underlying conviction that technological advances have altered the dominant form of war,[12] if not its very nature, is virtually identical in Brodie, Mitchell, and Douhet. To cite, if you will, the bottom line in the final chapter of *Strategy in the Missile Age*:

> Perhaps the most elementary, the most truistic, and yet the most important point one can make is that the kind of sudden and overwhelming calamity that one is talking about today in any reference to all-out or total war would be an utterly different and immeasurably worse phenomenon from war as we have known it in the past.[13]

Given the sheer magnitude of the damage and death recorded at Hiroshima,[14] to say nothing of the physical effects witnessed during early American thermonuclear weapon tests,[15] it is easy to understand how Brodie could have been led to such a conclusion. Although he was skeptical concerning the ability of analytic studies to make more than educated guesses for the various planning factors (including those pertaining to the physical effects of bomb explosions) that would determine the outcome of any all-out nuclear war between the United States and Soviet Union,[16] he was also persuaded that "the *minimum* of expected [American] fatalities" in such an exchange would probably fall in the tens of millions.[17] To put it mildly, the prospect of tens of millions of casualties on the first day is horrific, and it is hard to imagine such a possibility leaving anyone's thinking about future conflict unaffected.

Still, there was more behind Brodie's conclusion that "the atomic bomb came and changed everything"[18] than just the brute fact, first demonstrated at Alamogordo, New Mexico,[19] that a few pounds of uranium-235 or plutonium-239 had the power "to blow up the major part of a great city."[20] In his November 1945 arguments for the changed nature of war, Brodie meticulously identified two additional premises. Thus the explicit assumptions underlying his early views on deterrence were three:

(1) The atomic bomb compresses enormously the time needed to destroy targets like a modern city.[21]

(2) Atomic weapons will, in the hypothetical war of the future, be available to both sides (that is, to the United States and the Soviet Union) in large numbers relative to the number of appropriate targets.[22]

(3) Based upon present scientific knowledge, "devising effective tactical defenses" against atomic bombing attacks will continue to be a near impossibility.[23]

In assessing the plausibility of these assumptions, notice that the first and second are positive assertions, whereas the third denies that a certain military capability will be possible for the foreseeable future. The salient point is that positive assertions, whether about current or future matters of fact, have less stringent truth conditions than claims of future impossibility, however caveated. The single datum provided by the atomic bombing of Hiroshima in 1945 was sufficient to establish once and for all the empirical truth of Brodie's premise that atomic weapons greatly compressed the time needed to level a target like a large city. Similarly, subsequent advances in nuclear weapons technology and delivery means have amply borne out his hunch that both the United States and the Soviet Union would one day possess large quantities of atomic weapons deliverable over intercontinental distances.[24] Brodie's third premise, however, is another matter. Denying the feasibility of effective means to defend against strategic bomber attacks is the kind of claim that cannot be conclusively verified by any number of data points. By way of confirmation, I would note that while all three of Brodie's 1945 assumptions were carried forward without substantive change into *Strategy in the Missile Age*, he nonetheless also maintained, as we will see next, that meaningful defenses against the fission weapons of the 1950s had been possible after all.

FOUNDATIONS OF US AIR DOCTRINE

"LITTLE BOY" ATOMIC BOMB
This weapon is of the type detonated over Hiroshima, on 6 August 1945. It is 28 inches in diameter, 120 inches long, and weighs about 9,000 pounds. When detonated over Hiroshima, the Little Boy-type bomb produced a yield equivalent to approximately 20,000 tons of high explosives. (US Air Force Photo)

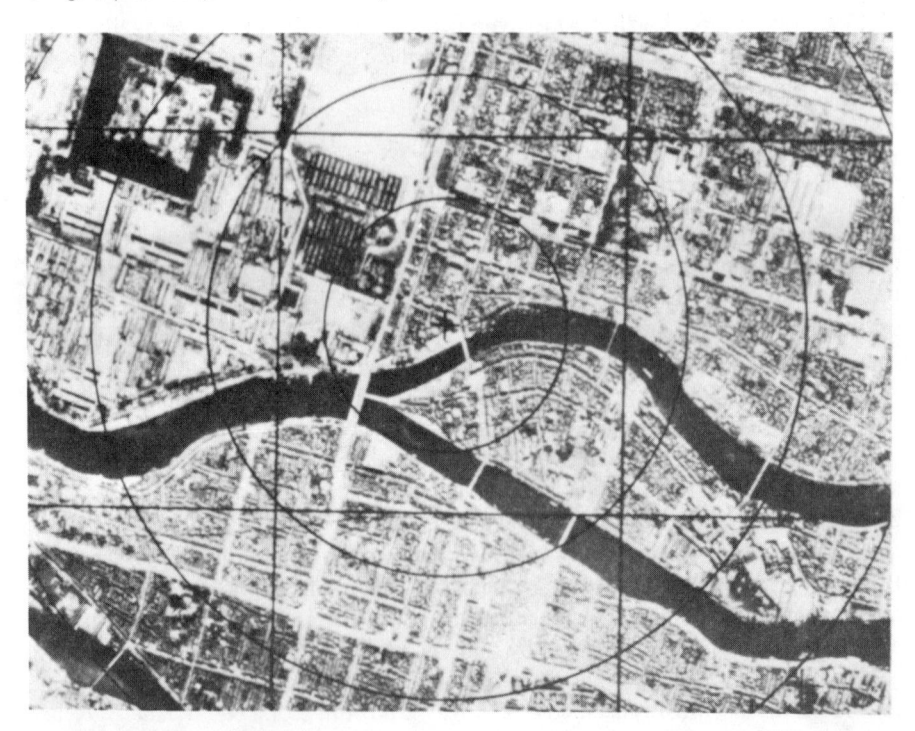

PRESTRIKE TARGET PHOTOGRAPH OF HIROSHIMA, JAPAN
The cross depicts ground zero, the spot directly below the explosion of the atomic bomb. The circles overlaid around ground zero are in 1,000-foot increments. (US Air Force Photo)

POLICY AND STRATEGY DETERRENCE

ATOMIC BURST AT HIROSHIMA, 6 AUGUST 1945
At the time this photograph was taken, the top of the mushroom cloud from the atomic burst had reached an altitude of 20,000 feet, and the smoke at the base extended over 10,000 feet horizontally. Two B-29s of the 509th Composite Group, part of the 303d Wing of the Twentieth Air Force, participated in this mission. One B-29 delivered the bomb, the other acted as escort. (US Air Force Photo)

FOUNDATIONS OF US AIR DOCTRINE

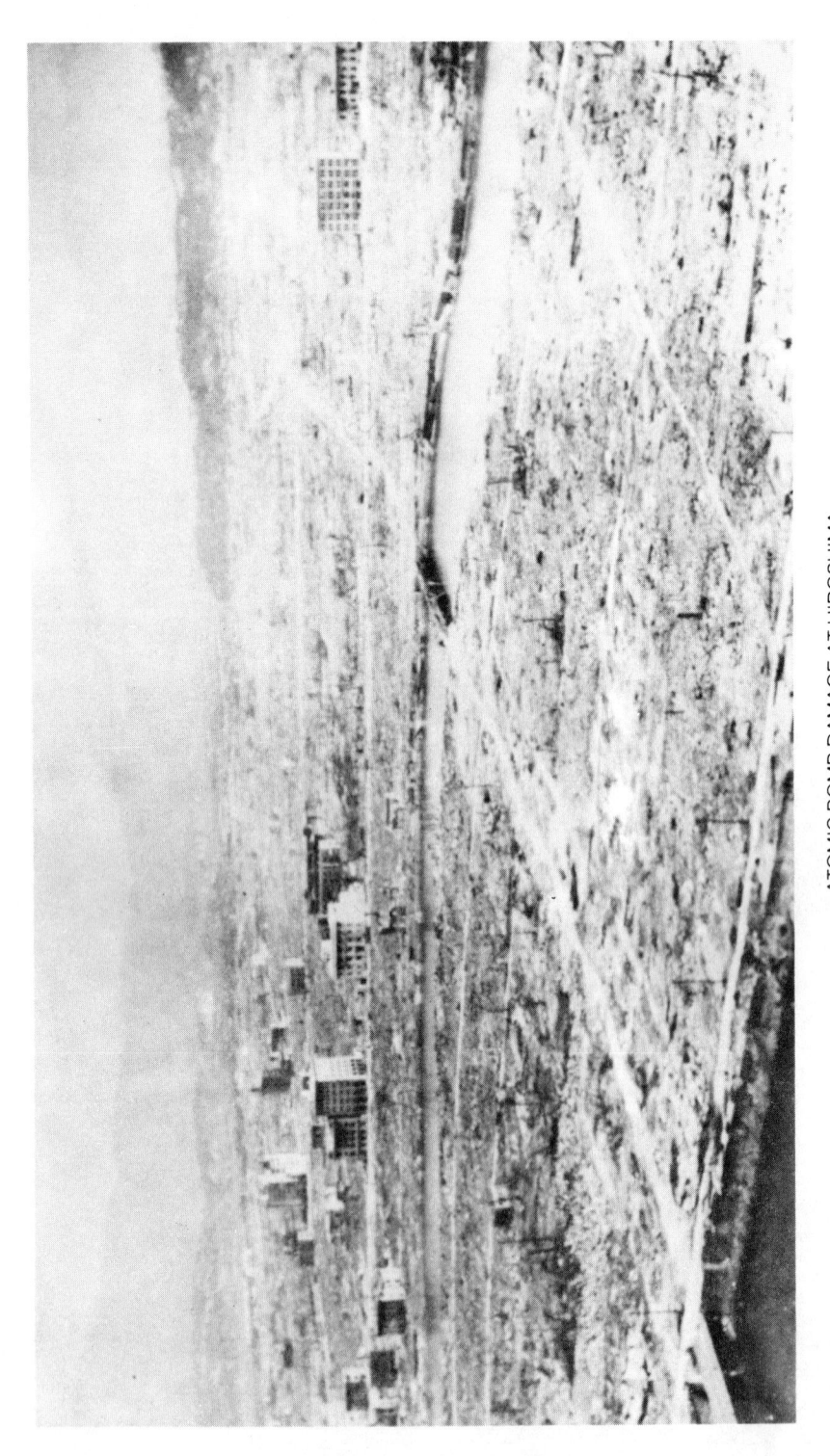

ATOMIC BOMB DAMAGE AT HIROSHIMA
(US Air Force Photo)

Written at a time when megaton-yield fusion devices had already been exploded and long-range missiles were on the brink of practicability,[25] the explicit discussion of nuclear weapons effects in *Strategy in the Missile Age* began by asking what differences, if any, thermonuclear (or fusion) bombs might make for earlier strategic projections based on fission (or atomic) bombs.[26] At first glance, Brodie's understated response may seem a masterful piece of persuasive argumentation. In both 1945 and 1946, Brodie had adamantly insisted that adequate defenses against the atomic bomb neither existed nor appeared very likely to exist in the future.[27] But by 1956 he was forced to concede that fission weapons alone were sufficiently limited in power to make it probable that substantial numbers would be needed to achieve decisive and certain results. This fact, in turn, "made it possible to visualize a meaningful even if not wholly satisfactory air defense, both active and passive" against atomic attack.[28] Hence, during the period following World War II in which only fission weapons were available to the United States and the Soviet Union, it was, Brodie confessed in retrospect,

> still necessary to think [of future all-out war] in terms of a struggle for command of the air in the old Douhet sense . . .[and] to apply, though in much modified form, the lore so painfully acquired in World War II concerning target selection for a strategic bombing campaign.[29]

Yet as reasonable as Brodie's willingness to admit past errors may appear, it did not count for much in the end. Despite having been once burned, so to speak, by the speculation that defenses against strategic attack would, in all likelihood, never be possible, Brodie immediately went on to claim that even the tenuous ties with previous forms of war conceivable in the fission era were called into question by the advent of high-yield fusion weapons inexpensive enough to manufacture in substantial numbers.[30] In *Strategy in the Missile Age,* therefore, the import of thermonuclear bombs, especially when married to ballistic missiles, was to validate even the most extravagant of the assumptions Brodie had made following the atomic bombings of Hiroshima and Nagasaki.[31]

Brodie's Image of All-Out War in the Missile Age

Douhet, as we have seen, envisaged future aerial warfare as unrestrained offense; and Mitchell foresaw a class of "aerial knights" capable of quickly and inexpensively shattering the heart of an enemy nation. The picture of all-out nuclear war between the United States and the Soviet Union that arose from Brodie's assumptions bears remarkable similarities to these earlier visions. Air attack, Brodie wrote,

> is intrinsically and radically different from ground attack. In form it consists not of a series of relocations of one's force, as is true of the advance of an army, but of a *series of sorties or shots,* each of which is *complete in itself* and *marvelously swift* in execution as compared with movements on land or sea [emphasis added]. They could be called swift even in Douhet's time;

today they involve supersonic aircraft and ballistic missiles. They are subject to no canalization by features of terrain. Aircraft have not only a wide latitude in choice of routes between base and target, within the limits of their range, but they also have a choice of altitudes, which can add tremendously to the bafflement of the defender. . . . Ballistic missiles, of course, offer even greater, almost insuperable, problems to the defender.[32]

This image of missile-age warfare constitutes virtually the antithesis of what American heavy bomber crews typically experienced during World War II. As the official history of the US Army Air Forces during that conflict has documented, the strategic bomber campaign was neither marvelously swift nor complete in itself:

The heavy bomber offensive was an impersonal sort of war and monotonous in its own peculiar way. Day after day, as weather and equipment permitted, B–17's and B-24's went out, dropped their deadly load, and turned homeward. The immediate results of their strikes could be photographed and assessed by intelligence officers in categories reminiscent of high school "grades"—bombing was excellent, good, fair, or poor. But rarely was a single mission or series of missions decisive. . . . The effects of the bombing were gradual, cumulative, and during the course of the campaign rarely measurable with any degree of assurance. Thus there was little visible progress, such as Allied troops could sense as they pushed Rommel's forces back from El Alamein toward Cap Bon, to encourage the Eighth Air Force. Bomber crews went back time and again to hit targets which they had seemingly demolished before. Only near the end of the war when the bottom dropped out of the German defense did the full results of the Combined Bomber Offensive become apparent; before that, the "phases" of the long-drawn-out campaign seldom achieved the sharp focus they had shown in the early plans.[33]

The actuality of most World War II strategic bombardment experience was not the only thing to fall by the wayside as Brodie unpacked the implications of the policy and strategy of deterrence. The traditional principles of war (mass or concentration, the objective, etc.[34]) were another early casualty of his image of modern total war. In Brodie's opinion, these principles had been overtaken by "the utterly unprecedented rate of change that has marked the weapons revolution since the coming of the first atomic bomb."[35] In their place he recommended the following triumvirate:

(1) A great nation that has forsworn the advantage of striking first must henceforth devote much of its military energies to cutting down drastically the advantage that the enemy might be able to derive from hitting first by surprise attack. "This entails doing a number of things, but it means above all guaranteeing . . . the survival of the retaliatory force under attack."[36]

(2) A nation that eschews preventive war, thus committing itself to a strategy of deterrence, needs "to provide a real and substantial capability for coping with limited and local aggression by local application of force."[37]

(3) Deterrence can fail: "the danger of total war is real and finite."[38]

There was, and remains, considerable irony about these "missile age" principles. They are open to the very same charge that, in the opening chapter of *Strategy in the Missile Age*, Brodie had leveled against the traditional military principles of war:

namely, that they represent essentially common sense propositions which are "too abstract and too general to be very useful as guides in war."[39]

Another victim of the thermonuclear bomb, as wielded by Brodie, was the long-standing concern of airmen like Wilson and Hansell over selecting the key target systems in the enemy's economy. In all-out nuclear conflict, Brodie maintained, the war potential of the combatants' economies could have practically nothing to do with the outcome.[40] This consequence followed directly from the conviction that in the missile age, strategic bombardment power had come to *dominate conflict absolutely*.[41] "The strategic air ascendancy which determines the outcome [of any all-out thermonuclear war between the United States and the USSR]," Brodie insisted, "is itself decided by the questions, (a) Who strikes first? (b) With what degree of surprise? (c) Against what preparations made by the other side to insure that its retaliatory force will survive and return the fire?"[42] From the perspective of *Strategy in the Missile Age*, modern total war had become little more than a spasmodic exchange of crushing blows.

The ultimate victim of Brodie's theorizing, however, was the notion that the central purpose of military forces is to win wars. As he put the point in 1946:

> The first and most vital step in any American security program for the age of atomic bombs is to take measures to guarantee to ourselves in case of attack the possibility of retaliation in kind. The writer, in making this statement, is not for the moment concerned about who will *win* the next war in which atomic bombs are used. Thus far, the chief purpose of our military establishment has been to win wars. From now on, its chief purpose must be to avert them. It can have almost no other useful purpose.[43]

There can be little doubt as to the radical intent of this passage or of the rationale behind it. Brodie fully meant to stand one of the bedrock values of the profession of arms on its head. The core ideas of the strategy of deterrence did not, he later wrote, spring from "traditional military axioms, to which they are in fact uncongenial," but from "the conviction that total nuclear war is to be avoided at almost any cost."[44] This, he went on to say,

> follows from the assumption that such a war, even if we were extraordinarily lucky, would be too big, too all-consuming to permit the survival of even those final values, like personal freedom, for which alone one could think of waging it. It need not be certain that it would turn out so badly; it is enough that there is a large chance that it would.[45]

Military men in all ages have instinctively put a high premium on victory, and from this perspective Brodie's conclusion that henceforth the chief purpose of America's military establishment must be to deter wars rather than to win them is a bitter pill to swallow.[46] Even Douhet might well have blanched at seeing his ideas about bombardment pushed to this extreme. Nevertheless, Brodie's conclusion must be recognized for what it is: Douhet's assumptions about aerial warfare propelled to their logical conclusion by the awesome destructive power of nuclear weapons.

A Paradox of Deterrence Theory

Pre-World War II bombardment enthusiasts, from Douhet and Mitchell to those of the Air Corps Tactical School, all broadly insisted that the bomber offered so unprecedented and decisive a weapon as to change, fundamentally, the nature of war. Brodie's assessment, in the aftermath of Hiroshima and Nagasaki, was that the airmen had been not so much wrong as premature. Nevertheless, it would be equally premature to infer that the advent of thermonuclear weapons and ballistic missiles left American strategic bombardment doctrine without flaws. On the contrary, the very technology that had, in Brodie's judgment, rescued Douhet, Mitchell, and Hansell from their errors also began to drive a wedge between any unrestricted use of military means and meaningful political objectives.[47] Since Brodie could foresee little hope of effective defense against nuclear bombardment even in the distant future, he concluded that the only *potentially perfect* way to avoid such an attack on the United States lay in deploying an unassailable retaliatory capability to mount nuclear strikes against the attacker's homeland.[48] Conversely, if deterrence failed, then all-out war between the United States and the Soviet Union seemed to boil down to a massive exchange of blows that, under the conditions of 1959, would be so destructive as to spell the end of both belligerents as viable societies.[49] Hence, the essence of deterrence lay in the outwardly irrational stratagem of maintaining an assured capability to wreak on the Soviet Union the very nuclear holocaust that the policy of deterrence sought to avert for the United States.

Further, in the event that deterrence should fail—which in 1959 Brodie saw as a genuine possibility[50]—this appearance of irrationality gave way to outright paradox. Brodie's own formulation of the dilemma is still one of the best. "The rub comes from the fact that what looks like the most rational *deterrence* policy involves a commitment to a strategy of response which, if we ever had to excuse it, might then look very foolish."[51]

> Suppose, for example, the enemy attacked our retaliatory forces with great power but took scrupulous care to avoid major injury to our cities. . . . If his attack is successful to any serious degree, we should be left with a severely truncated retaliatory force while his remained relatively intact. These hardly seem propitious circumstances for us to *initiate* an exchange of city destruction which would quickly use up our remaining power, otherwise useful for bargaining, in an act of suicidal vindictiveness. Our hitting at enemy cities would simply force the destruction of our own, and in substantially greater degree.[52]

But, for the sake of deterrence before hostilities, we must make our retaliation as *certain* and *horrible* as possible.

> The enemy must expect us to be vindictive and irrational if he attacks us. We must give him every reason to feel that that portion of our retaliatory force which survives his attack will surely be directed against his major centers of population.[53]

Brodie had little to offer in the way of a solution to this disturbing conflict between what seemed to be the most rational deterrence strategy before hostilities, and the course of action that might best serve American national interests should deterrence fail. Beyond the unsatisfying observation that "wartime decisions [about nuclear conflict] may be very different from those we presently like to imagine ourselves making,"[54] he was content to leave the matter open and unresolved.[55]

That Brodie could, with his own pen, expose so elementary a paradox at the core of deterrence theory and then brush it aside by cavalierly pressing on to other topics is, to say the least, troubling. Yet, as we shall see in the next chapter, a signal unwillingness to face squarely the practical difficulties of applying strategic bombardment doctrines and strategies in the real world has been a persistent weakness of air power theorists ever since Douhet.

NOTES

CHAPTER 4

1. Brodie, *Strategy in the Missile Age*, p. 73. This sentiment on Brodie's part goes back at least to 1952. In fact, the cited version of this sentence differs only slightly from the original wording (see Bernard Brodie, *The Heritage of Douhet* (Santa Monica, California: Rand research memorandum RM-1013, 31 December 1952), p. 2).

2. Brodie, *Strategy in the Missile Age*, p. 185; the emphasis is in the original. This portion of the book first appeared in Brodie's confidential Rand research memorandum *Is There a Defense?* (Santa Monica: Rand research memorandum RM-1781, 16 August 1956).

3. John Keegan, "The Human Face of Deterrence," *International Security*, Summer 1981, p. 142.

4. Again, a recurring theme of air power thinkers between the two world wars was that nations equipped with air fleets could escape the terrible human costs paid at places like Paschendael, the Somme, and Verdun (Murray, *Strategy for Defeat: The Luftwaffe, 1933–1945*, pp. xxiii and 302). In the context of American bombardment theory, however, this suggestion appears naive given the obvious fact that the economic sinews of 20th century industrialized societies have largely been collocated with their urban population centers. In any event, the scope and magnitude of the destruction that conventional bombing imposed upon cities like Hamburg, Dresden, and Tokyo certainly argues that air power did little to render warfare less costly for cities and their civilian inhabitants. For example, the "Gomorrah" series of Allied bombing attacks on Hamburg in late July 1943 precipitated, on the evening of the 27th, a fire storm that burned out a 4-square-mile hole in the city and killed 30–40,000 people in a single night (pp. 167–68).

5. David MacIsaac, "Voices From the Central Blue: Theories of Air Warfare," April 1980 draft of work in progress. While the thought here was originally MacIsaac's, I have modified his wording and somewhat tempered his enthusiasm for Brodie's 1959 book as the *only* legitimate classic on missile age strategy. Obviously there are other works that might be considered to rank with *Strategy in the Missile Age*. One such candidate would undoubtedly be Henry A. Kissinger's *Nuclear Weapons and Foreign Policy* (New York: Harper for the Council on Foreign Relations, 1957). But for sheer breadth, hard-nosed pragmatism, and explicit grounding in pre-atomic military thought, *Strategy in the Missile Age* is hard to beat.

6. 'Rand' is an acronym for 'Research and Development' (Brodie, *Strategy in the Missile Age*, p. 384). The Rand Corporation was founded in 1948 as a nonprofit research organization. According to Brodie, Rand's purpose was to employ scientific methods, notably system analysis and mathematical wargaming, to assist the Air Force in choosing among competing weapon systems (pp. 384–5). However, General H. H. Arnold's aim in September 1945, when he first decided to begin funneling Army Air Forces money to the portion of Douglas Aircraft that would evolve into Rand, appears to have been primarily "to set up a special aircraft R&D effort" (David MacIsaac, *The Air Force and Strategic Air Power 1945–1951* (Washington, DC: Woodrow Wilson International Center, working paper Number 8, 21 June 1979), p. 23).

7. In the preface to *Strategy in the Missile Age*, Brodie remarked: "Most of my Rand colleagues, I am sure, agree with most of what I say, and many agree essentially with the whole of it" (p. vi). Those specifically mentioned as either having contributed to the general environment of thought in which the book was written, or else having helped directly with the manuscript, included Herman Kahn, William

W. Kaufmann, Andrew W. Marshall, Henry S. Rowen, Thomas C. Schelling, Albert J. Wohlstetter, and Fred C. Iklé. Andrew Marshall's recollections, during a 13 November 1981 conversation about the writing of *Strategy in the Missile Age*, generally confirm the impression given by Brodie's preface. According to Marshall, Brodie came to Rand with the idea of providing fresh perspectives on air strategy in the nuclear era, and at least one early chapter of *Strategy in the Missile Age* was completed by December 1952. Brodie, however, then hit a long dry spell. Indeed, the next chapter to emerge as a Rand memorandum did not appear until August 1956, although Brodie later indicated that not all chapters were issued separately (Bernard Brodie, *The Anatomy of Deterrence* (Santa Monica: Rand research memorandum RM-2218, 23 July 1958), p. iii). But when Brodie finally resumed work, the book assumed a different tack than initially envisaged. Instead of offering fresh thoughts on nuclear strategy, Brodie's focus became that of articulating the dominant thinking at Rand on deterrence and related issues.

8. Brodie, *Strategy in the Missile Age*, p. 19.

9. Brodie, *The Anatomy of Deterrence*, RM-2218, p. iii. For earlier instances of this description, see Bernard Brodie, *The Implications of Nuclear Weapons in Total War* (Santa Monica: Rand research memorandum RM-1842, 17 December 1956), p. ii; also Bernard Brodie, *Strategic Air Power in World War II* (Santa Monica: Rand research memorandum RM-1866, 4 February 1957), p. ii.

10. Brodie, *Strategy in the Missile Age*, p. 106. One of Brodie's most elementary conclusions about nuclear war in *Strategy in the Missile Age* was that with the advent of atomic weapons, strategic bombing had become, "incontrovertibly, the dominant form of war" (p. 152). But as Brodie's exposition of Douhet emphasized, the Italian airman's basic thesis consisted of the twofold argument that, first, the nature of air power required command of the air to be won by aggressive bombing action (rather than by aerial fighting), and that, second, command of the air, once obtained, would then ensure victory all down the line (p. 82). On this reading of Douhet, it is clear that both men embraced, as a fundamental tenet, the proposition that strategic bombing had become the dominant form of war.

11. Mitchell, *Winged Defense*, pp. xiv and 4; Douhet, p. 3. Later, in the hands of ACTS bombardment theorists, this point of departure produced the doctrine that air forces alone, in contrast to ground and naval forces, were capable of ignoring *all* hostile combat units, *directly* attacking the enemy's means and will to resist, and being *immediately decisive* (Fabyanic, *The Development of Airpower Between the Wars*, p. 18).

12. Brodie, *Strategy in the Missile Age*, p. 152. For Brodie's early accounts of the features of atomic weapons that are of military importance, see Bernard Brodie, *The Atomic Bomb and American Security* (New Haven, Connecticut: Yale Institute of International Studies, Memorandum Number 18, 1 November 1945), pp. 1–5; also Frederick S. Dunn et al., Bernard Brodie ed., *The Absolute Weapon: Atomic Power and World Order* (Freeport, New York: Books for Libraries Press, 1972 reprint of 1946 Yale Institute of International Studies ed.), pp. 24–27. In the latter case, the referenced section is captioned: "*The power of the present bomb is such that any city in the world can be effectively destroyed by one to ten bombs*" (p. 24).

13. Brodie, *Strategy in the Missile Age*, p. 391.

14. Historical accounts of the 6 August 1945 atomic attack on Hiroshima typically include the following facts. The majority of Hiroshima's more than 300,000 inhabitants were in the open, without protection, when the bomb detonated over the center of the city; two-thirds of the city was destroyed; 78,150 civilians were killed (most of them outright, in explosions or in fires, though some died later from radiation effects); nearly 70,000 more people were injured; and most of the remainder of Hiroshima's inhabitants suffered long-term radiation damage (R. Ernest Dupuy and Trevor N. Dupuy, *The Encyclopedia of Military History from 3500 B.C. to the Present* (New York, Hagerstown, San Francisco, and London: Harper and Row, rev. ed. 1977), pp. 1197–98). While the rough magnitude of damage to city structures at Hiroshima is evident from photographic and other records, the number of people killed by the atomic explosion there is not known with much precision. Primary reports on the total number of civilian dead and missing at Hiroshima range from a low of 42,550 up to 151,900–165,900 (Committee for the Compilation of Materials on Damage Caused by the Atomic Bombs in Hiroshima and Nagasaki, *Hiroshima and Nagasaki: The Physical, Medical, and Social Effects of the Atomic Bombings*, trans. Eisei Ishikawa and David L. Swain (New York: Basic Books, 1981), Table 10.11 on p. 364). Because few of these primary reports were clear about their sources and methods, the true number of dead appears likely to remain obscured by considerable uncertainty (pp. 363–64).

15. The "Mike" thermonuclear shot of 7 November 1952, whose yield was reported as the equivalent of over 5 million tons of TNT, caused the complete disappearance of the small island of Elugelab and left an underwater crater over 1 mile across and about 175 feet deep at the center (Brodie, *Strategy in the Missile Age*, p. 154).

16. Brodie, *Strategy in the Missile Age*, p. 164.

17. Brodie, *Strategy in the Missile Age*, p. 220.

18. Brodie, *Strategy in the Missile Age*, p. 150.

19. The first experimental atomic bomb was detonated at Alamogordo, New Mexico, on 16 July 1945 (Dupuy and Dupuy, p. 1197).

20. Brodie, *The Atomic Bomb and American Security*, p. 5.

21. In Brodie's eyes, it was the potential to concentrate great damage in unprecedentedly short spaces of time that was the nub of the atom bomb's epochal implications for future war: "The essential change introduced by the atomic bomb is not that it will make war more violent—a city can be as effectively destroyed with TNT and incendiaries—but that it will concentrate the violence in terms of time" (*The Atomic Bomb and American Security*, p. 3).

22. Brodie, *The Atomic Bomb and American Security*, footnote 2 on p. 2.

23. Brodie, *The Atomic Bomb and American Security*, p. 2. Brodie's case for the near-impossibility of effective tactical defenses against atomic bombing attacks can be found on pages 5 to 7.

24. As of early 1983, the United States reportedly possessed 9,975 strategic warheads and bombs, the Soviet Union 7,750 (Fred Kaplan, "Why We Decided Not to Nuke the Soviets," *Washington Post*, 29 May 1983, p. C1; also *Whence the Threat to Peace* (Moscow: Military Publishing House, USSR Ministry of Defense, 2d rev. ed., 1982), p. 8).

25. Chapter 5 of *Strategy in the Missile Age*, which appears in the 1959 book under the title "The Advent of Nuclear Weapons" and begins Brodie's treatment of the impact of nuclear weapons on war, was originally issued in December 1956 as *The Implications of Nuclear Weapons in Total War* (Rand research memorandum RM-1842).

26. Brodie, *Strategy in the Missile Age*, p. 152.

27. Brodie, *The Atomic Bomb and American Security*, p. 6; Brodie, *The Absolute Weapon: Atomic Power and World Order*, p. 28.

28. Brodie, *Strategy in the Missile Age*, p. 153. Brodie's explanation of the difference between the two basic forms of defense, active and passive, does not occur until Chapter 6 (pp. 180–84).

29. Brodie, *Strategy in the Missile Age*, p. 153.

30. Brodie, *Strategy in the Missile Age*, pp. 153–54.

31. Brodie, *Strategy in the Missile Age*, pp. 152–55.

32. Brodie, *Strategy in the Missile Age*, p. 180.

33. Wesley F. Craven and James L. Cate ed., *The Army Air Forces in World War II*, Vol. 2, *Europe: TORCH to POINTBLANK, August 1942 to December 1943* (Chicago: University of Chicago Press, 1949), p. ix. Craven's and Cate's description is remarkably evocative of my own experiences as an F–4 crewmember during the ROLLING THUNDER bombing campaign against North Vietnam.

34. Brodie's formulation of the traditional principles of war can be found on page 24 of *Strategy in the Missile Age*. There, for example, he explicates the principle of mass (or concentration) as meaning that it is desirable to avoid "undue dispersion of strength in order to maximize the chances for superiority at the decisive point."

35. Brodie, *Strategy in the Missile Age*, p. 407.

36. Brodie, *Strategy in the Missile Age*, p. 394.

37. Brodie, *Strategy in the Missile Age*, p. 396.

38. Brodie, *Strategy in the Missile Age*, p. 397.

39. Brodie, *Strategy in the Missile Age*, p. 26.

40. Brodie, *Strategy in the Missile Age*, p. 402.

41. Brodie, *Strategy in the Missile Age*, p. 402.

42. Brodie, *Strategy in the Missile Age*, p. 403.

43. Brodie, *The Absolute Weapon: Atomic Power and World Order*, p. 76.

44. Brodie, *Strategy in the Missile Age*, pp. 268–69.

45. Brodie, *Strategy in the Missile Age*, p. 269.

46. As Brodie remarked near the end of his life, "To the military man deterrence comes as the by-product, not the central theme, of his strategic structure. Any philosophy which puts it at the heart of the matter must be uncongenial to him" (Bernard Brodie, "The Development of Nuclear Strategy," *International Security,* Spring 1978, p. 67).

47. "It is precisely the fact," Brodie commented in 1978, "that one finds it difficult if not impossible to find a valid political objective that would justify the destruction inevitable in a strategic nuclear exchange that makes the whole concept of nuclear deterrence credible" ("The Development of Nuclear Strategy," p. 73).

48. Brodie, *Strategy in the Missile Age*, p. 185.

49. On the issue of whether the United States or the Soviet Union could in some meaningful sense win an unrestricted nuclear war with the other, Brodie's position in *Strategy in the Missile Age* remains, at best, hard to discern. Despite his emphasis on averting war, Brodie denied being uninterested in how a nuclear conflict might be fought and for what objectives: "*So long as there is a finite chance of war, we have to be interested in outcomes; and although all outcomes would be bad, some would be very much worse than others*" (*Strategy in the Missile Age*, p. 278). Elsewhere, however, Brodie not only asserted that it might be impossible, due to circumstances beyond our control, for the United States to win a nuclear war with the Soviets (p. 277), but he also insisted: (a) that the careful and detailed studies of civil defense that would be necessary to determine the truth of whether a nuclear war would be the end of the world for us, let alone for all humanity, have not been done (p. 298); (b) that even a total war that began with a surprise enemy attack need not, if we have taken the adequate precautions beforehand, result in the political extinction of the United States (p. 392); and (c) that the unsolved problem of nuclear war is "how to stop, quickly, once it is decided" in order to avoid grandiose, wanton destruction (p. 404).

50. Brodie, *Strategy in the Missile Age*, pp. 213 and 397. As we will see in the second part of Chapter 6, though, Brodie later developed reservations as to how genuine the risk of US-USSR nuclear war had been, or could be.

51. Brodie, *Strategy in the Missile Age*, p. 292.

52. Brodie, Strategy in the Missile Age, pp. 292-93.

53. Brodie, *Strategy in the Missile Age*, p. 293.

54. Brodie, *Strategy in the Missile Age*, p. 294.

55. Brodie did not consider disarmament a viable, long-term alternative to living under the shadow of the bomb. "It seems by now abundantly clear," he wrote in *Strategy in the Missile Age,* "that total nuclear disarmament is not a reasonable objective" (p. 300). About the only utility Brodie saw in arms control agreements was to help ourselves and the Soviets avoid wasteful expenditures ("The Development of Nuclear Strategy," p. 71). Thus, although he considered the great problem of his age to be that of finding a way to cope with nuclear weapons, Brodie's solution was, to recall his original metaphor, for the American people to live indefinitely under "the shadow of a sword of Damocles" *(The Atomic Bomb and American Security,* p. 1).

CHAPTER 5

A Clausewitzian Critique

Since all information and assumptions are open to doubt, and with chance at work everywhere, the commander continually finds that things are not as he expected.[1]

Carl von Clausewitz, 1832

There is no panacea. A formula is harmful. Everything must be applied according to the situation.[2]

Crown Prince Rupprecht, 1919

Improvisation is the natural order of warfare. The perfect formulas will continue to be found only on charts.[3]

S. L. A. Marshall, 1947

A veil of uncertainty [is] the one unvarying factor in war. . . .[4]

Erich von Manstein, 1956

This study has been organized around the question: To what extent has air power theory in the United States envisaged war as an engineering enterprise whose main elements are, in their essentials, as determinate and calculable as the stress loadings on a dam or bridge? The present chapter will begin to formulate an answer.

The Core Beliefs of Mainstream US Air Doctrine

The first order of business is to state, concisely, the basic beliefs about the air weapon that have constituted the foundation of mainstream US air doctrine. What I would propose is that the core ideas which, by 1940, dominated Air Corps Tactical School thinking about industrial bombardment and, after Hiroshima, formed the foundation of American theorizing about deterrence can be captured in four statements.

FOUNDATIONS OF US AIR DOCTRINE

(1) *Technological advances* have created—first in the long-range bomber and, later, in the thermonuclear-tipped ballistic missile—offensive weapons of such unprecedented destructive power as to *change the dominant form,* if not the very nature, of *all-out* war between industrialized societies.

(2) Since there appears to be no effective defense against a well-planned and well-conducted bombardment attack, *air forces can,* in contrast to armies and navies, leap over traditional obstacles (oceans, vast distances, opposing forces, etc.) and *swiftly destroy* the *will* or *means* of an enemy society to wage war.[5]

(3) In any warfighting application of the air weapon, *aerial strategy* reduces to *selecting* those key *targets* whose destruction will secure the military objectives sought, and *aerial employment* consists of *allocating* the necessary *sorties* to impose the desired levels of destruction.

(4) If the only thinkable political objective for nuclear-armed adversaries is to deter unrestricted conflict, then a *known capability* for *certain,* horrific *retaliation* becomes the only *theoretically perfect defense,* especially fore a nation that has foresworn the advantage of striking first.

Are these four propositions a fair distillation of the fundamental beliefs about the air weapon articulated by the theorists examined in Chapters 2, 3, and 4? I believe that they are. In the case of Propositions 1 and 3, this claim does not go much beyond reiterating obvious matters of fact. The idea that technological innovations in weaponry can transform the nature of war (Proposition 1) was, without a doubt, taken as a cornerstone and intellectual point of departure for air doctrine by Douhet, Mitchell, Hansell, and Brodie. Similarly, all four of these men eventually embraced the view that bombardment would one day be—if it had not already become—the dominant form of war (Proposition 3).

The concept of deterrence embodied in Proposition 4 requires a bit more of an argument. While it unquestionably applies to Brodie, who was one of the architects of nuclear deterrence, the theories of Douhet, Mitchell, and Hansell were worked out long before the advent of atomic weapons. Nonetheless, Proposition 4 can be plausibly extended to Douhet, Mitchell, and Hansell on the following grounds. When Proposition 4 is seen for what it is—an updating of Douhet for the nuclear age under the further assumption that there is no effective defense against bombardment attacks (Proposition 2)—it becomes as unavoidably a consequence of the air power ideas of Mitchell and Hansell as it was of Douhet's.

Proposition 2, however, presents a more difficult problem. Douhet, Hansell, and Brodie, of course, all stressed the offense's theoretical preponderance over the defense. Indeed, this idea was pushed to the point in AWPD–1 that air superiority became little more than a hedge against the possibility that the *Luftwaffe* might pose enough of an obstacle to American bombing operations to warrant attention as an intermediate target system. By contrast, Mitchell was more realistic about the need for fighter (or pursuit) aviation. Not only did he warn in his 1923 *Notes on the Multi-Motored Bombardment Group Day and Night* that a bomber formation, despite its formidable defensive firepower, would be certain to suffer heavy casualties if subjected to incessant attack by a greatly superior force of fighters, but in his 1925 *Winged Defense* he repeated this caution, underscoring it with the insistence that if enemy pursuit aviation could not be defeated, then everything else would fail.[6] So the Billy Mitchell of the early 1920s would surely have resisted the idea, implicit in Proposition 2, that pursuit aviation could not offer any effective defense against bomber attacks.

Yet even this lone exception to the claim that Propositions 1–4 represent an accurate distillation of Douhet, Mitchell, Hansell, and Brodie is less telling than it may seem. After his court-martial in 1925, Mitchell began to campaign "for the incorporation of the strategic bombardment idea into national military policy,"[7] and the harder he strove to lay before the American public the best case possible for strategic bombardment, the more closely his pronouncements approached those of Douhet. Granted, unlike Douhet, Mitchell never shut the door completely on pursuit aviation.[8] But by the time of his 1930 aeronautical textbook *Skyways,* he considered it "a serious question" whether any defense against attacking aircraft could be effective, so great was the airplane's potential for concealment in the vast spaces of the air.[9] And in the end, Mitchell came to embrace virtually all of Douhet's main points, including the overall thrust of Proposition 2, that in future wars there probably would not be any way to stop a determined bombardment attack.[10] On balance, therefore, I do not think it stretches the evidence to assert that Propositions 1–4 express the broad spirit of the fundamental tenets about the air weapon that Douhet, Mitchell, Hansell, and Brodie all accepted.

Some Ramifications

This near unanimity on fundamentals has several ramifications. Possibly the most obvious is that seminal beliefs of US air power theorists underwent little evolution from the late 1920s through the early 1960s. The core precepts about aerial warfare that Billy Mitchell began to embrace by the late 1920s were essentially those that Army Air Corps bomber enthusiasts carried with them into World War II. After Hiroshima, these same tenets largely recurred in the framework of the theory of deterrence elaborated by civilian academics such as Bernard Brodie.

Have American doctrinal precepts about aerial warfare departed greatly from Propositions 1–4 since the era in which *Strategy in the Missile Age* was conceived? I think not. The swift rise and continuing importance of the Strategic Air Command within the US Air Force offer persuasive evidence of an enduring institutional commitment to all four propositions, at least within the context of general war. As for fundamental Air Force thinking about conventional conflict since service independence in 1947, neither the Korean nor Vietnam Wars saw any real falling away from Air Corps Tactical School beliefs about the unprecedented decisiveness of well-targeted, well-executed bombardment attacks. Consider, in the case of Korea, Major General Emmett O'Donnell's personal hopes for a quick, decisive strategic air campaign against North Korea in the summer of 1950. "It was my intention and hope . . . " said General O'Donnell,

> that we would be able to get out there and to cash in on our psychological advantage in having gotten into the theater and into the war so fast by putting a very severe blow on the North Koreans, with an advance warning, perhaps, telling them that they had gone too far in what we all recognized as being an act of aggression . . . and go to work burning five major cities in North Korea to the ground, and to destroy completely every one of about 18 major strategic targets.[11]

The commitment in General O'Donnell's words to Propositions 1–3 is clear, and, subsequently, even the Vietnam War did not lessen enthusiasm for these precepts among Air Force leaders. Indeed, the preeminent lesson drawn by senior airmen like General William W. Momyer from the protracted air war against North Vietnam—namely, that air power "can be strategically decisive if its application is intense, continuous, and focused on the enemy's vital systems"[12]—was identical to that derived by General Hansell from the Combined Bomber Offensive's failure to bring about the collapse of the Third *Reich* prior to the Normandy invasion.[13] Thus, the breathtaking technological advances that have occurred in the means of aerial warfare since Mitchell's First Provisional Air Brigade sank the *Ostfriesland* in 1921 have not been accompanied by a comparable evolution in the basic tenets of mainstream US air doctrine.

A rather similar picture flows from the image of war bound up in Propositions 1–4. Take AWPD–1. Again, the military objective of this first US strategic air plan was to defeat Germany and her allies; in turn, the air task that the AWPD–1 planners derived from this strategic objective encompassed the operational goals of destroying German industrial capacity, restricting Axis air operations, and, if necessary, permitting and supporting a final invasion of Germany;[14] lastly, it was the conclusion of George, Walker, Hansell, and Kuter that the action needed to accomplish this threefold air task was the precision bombardment of 154 scientifically selected targets. What is so extraordinary in this line of thought is the presumption of a direct, causal linkage between the existence of a certain size bombardment force and the attainment of specifiable results in combat. As the AWPD–1 planners wrote at the time:

> The *exact number of airplanes* required to assure the complete destruction of these 154 selected targets has been determined by a detailed study of bombing accuracy in wartime operations including pursuit and antiaircraft opposition [emphasis added]. This approach and analysis has [sic] established the requirement that 6,834 operating bombardment airplanes are required to accomplish the task during the six-month period that weather conditions favor operations over Germany.[15]

To be sure, Hansell and his colleagues conceded that in the absence of adequate bases, or the time required to design and manufacture the needed number of 4,000 mile radius-of-action bombers, a somewhat smaller "Interim Expedient Force" based in the United Kingdom could do the job.[16] Still, their commitment to an image of war as a phenomenon whose processes are subject to predictable, if not mathematical, relationships is unmistakable. Baldly stated, the essence of AWPD-1 was that aerial warfare could well be reduced to pat formulas and engineering calculations; further, given a bombardment force of the requisite size and technical characteristics, certain results were thought to follow predictably should that force be brought to bear against the enemy.

This American propensity to see war as an engineering science does not appear to have lessened appreciably in the four decades since AWPD-1. For instance, the Army Air Forces (from August 1945 to September 1947) and the United States Air Force (from September 1947 until the initiation of the Korean War) argued "that 70 air groups were necessary to ensure the national security of the United States"[17]— the tacit assumption being, much as in AWPD-1, that the existence of a technologically superior force of a specific size (105 groups) would guarantee certain results (US domination of the postwar world.)[18] Similarly, the virtual obsession of most American strategic (bombing) analysts since 1945 with various baseline (or canonical) calculations about prospective US-Soviet nuclear exchanges—especially as a definitive basis for determining force structures[19]— suggests that the impulse to believe that war can be reduced to engineering formulas and calculations has continued to dominate thinking not just within the Air Force, but throughout the American defense community as well.

This last thought raises one other aspect of Propositions 1–4: their close-knit unity, whether considered in a conventional or a nuclear context. From a missile-age perspective, these four precepts are, thankfully, speculative in that the world, as yet, has no direct experience with all-out war between nuclear-armed adversaries. To this extent, little direct confirmation of the empirical validity of Propositions 1–4 is possible. Nonetheless, there is evidence that can be used to judge their soundness, namely the history of industrial bombardment using conventional munitions. Should existing combat experience with industrial bombardment turn out to challenge Propositions 1–4 within the realm of conventional warfighting, then this same experience must raise doubts about their validity in the nuclear missile age.

Friction

With the fundamental precepts about aerial warfare of Douhet, Mitchell, the AWPD-1 planners, and Brodie now clearly before us, it is possible to begin a balanced assessment of their theories. I indicated in Chapter 1 that the *sine qua non* of a successful military organization is the capacity to adapt to changing conditions better than the enemy, the implication being that sound theory can do much to facilitate such adaptation.[20] In this context, it seems appropriate—indeed imperative—for US airmen today to ask: How suited are Propositions 1–4, along with their implicit image of war as an engineering science, to the likely demands of US security in the 1980s and beyond? Simply answered, this doctrinal heritage does not appear well suited to the future; in fact, it does not even seem well suited to the present. Why not? Because it omits the most important ingredient of all: the complex amalgam that Clausewitz called "friction in war."

To grasp what is being suggested here, we must look more closely at the reasoning behind Book One of Clausewitz's *Vom Kriege (On War)*. Structurally, this book consists of eight chapters. But while the first three represent over three-quarters of Book One in length, Chapters 4 through 8 are devoted exclusively to friction.[21] There, in five terse chapters, a topography for friction is sketched. Four broad categories or sources of *general friction* are elaborated:

(1) The paralyzing, visceral impact of *danger* in war.[22]

(2) The extraordinary demands for *exertion* that combat imposes.[23]

(3) The irreducible *distortions* and *uncertainties* inherent in the diverse information on which action in war must be based.[24]

(4) The inevitable obstacles to action that arise from the *play of chance* and the *enemy's unpredictability*.[25]

In Clausewitz's estimation, these four elements—danger, exertion, uncertainty, and chance—"coalesce to form the atmosphere of war."[26] Explicitly, the concept of general friction is for Clausewitz the only notion "that more or less corresponds to the factors that distinguish real war from war on paper."[27]

It would be hard to overstate the importance of friction in *Vom Kriege*. The insight that general friction makes up the fundamental *atmosphere* of war is one of a handful of themes that run the length of breadth of Clausewitz's masterpiece. War, Clausewitz wrote,

> is more than a true chameleon that slightly adapts its characteristics to the given case. As a total phenomenon its dominant tendencies always make war a remarkable trinity—composed of primordial *violence*, hatred, and enmity, which are to be regarded as a blind natural force; of the *play of chance* and probability, within which the creative spirit is free to roam; and of its element of *subordination, as an instrument of policy*, which makes it subject to reason alone [emphasis added].[28]

The essential thing to notice in this passage is that all three of the outward manifestations that Clausewitz underscored as expressing the dominant tendencies of war are bound up with *Friktion*. Primordial violence and enmity give rise to the dangers, psychological stresses, and demands for physical exertion that so profoundly affect individuals engaged in war; chance is explicitly portrayed in *On War* as a generic cause of the usually enormous gulf between intended and actual

A CLAUSEWITZIAN CRITIQUE

FRICTION IN WAR: WEATHER, WEARINESS

Returning from a daylight bombing mission against synthetic oil plants and communications centers behind German lines, two B-17s collide in midair and disintegrate. The accident occurred only a few hundred feet off the ground as the formation roared through the thick blanket of clouds that obscured the base and reduced visibility to almost zero. The density of the overcast is indicated by the fact that only a few of the B-17s in the formation, which numbered more than a score, are visible. None of the crewmembers from either of the ill-fated bombers escaped. (US Air Force Photo)

FOUNDATIONS OF US AIR DOCTRINE

FRICTION IN WAR: THE UNEXPECTED
The sequence of four photographs on this page and the next were taken over Berlin on 19 May 1944. In the first, a B–17 in a lower group has slid directly underneath the upper B–17 just as the bombardier released his bombs. In the second, a bomb has already carried away the lower B–17's horizontal stabilizer. (US Air Force Photos)

FRICTION IN WAR: THE UNEXPECTED (continued)
Eighth Air Force's comment when these pictures were carried in the September 1944 issue of the Army Air Forces' confidential magazine *IMPACT* was: "heads-up-and-locked in the ship above, the lower plane out of position." Thus, the caption continued, "what the Germans failed to accomplish, we somehow managed to bring about. The plane had arrived at a distant target through intervening flak and safely past German fighters. It carried a crew trained individually at many places and now brought together to form, with the plane, a striking unit of fine balance and power. Then at the instant of potential impact, it was betrayed by slips in air discipline—a discipline in itself the fruition of endless plans and study, as essential in the air as in any other form of attack, both to avoid enemy defenses and to make possible the massive concentrations of our planes in the missions of today."
(US Air Force Photos)

FOUNDATIONS OF US AIR DOCTRINE

FRICTION IN WAR: GERMAN FLAK OVER VIENNA, AUSTRIA
In early 1944, German fighters were downing two-to-three times as many US heavy bombers as German antiaircraft artillery fire (flak). For example, on Eighth Air Force's 6 March 1944 mission to Berlin, 42 of the 69 bombers missing in action were probably or certainly lost to *Luftwaffe* fighters. Nevertheless, at this stage American bomber crews dreaded German flak more than the fighters (Ethell and Price, *Target Berlin, Mission 250: 6 March 1944*, p. 91). The reason was psychological: US bomber crews could normally shoot back at the German fighters, whereas in massed formations they, as a rule, could not even attempt to dodge the flak. (US Air Force Photo)

performance on the battlefield; and the harmonious subordination of military means to the political ends of the state[29] remains as much of an enigma and source of friction for generals and politicians today as it was in the time of Napoleon. *Friktion,* in short, is the logical *Schwerpunkt* (focus of main effort) of *Vom Kriege*.[30] And if Clausewitz was correct in singling out friction as the inescapable atmosphere of war, then any attempt to come to grips with war that generally omits friction[31] is incomplete in that it fails to deal with the phenomenon of war as it actually occurs.[32]

Collective Risk

The gravity of the omission I have identified in the air power theories of Douhet, Mitchell, the AWPD–1 planners, and Brodie should now be more apparent than it may have been at first. Broadly speaking, the essential import of general friction is that the elemental processes of war are too uncertain, too riddled with chance and the unforeseeable to be wholly, or even mostly, captured by pat formulas and engineering calculations. To the extent that air power thinkers from Douhet to Brodie ignored friction, their theories appear to be fundamentally flawed. Indeed, insofar as *Friktion* remains, even late in the 20th century, the inexorable atmosphere of war, the air power precepts elaborated in *Command of the Air, Winged Defense,* Hansell's *The Air Plan that Defeated Hitler,* and *Strategy in the Missile Age* appear about as useful in guiding the conduct of real war as the abstract ideal of military violence as an end in itself, unrestrained by policy or any other consideration.[33]

As stated, this Clausewitzian critique is rather sweeping. It also does little to illuminate the cumulative or collective nature of general friction. Consequently, before turning to the main problem of Chapter 6 (whether friction remains as important in war today as it was on the Napoleonic battlefields of Clausewitz's time), I want to recast the critique of the present chapter in more specific terms.

The assumptions of Air Corps Tactical School precision bombardment theory seem particularly useful in this regard since they were later subjected to the test of actual combat. Colonel Thomas A. Fabyanic's incisive critique of US air planning during the years 1941–44 indicates that AWPD–1 and the 1943 plan for the combined bomber offensive from the United Kingdom were largely predicated on five assumptions.

(1) SIZE AND COMPOSITION OF THE AIR FORCES NECESSARY TO DEFEAT GERMANY: There will be no appreciable competing demands for heavy bomber resources beyond the strategic air campaign itself, and, under combat conditions, each heavy bomber will be able to launch about 50 percent of its 70 combat aircraft on any given day.[34]

(2) BOMBING ACCURACY: If peacetime bombing scores indicate, for example, that 30 B-17 groups might be needed to take out a given target, then five times that number (150 groups) will do the job in combat.[35]

(3) BOMB EFFECTIVENESS: Peacetime testing of munitions effects is an adequate substitute for operational experience.[36]

(4) PENETRATION: In the hands of properly trained American crews, the B-17's technical superiority, especially its formidable defensive armament, will enable well-flown formations to penetrate German defenses with acceptable losses.[37]

(5) EXISTENCE AND VULNERABILITY OF VITAL TARGETS: Industrial target systems can be identified that are vital to Germany's economy; these targets are so vulnerable that no effective enemy workarounds or countermeasures will be possible in the face of bombardment attacks.[38]

On first glance, each of these assumptions appears quite plausible. Assuming a 50-percent bomber launch rate under combat conditions, or that 150 bomber groups can achieve in combat the amount of target destruction that 30 groups could theoretically accomplish with peacetime bombing accuracies, seems so conservative that it is tempting to conclude that friction has been adequately taken into account. But there is a collective sense in which I would insist that friction has, in fact, been ignored. As Colonel Fabyanic has pointed out:

> The planners recognized that in each one of these assumptions, there were certain positive and negative aspects. But in their minds, if the positive aspects outweighed those of the negative, they tended to accept the assumption as a fact and moved to the next assumption more or less with a clean slate, thus avoiding the accumulation of potential difficulties.... By doing so, they ignored the cumulative effect of the residual negative aspects in each of these assumptions.[39]

In other words, the Army Air Corps planners overlooked general friction in the sense of Fabyanic's notion of *collective risk,* meaning the aggregate accumulation of potential difficulties that are inherent in any set of assumptions.

To generalize, it is this ubiquitous, cumulative aspect of actual combat operations that I take to be the core meaning of Clausewitz's contention that *Friktion*[40] constitutes the very atmosphere of war. Thus, when I assert that the theories of air power thinkers from Douhet through Brodie are fundamentally flawed in that they ignored general friction, it is primarily this collective dimension of frictional difficulties that I have in mind.

NOTES

CHAPTER 5

1. von Clausewitz, p. 102.

2. Timothy T. Lupfer, *The Dynamics of Doctrine: The Changes in German Tactical Doctrine During the First World War* (Fort Leavenworth, Kansas: US Army Command and General Staff College, July 1981), p. 58. Clausewitz tended to be even blunter concerning the value of rules and formulas: "Rules are not only made for idiots, but are idiotic in themselves" (von Clausewitz, p. 184).

3. Samuel Lyman Attwood Marshall, *Men Against Fire: The Problem of Battle Command in Future War* (New York: Morrow, 1947), p. 20.

4. von Manstein, p. 137.

5. A simpler statement of my Proposition 2 would be that strategic bombardment is the only form of warfare that is decisive. However, the meaning of the term 'decisive' has come to be so emotion-laden for US airmen and military historians alike that its use tends to undermine rational discussion.

6. Mitchell, *Notes on the Multi-Motored Bombardment Group Day and Night*, p. 105; Mitchell, *Winged Defense*, p. 164.

7. Alfred F. Hurley, *The Aeronautical Ideas of General William Mitchell* (Princeton University: PhD dissertation, May 1961), p. 184. Regarding Mitchell's crusade for strategic air power, Hurley went so far as to suggest that Mitchell deserved much credit for "the so-called 'deterrence' concept which has been the cornerstone of [US] military policy in the 'Cold War' " (p. 249).

8. Hurley, *Billy Mitchell: Crusader of Air Power*, p. 129.

9. General William Mitchell, *Skyways* (Philadelphia and London: J. B. Lippincott, 1930), p. 289.

10. Raymond R. Flugel, *United States Air Force Doctrine: A Study of the Influence of William Mitchell and Giulio Douhet at the Air Corps Tactical School, 1921–1935* (University of Oklahoma, Norman, Oklahoma: PhD dissertation, 1965), pp. 217–18 and 254. Even in *Skyways*, Mitchell had pointed out that during World War I, the Allies' best defense against German bombardment had been "to keep bombing their aerodromes" (p. 287).

11. Robert F. Futrell, *The United States Air Force in Korea 1950–1953* (New York: Duell, Sloan and Pearce, 1961), p. 177. General O'Donnell's initial concept included area bombardment of North Korean cities with incendiaries, a tactic that the Joint Chiefs of Staff refused to authorize. Nevertheless, from 13 July through 26 September 1950, Far East Air Forces Bomber Command B–29s, operating virtually unopposed, were able to effect an average of 55 percent destruction against all of the strategic targets supporting the North Korean People's Army save one: the naval oil-storage tanks at Rashin, which were proscribed for political reasons (pp. 177 and 184–5). The US Air Force did not mount another strategic bomber offensive of this sort until December 1972.

12. William W. Momyer, *Airpower in Three Wars (WW II, Korea, Vietnam)*, A. J. C. Lavalle and James C. Gaston eds. (Washington, DC: US Government Printing Office, 1978), p. 339. In both late 1964 and early 1965, senior Air Force generals such as Curtis LeMay and John McConnell repeatedly advocated (not without justification) a brief, intensive bombing campaign as the best way to force North Vietnam to negotiate a settlement in the south (pp. 17–18). Their advice was long ignored. Particularly during the ROLLING THUNDER phase of the air war against North Vietnam (March 1965 to March 1968), the preference among key decision makers like (then) Secretary of Defense Robert S. McNamara was for a more limited application of air power in which the size and frequency of US air strikes, as well as individual targets, were selected in Washington (pp. 18–19), and it was not until December 1972 that an all-out air campaign against North Vietnam's heartland was attempted. Of President Richard M.

Nixon's decision to initiate such a campaign, General Momyer wrote in 1978: "For the first time, B-52s were used in large numbers to bring the full weight of airpower to bear. What airmen had advocated as the proper employment of airpower was now the President's strategy—concentrated use of all forms of airpower to strike at the vital power centers, causing maximum disruption in the economic, military, and political life of the country'' (p. 33).

13. As of 1972, Hansell's assessment of the heavy bomber effort in Europe during World War II was as follows: "In looking back at the strategic air plans, it seems clear that AWPD-1 *could* have been carried out as planned. This would have required strict adherence to military operations and production priorities proposed. But if (1) the forces had been deployed as stated under the agreed strategy, avoiding major strategic diversion; (2) the airplane build-up schedule established in AWPD-42 had been met (which was possible); (3) the strategic bombing effort had been concentrated on the top three priority objectives of AWPD-1 and AWPD-42, after the defeat of the *Luftwaffe* (electric power, synthetic oil, and German transportation); and (4) the long-range escort fighter force had been available earlier (which was also possible), there would have been enough force available to carry out the appropriate missions *prior to the invasion,* and to achieve destruction of the primary target systems before the Normandy assault.'' (Hansell, *The Air Plan that Defeated Hitler,* p. 267.)

14. *Graphic Presentation and a Brief: AWPD-1, Munitions Requirements of the Army Air Forces to Defeat Our Potential Enemies.*

15. *Graphic Presentation and a Brief: AWPD-1, Munitions Requirements of the Army Air Forces to Defeat Our Potential Enemies.* The map from which the cited quotation was taken appears as Figure 1 on page 28 of the present study.

16. *Graphic Presentation and a Brief: AWPD-1, Munitions Requirements of the Army Air Forces to Defeat Our Potential Enemies.* The Interim Expedient Force assumed an operating force of 3,842 heavy and medium bombers augmented by 1,288 monthly replacements (Ibid.).

17. Smith, *The Air Force Plans for Peace: 1943-1945,* p. 54. The 70-group plan was the fifth and most important produced by the Air Staff's Post-War Division and other agencies with the aim of planning for Air Force independence from the US Army in the postwar period (pp. 14 and 54).

18. Smith, *The Air Force Plans for Peace: 1943-1945,* p. 104. "General Arnold believed—and the postwar planners were in complete agreement with him—that as long as the United States maintained its technological lead in aviation, in general, and in strategic bombardment, in particular, there would be little to fear from any potential aggressor'' (p. 106).

19. A good recent example of the canonical nuclear exchange calculations that have long obsessed US strategic analysts can be seen in the table reproduced below from Lawrence J. Korb's article "The Case for the MX," *Air University Review,* July-August 1980. Based on these pessimistic calculations, Korb constructed the following argument for building and deploying the MX missile: "Presently 15 percent of our fixed silo Minuteman force [of 1,000 launchers] may be able to survive a Soviet attack that targets each silo with two warheads. (See Table I.) Within the next few years, the number of surviving silos could drop to about 5 percent. . . . Moveover, the Soviets can inflict this vast damage upon our ICBM force by firing only one-third of their own supply of ICBM warheads. Therefore, unless one is willing to adopt the destabilizing launch on warning or launch under attack strategy, the ICBM force must be made mobile if it is to survive a preemptive Soviet strike'' (pp. 4-5). Korb's argument obviously requires the additional assumption that effective defense against nuclear ballistic missiles will remain impossible.

Table I. SURVIVING US SILOS (Minuteman and Titan) 1980-1990						
Fiscal Year	1980	1982	1984	1986	1988	1990
Scenario*						
OPTIMISTIC	360	350	210	160	50	25
PESSIMISTIC	150	120	50	40	0	0
REALISTIC	200	180	135	75	25	10

*Depends on uncertainties concerning yields, accuracy, and reliability of Soviet strategic forces.

20. Although the role of theory in adaption by military organizations has never been easy to articulate, Lupfer's insights into German attitudes toward evidence surely touch on one of the keys to German operational genius in this century. "For the Germans all tactical solutions were tentative; the Germans developed tactical doctrine inductively, and applied and refined it in the same spirit. This process still demands much talent and ability, and it still requires *a deliberate search for evidence* [emphasis added]. Glib solutions do not replace hard work" (Lupfer, p. 58).

21. As John Guilmartin has pointed out on several occasions, few theorists of war have had as much *firsthand* experience with actual military operations as Clausewitz. Why do I emphasize such experience? Because, beyond a certain point there may literally be no substitute for having been in battle. As Thomas Keneally has so poignantly written of Usaph Bumpass, the protagonist in his recent Civil War novel *Confederates:* Before the battle of Kernstown Usaph had "experienced skirmishes, and he thought that a battle would be just a skirmish times five or ten. But he had not been ready for the real elements of battle—the cannon shrieks, the feel of the air when it is raddled with musket balls and you feel that if you sniff you'll breath one in. You could not ready yourself for the wild varieties of damage men suffered or the range of grunts and groans and roars they uttered. You couldn't picture to yourself beforehand the thirst or the terrible daze you stayed in while you held a line of fence, or the speed you would panic with. You couldn't guess the craziness with which you might roar up towards artillery if ordered to or the equal craziness with which you would run. And you couldn't most of all imagine how it was to live through your first battle and look back on it" (Thomas Keneally, *Confederates* (New York: Berkeley, 1980), p. 89).

22. Confronted with imminent danger of death or mutilation, particularly when this prospect is driven home by the sight of others being killed and mutilated, "even the bravest can become slightly distracted" (von Clausewitz, p. 113). "It is an exceptional man who keeps his powers of quick decision intact if he has never been through this experience" (p. 113). "Danger dominates the commander not merely by threatening him personally, but by threatening those entrusted to him . . .[A]ction in war . . . is never completely free from danger" (p. 138).

23. "If no one had the right to give his views on military operations except when he is frozen, or faint from heat and thirst, or depressed from privation and fatigue," Clausewitz wrote, "objective and accurate views would be even rarer than they are. But they would at least be subjectively valid, for the speaker's experience would precisely determine his judgment" (p. 115).

24. "War is the realm of uncertainty; three-quarters of the factors on which action in war is based are wrapped in a fog of greater or lesser uncertainty. A sensitive and discriminating judgment is called for; a skilled intelligence to scent out the truth" (von Clausewitz, p. 101).

25. "Countless minor incidents—the kind you can never really foresee—combine to lower the general level of performance, so that one always falls short of the intended goal"; these "difficulties accumulate and end by producing a kind of friction that is inconceivable unless one has experienced war" (von Clausewitz, p. 119). Later, in Book Two, Clausewitz expanded this fourth component of friction by arguing that "the very nature of interaction [with the enemy] is bound to make it unpredictable" (p. 139).

26. von Clausewitz, p. 122. This passage should be compared with Clausewitz's earlier statement that danger, exertion, uncertainty, and chance "make up the climate of war" (p. 104). Note, however, that in the original Clausewitz used *Atmosphare* in both places (Carl von Clausewitz, *Vom Kriege* (Bonn: Ferd. Dummlers, 1980), pp. 237 and 265).

27. von Clausewitz, p. 119. Clausewitz's definitive characterization of friction (as those factors that more or less distinguish real war from war on paper) occurs in Chapter 7 of Book One. The initial focus of this chapter seems to be on the component of general friction that Paret and Howard tend to translate as "chance." But after two paragraphs, the discussion appears to shift to friction in general. And because the title of Chapter 7 is not 'Chance' *(Zufall)* but *Friktion im Kriege* (literally 'Friction in War'), such a shift cannot be considered out of place *(Vom Kriege,* p. 261). Hence, I do not feel I am straining Clausewitz's text in construing this characterization to mean the general concept of friction rather than one of its components.

28. von Clausewitz, p. 89.

29. The passage under interpretation here comes from the first chapter of Book One. As of 1830, the year before Clausewitz died, this chapter was the only part of *On War* that he regarded as finished (von

Clausewitz, p. 70). The components of general friction delineated in later chapters of Book One do not, of course, specifically include the possibility of divergence between military operations and the political aim they seek to serve. However, this external kind of friction not only exists and satisfies the general characterization of friction given in Chapter 7 of Book One, but in the single finished chapter of *On War* (Chapter 1 of Book One) Clausewitz specified conditions under which the political and military aims would tend to be at variance (p. 88). Consequently, it does not seem unreasonable to think that the thorny problem of subordinating the military instrument to political goals might well have expressly emerged as a variety of friction had Clausewitz lived long enough to finish revising his draft.

30. At first glance, portraying friction as *the* focus of *On War* may strike the reader as an exaggeration. But the longer I have wrestled with the logical underpinnings of *On War*—especially from the standpoint of reading Clausewitz's manuscript as a concerted attempt to understand the total phenomenon of war—the more central and enduring the issue of friction has seemed.

31. Perhaps the most vociferous critic of Clausewitz in the last half century has been the British historian B. H. Liddell Hart. Among other charges, Liddell Hart has consistently laid much of the blame for "both the causation and the character of World War I" at Clausewitz's feet on the grounds that Clausewitz's passion for pure theory at the expense of common sense fostered in his disciples a conception of war so utterly mistaken as to lead them to lose all grip on reality (B. H. Liddell Hart, *Strategy* (New York and Washington: Praeger, 2d. rev. ed., 1967), p. 357; B. H. Liddell Hart, *The Ghost of Napoleon* (London: Faber and Faber, 1933), p. 124). But as John Boyd first pointed out to me, the word 'friction' does not occur *even once* in Liddell Hart's original account of Clausewitz's thought in *The Ghost of Napoleon* (pp. 118–129), or in the final revised edition of his widely read *Strategy* (pp. 352–57)!

32. The insight in this sentence are John Boyd's.

33. Clausewitz noted early in *On War* that the *pure concept* of war as an act of force aimed at overcoming the enemy leads, in abstract theory, to the extreme conclusion that "there is no logical limit to the application of that force" (von Clausewitz, p. 77). In actual practice, things are altogether different because it is obligatory to subordinate the military instrument to political aims. Clausewitz's argument for the necessity of such subordination is both clear and compelling. Otherwise, the use of military violence by the state fails to be a rational—or morally defensible—enterprise (p. 89).

34. Fabyanic, *The Development of Airpower Between the Wars*, p. 20. In the fall of 1943, Eighth Air Force's actual launch rate for assigned heavy bombers was about 33 percent, not the 50 percent assumed in AWPD–1 (Ibid.).

35. Fabyanic, *The Development of Airpower Between the Wars*, p. 21. As mentioned in note 20 to Chapter 3, this premise about bombing accuracy required the further assumption that each individual bomb be independently targeted, sighted, and released—a condition that German air defenses seldom permitted the American bombers to satisfy. For example, the typical B–17 load of eight bombs would have required eight separate passes over the target and, hence, eight successive exposures to German flak.

36. Fabyanic, *The Development of Airpower Between the Wars*, p. 21.

37. Fabyanic, *The Development of Airpower Between the Wars*, p. 21. The validity of ACTS assumptions about the bomber's ability to penetrate enemy air defenses without unacceptable losses is discussed at length in Chapter 6.

38. Fabyanic, *The Development of Airpower Between the Wars*, p. 22.

39. Fabyanic, *The Development of Airpower Between the Wars*, p. 22

40. Clausewitz's use of the term '*Friktion*' tends to be metaphorical. While connotation of friction in the more everyday sense of one thing rubbing mechanically against another is often present in *On War*—as when Clausewitz speaks of a military unit no longer running "like a well-oiled machine" (p. 104)—his core meaning seems more figurative—as when, in describing friction's effects, he likens action in war to trying to run underwater (p. 120).

CHAPTER 6

FRICTION IN 20TH CENTURY WARFARE

The strongest contribution of Clausewitz to military theory—that war is an instrument of policy whose only purpose is to achieve a political objective—is least understood in the American military tradition. The American warrior isolates war from policy [and] pursues war as a crusade in a strategy of annihilation too little related to the peace which must follow.[1]

Captain Paul R. Schratz

History strengthens critical judgment by forcing one to recognize that objective evidence, regardless of its relevance, and rational behavior, despite its intellectual appeal, represent only a part of the process of evaluating conflict. At least equally important is a good sense of history that alerts [one] to such unquantifiable aspects of behavior as free will, emotion, chance, and uncertainty.[2]

Colonel Thomas A. Fabyanic

The critique of Chapter 5 took a conditional form. If the elemental processes of war truly are riddled with chance, uncertainty, and the enemy's unpredictable reactions, then the air power theories of Douhet, Mitchell, Hansell, and Brodie are flawed to the extent that they ignore general friction. To complete the argument begun, I must show that friction remains as central to the use of military force today as it was during the Napoleonic era in which Clausewitz experienced war.

The more straightforward part of this task is to document the persistence of friction-related discrepancies between the actual practice of war and its pure theory in this century. Toward this end, the first part of this chapter examines the gap between the pre-World War II doctrine of strategic bombardment described in Hansell's *The Air Plan that Defeated Hitler* and its application during the Combined Bomber Offensive against Hitler's Third *Reich;* the second considers the role of friction in the nuclear era.

There is, however, a more ambitious part to the task of completing the argument begun in Chapter 5. Beyond merely documenting that friction remains *a* factor in contemporary war, I want to insist that general *Friktion* is *the* overriding dimension. Thus, in the case of the Combined Bomber Offensive, I have sought to highlight the great price in blood that American airmen paid because the Air Corps Tactical

School's theory of industrial bombardment gave so little consideration to friction. Similarly, the discussion of Brodie's 1978 article "The Development of Nuclear Strategy" in the second part of this chapter argues that even in the age of nuclear-tipped intercontinental missiles, frictional considerations continue to form the fundamental atmosphere of war.

PART 1

Friction in the Combined Bomber Offensive World II

There is a thin line between stubborn and stupid adherence to a preconceived idea on the one hand, and courageous persistence in the face of initial reverses on the other.[3]

Even if we penetrated to the selected targets without unacceptable losses, and destroyed those targets, how could we predict with assurance the effect upon the viability of the German nation?[4]

Major General Haywood S. Hansell, Jr.

The essence of real war is that nothing develops strictly according to plan.[5]

Colonel Thomas A. Fabyanic

It should not be surprising that pre-World War II American thinking about the air weapon exhibited little appreciation of friction, especially as a collective phenomenon. In the first place, the Air Corps Tactical School doctrine of strategic bombardment described in the second chapter of *The Air Plan that Defeated Hitler* was, at best, speculative theory, not something firmly based on evidence. As General Hansell wrote in 1972 of Air Corps bombardment doctrine at the time AWPD–1 was drafted, the feasibility of effective and sustained air attack as the key to victory had not then been demonstrated by experience; in 1941 at least, "victory through air power alone was pure theory."[6] In the second place, the cause of air power had by then acquired a messianic coloring in the eyes of many American airmen.[7] Particularly in the case of dedicated proponents like Hansell, who had endured long years of frustration under Army domination, there was little inclination to search for shortcomings in Air Corps doctrine. On the contrary, by the fall of 1941 the AWPD–1 planners were confident that they had developed ready answers to the manifold problems of putting the abstract theory of industrial bombardment into practice against Hitler's Germany.

By comparison, Clausewitz's attitude concerning the prospects of easily translating pure concepts, however ideal, into effective practice was fundamentally at odds with the brash confidence of US Army Air Corps staff planners.

> From a pure concept of war, you might try to deduce absolute terms for the objective you should aim at and for the means of achieving it; but if you did so, the continuous interaction would land you in extremes that represented nothing but a play of the imagination issuing from an almost

invisible sequence of logical subtleties. If we were to think in purely absolute terms, we could avoid every difficulty by a stroke of the pen and proclaim with inflexible logic that, since the extreme must always be the goal, the greatest effort must always be exerted. Any such pronouncement would be an abstraction and would leave the real world quite unaffected.... But move from the abstract to the real world, and the whole thing looks quite different. In the abstract world, optimism was all-powerful and forced us to assume that both parties to the conflict not only sought perfection but attained it. Would this ever occur in practice? Yes, it would if: (a) war were a wholly isolated act, occurring suddenly and not produced by previous events in the political world; (b) it consisted of a single decisive act or a set of simultaneous ones; (c) the decision achieved was complete and perfect in itself, uninfluenced by any previous estimate of the political situation it would bring about.[8]

Did Clausewitz feel that any of the conditions necessary for practice to attain the perfection of pure theory were likely to be realized in the real world? Clearly he did not. Among other things, the subsection of Book One of *Vom Kriege* just cited was immediately followed by three more arguing, respectively, that war is never a wholly isolated act, does not consist of a single short blow, and is a phenomenon whose results cannot be final.[9] In sum, whereas airmen like Hansell treated the conduct of war as a series of engineering problems amenable to precise, optimal solutions, Clausewitz took the opposite view, explicitly arguing that pat formulas would never provide a firm basis for military practice.[10]

Weather

Nevertheless, it would be a mistake to think that friction did not rear its unseemly head in *The Air Plan that Defeated Hitler*. Hansell's book covered not only the speculative theory of strategic bombardment but the Army Air Forces' efforts to employ this doctrine against the industrial heartland of Hitler's Germany as well. The point I want to begin documenting, therefore, is the extent to which *Friktion* affected the very atmosphere in which the US strategic air campaign unfolded.

Consider the fickle European weather. As Hansell later summarized the effects that this ever-present factor had on American heavy bomber operations:

> If the weather at the target area was not suitable to bombing, then a whole mission had been wasted and perhaps the lives of many crewmen had been lost to no effect. If the weather on return to base was "socked in," then disaster could ensue. As any visitor to England and all members of the Eighth Air Force will recall, England is occasionally hit by dense fog over large areas, and that fog can be so dense that it is difficult to walk from the mess to the operations office—to say nothing of finding hardstands and the airplanes.... It was quite possible that the entire Eighth Air Force could be lost on a single afternoon by returning to England and finding all bases "socked in." And bombing accuracy was heavily degraded by even partial cloud cover of the target. The weather was actually a greater hazard and obstacle than the German air force.[11]

While Hansell's closing sentence may seem overstated, it is not. Despite the recurring hope among American bomber leaders that technological advances would eventually overcome the many difficulties poor weather posed for precision bombardment operations during World War II, weather remained an impediment of the first order to the very end.

October 1943: Information, Doctrinal Rigidity, Enemy Countermeasures

One could, of course, continue documenting friction's impact on the daylight bomber offensive against Hitler's *Reich* by simply enumerating specific frictional difficulties that occurred. For example, a category of friction repeatedly singled out by Clausewitz concerned the gaps, errors, and uncertainties that infect the information on which action in war must be based, and numerous instances of such difficulties impeding American daylight bomber operations in World War II can be cited.[12] However, the importance attached in Chapter 5 to friction's collective aspects argues that a better approach would be to concentrate on historical episodes in which difficulties accumulated from several sources.

The Combined Bomber Offensive (CBO) plan of May 1943 identified German fighter strength in Western Europe as "an *Intermediate* objective second to none in priority,"[13] and "from June 1943 through the spring of 1944, the main effort of the Eighth Air Force, and of the combined [air] forces for that matter, was directed against the German air force."[14] Eaker's CBO plan envisaged two primary mechanisms for defeating the *Luftwaffe:* the destruction by precision bombardment of the fighter and engine factories believed essential to keeping German air force units supplied with operational airframes; and the "accelerated rate of combat wastage" that increased bomber forces would impose on the Germans in the air.[15] While circumstances eventually would compel the Eighth Air Force to add a third major mechanism—the long-range, deep escort fighter—I want to focus initially on how imperfect information, rigid adherence to prewar bombardment doctrine, and the enemy's unpredictability combined to disrupt American efforts to engineer the *Luftwaffe*'s defeat through the mechanisms of air battle wastage and heavy bombardment of Germany's aviation industry.

I have chosen the fall of 1943 for a couple of reasons. At this early stage in the US daylight bombing effort, the only attrition mechanism that appears to have had much impact on the German air force was the defensive firepower of American bombers. The effects of the others—bombardment of the key links in the *Reich's* aviation industry (sporadically augmented by heavy bomber attacks on *Luftwaffe* airfields) and attrition by allied fighters—on the overall course of the daylight air campaign were relatively minor. Further, in the second week of October 1943, Eighth Air Force made four attempts "to break through the German fighter defenses unescorted."[16] These missions proved so costly that the American objective of smashing the *Luftwaffe* with deep penetration, precision bombing had to be abandoned until early 1944; moreover, rampant inflation in American estimates of the losses that US heavy bombers were inflicting on the German fighter force in aerial combat played a pivotal role in obfuscating the relative costs versus benefits of this attrition-type warfare.

The subject of claim inflation by American bomber crews during World War II remains an emotional issue to this day. In the official history of the Army Air Forces in World War II, Craven and Cate have stated that as early as the autumn of 1942, Eighth Air Force leaders recognized that "accepted claims of German fighters destroyed or damaged by heavy bomber crews were too optimistic."[17] But despite recurring measures to prevent excessive claim inflation by Eighth Air Force bomber crews, "the problem never was satisfactorily solved."[18]

In the fall of 1943, the magnitude of this claim inflation seems to have been truly staggering. During the watershed month of October 1943, Eighth Air Force heavy bombers flew seven daylight missions against German targets.[19] Five of these attacks, culminating with the infamous second Schweinfurt raid of 14 October 1943, drew sizeable reactions from the *Luftwaffe*.[20] For these five air battles, Army Air Forces documents from September 1945 credited Allied bombers and fighters with 983 German aircraft definitely or probably destroyed in the air, of which less than 10 percent were due to British and American fighters.[21]

Actual *Luftwaffe* losses in the West (destroyed and written off) came to only 284 aircraft.[22] For the five major daylight air battles of October 1943, Eighth Air Force's estimate of the combat wastage bombing had imposed on the German *Jagdgeschwaders* (fighter wings) was approximately 340 percent too high. Indeed, on the further assumption that the air-to-air claims of Allied fighter pilots were fairly accurate in October,[23] the definite and probable kills credited to US heavy bomber crews for the month must, on average, have been exaggerated by a factor of better than four. In the case of the 14 October mission against the Schweinfurt ball bearing plants, the inflation rate of enemy kills was 430 percent![24] Consequently, there seems little doubt that throughout this period, US bomber leaders had a highly optimistic impression of the attrition that their efforts to break through the *Reich*'s defenses unescorted were inflicting on the *Luftwaffe* in the air.

Why should this optimistic impression have materially affected the course of the air battle in the fall of 1943? After all, while American claims of German aircraft destroyed in action were greatly exaggerated, the fact remains that the *Luftwaffe*'s attrition over central Germany during September and October of 1943 was not negligible. *Reich* Air Ministry wartime records show that in September of that year, the German air force lost 276 fighters in Western Europe (17.4 percent of its total fighter force as of 1 September 1943), and 284 more were destroyed or written off in October (17.2 percent); the defense against the 14 October Schweinfurt mission alone cost the *Luftwaffe* between 3.5 percent and 4 percent of its total fighter aircraft in the West.[25]

The answer can be found in comparing actual US attrition during this period with that of the German fighter force. If anything, American losses were even less supportable than the *Luftwaffe*'s. Just for the four deep penetration raids of 8, 9, 10, and 14 October 1943, Eighth Air Force listed 148 B–17s and B–24s missing in action, and another 15 heavies were written off as beyond economical repair.[26] These losses amounted to about 30 percent of the fully operational B–17s and B–24s in Eighth's tactical units during October and 35 percent of its combat effective heavy bomber crews.[27] In short,

FOUNDATIONS OF US AIR DOCTRINE

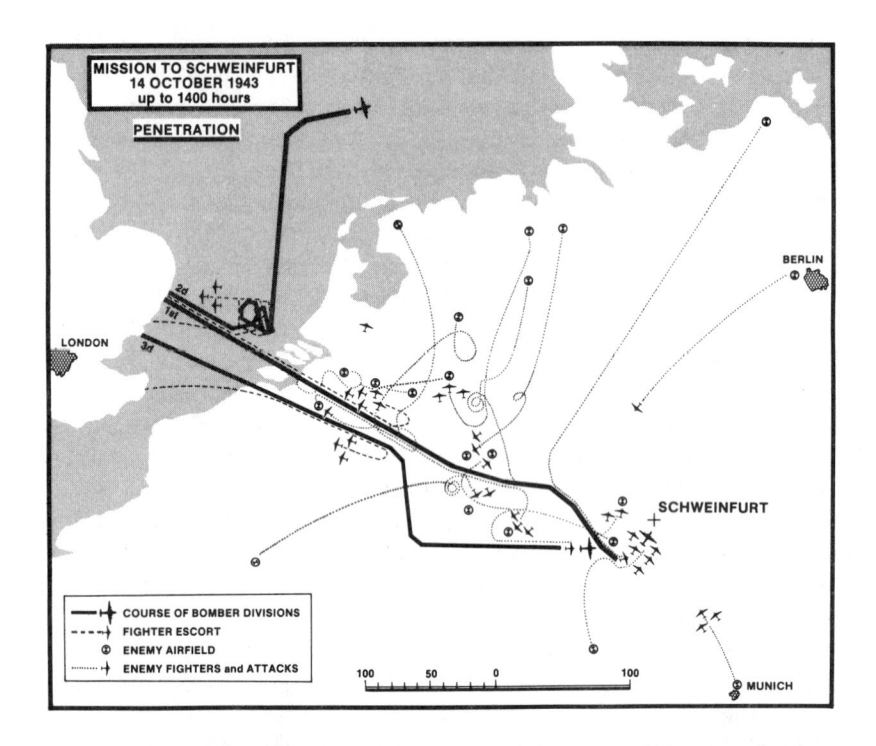

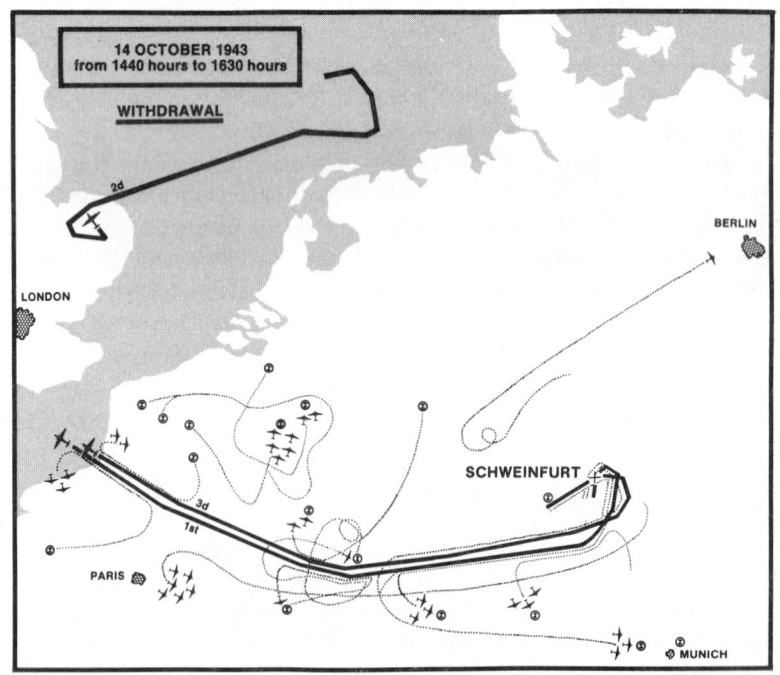

Figure 2. Mission to Schweinfurt, 14 October 1943

SCHWEINFURT, 14 OCTOBER 1943: FIRST WAVE
This photograph is the first of several taken during Eighth Air Force's 14 October 1943 mission against the German ball bearing plants at Schweinfurt. It was snapped just as the bombs from the first wave of American B–17s exploded. The dotted lines outline the locations of specific factories; the arrows labelled 'AP' point to aim points within specific plant areas. (US Air Force Photo)

FOUNDATIONS OF US AIR DOCTRINE

SCHWEINFURT, 14 OCTOBER 1943: THIRD WAVE
This photograph was taken as the third wave of B–17s came over Schweinfurt. Said General H. H. "Hap" Arnold of this target: "We know the ball bearing industry represents a potential war production bottleneck, for it is impracticable to assemble any considerable stockpile of ball bearings." (US Air Force Photo)

FRICTION IN 20TH CENTURY WARFARE

SCHWEINFURT, 14 OCTOBER 1943: HEADING HOME
Heading for home, American B-17 crews could look back and see Schweinfurt in flames. Eighth Air Force listed 60 B-17s, 1 P-47, and their 595 crewmembers "missing in action" on this mission. The feelings of the airmen who survived are perhaps best summarized on a memorial plaque that hangs on the 10th corridor of the 4th floor of the Pentagon: "To the memory of the airmen of the United States Army Eighth Air Force who, against overwhelming odds and savage defiance, attacked and destroyed the ball bearing factories in Schweinfurt, Germany, 14 October 1943. Known officially as Mission No. 155; known by all those who were there as BLACK THURSDAY." (US Air Force Photo)

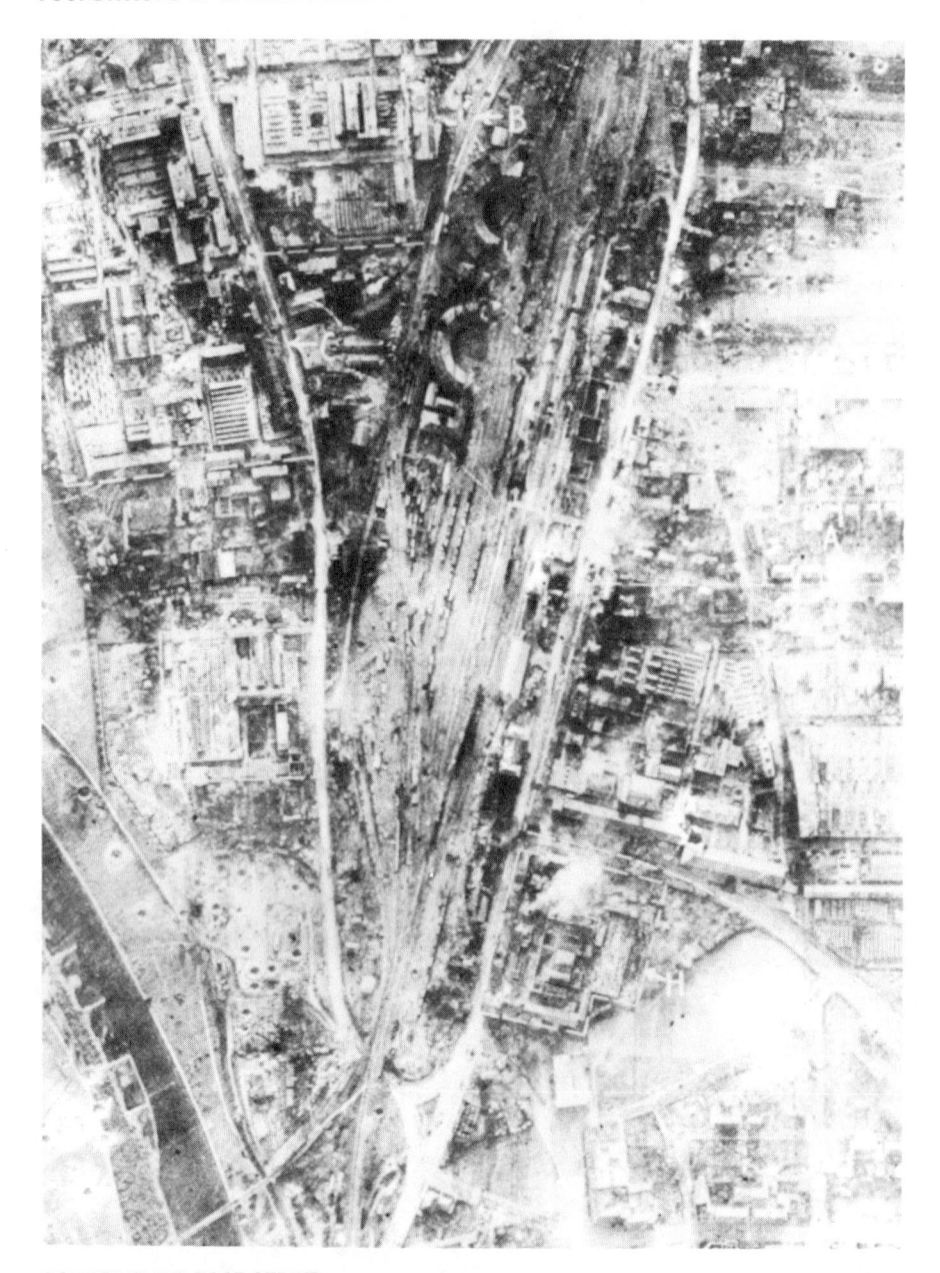

SCHWEINFURT: POST-STRIKE
After the 14 October 1943 raid, General Arnold enthused: "We did it in daylight, and we did it with the care and accuracy of a marksman firing a rifle at a bullseye. We moved in on a city of 50,000 people and destroyed the part of it that contributed to the enemy's ability to wage war against us. When that part of it was a heap of twisted girders, smoking ruins, and pulverized machinery, we handed it back, completely useless, to the Germans." For a more thoughtful assessment of the merits of Eighth Air Force's two assaults on Schweinfurt in 1943, by a B-17 crewman who survived both missions, see Chapter 14 of Elmer Bendiner's *The Fall of Fortresses* (New York: G. P. Putnam's Sons, 1980). (US Air Force Photo)

FRICTION IN 20TH CENTURY WARFARE

BOEING B-17 GOING DOWN SOUTH OF DUNKIRK, FRANCE
(US Air Force Photo)

B-17 HIT BY NAZI AIR-TO-AIR ROCKET
This photo was taken after the bombers had attacked German railway marshalling yards at Munich. (US Air Force Photo)

FOUNDATIONS OF US AIR DOCTRINE

B-24 LIBERATOR DOWNED BY GERMAN FLAK
(US Air Force Photos)

the level of attrition for both Germany's fighter forces as well as Eighth Air Force during September and October [1943] bordered on the point where both were close to losing cohesion and effectiveness as combat forces.[28]

The implication that emerges, then, is that in the second week of October 1943, Eighth Air Force pushed its heavy bombardment groups at least one target too far, thereby ending large-scale, deep-penetration bombing of Germany for the rest of the year. What role did friction play in this outcome? Prewar Air Corps Tactical School theory held that large formations of heavily armed bombers could be self-defending, and Eaker had concluded, as early as October 1942, that a minimum force of 300 B-17s could "effectively attack any German target and return without excessive or uneconomic losses."[29]

What constituted excessive or unacceptable losses? Here friction came into play. Exaggerated kill claims masked how little Eighth Air Force was getting in return for the heavy bomber attrition its units were suffering on raids against targets deep in Germany.

In turn, this friction fed another. Behind the abstract doctrine that enough mass, defensive firepower, and the proper formations would enable unescorted bombers to penetrate any defense lay a refusal to admit that the enemy's reactions could fundamentally threaten bomber operations. As a result, misled by a highly inflated picture of the damage they were inflicting on the German *Jagdgeschwaders*, US bomber leaders persisted in the conceit that they had forged a tactical instrument to which no adversary could adapt. The second Schweinfurt raid, which saw a total of 291 B-17s dispatched,[30] proved otherwise. By concentrating on one formation at a time, using rockets fired from beyond the effective range of B-17 machineguns to break up the American bomber boxes, and aggressively pressing home fighter attacks, the Germans demonstrated once and for all that unescorted bombers were not invulnerable to attack by determined, resourceful opponents.[31]

In retrospect, so costly a demonstration that a reactive enemy can induce unforeseen frictions probably should have been unnecessary. Yet the very fact that unescorted American bomber formations had to experience tactical defeat for Eighth Air Force's leaders to learn this lesson is itself eloquent testimony as to the ubiquitous role of *Friktion* in warfare.

Big Week and the Problem of Industrial Impact Assessments

The fall of 1943 was not the only period in which doctrinal rigidity, imperfect information, and the enemy's unpredictable reactions affected the daylight bomber offensive. The preeminent mechanism that American airmen hoped to employ against the German air force was the precision bombardment of industrial targets vital to the Third *Reich*'s aircraft production. However, accurately assessing the aggregate industrial consequences of physical bomb damage against targets like airframe assembly plants proved as insoluble a problem as had the elimination of inflation in bomber crew claims, and for many of the same reasons.

By the third week of February 1944, a break in the extended period of bad weather that had hamstrung precision bomber operations since January finally permitted US heavy bombers to initiate a series of maximum effort missions against the German fighter industry. These raids, which came to be known as "the Big Week" (20–25 February 1944),[32] signalled a resumption of the American drive to break through the German fighter defenses that had ended with the second trip to Schweinfurt the previous October.

The level of American effort in Big Week was impressive. On the opening mission of 20 February 1944, the newly created US Strategic Air Forces in Europe (USSTAF)[33] dispatched 16 combat wings of B–17s and B–24s numbering over 1,000 heavy bombers. Besides initiating what would prove by late April to have been the largest air battle of World War II,[34] Big Week saw over 3,800 American bomber sorties deliver a total of almost 10,000 tons of bombs on the main POINTBLANK (or CBO) targets—a level of effort roughly equal to that of the Eighth Air Force throughout its entire first year of operations.[35]

Still, as impressive as such statistics may seem, they tell us precious little about Big Week's effects on the capabilities of *Luftwaffe Jagdgeschwaders* to contest Allied control of the skies over central Germany during the daytime. The thrust of the US strategic bombing campaign at this stage was to run the *Luftwaffe* out of planes, and efforts like Big Week strove to do so by the concentrated bombardment of industrial facilities that were thought to be critical to German fighter production. Implicit in this approach was the presumption that getting from the visible effects of bombing to its actual effectiveness in disrupting particular economic target systems was fairly straightforward. But though physical damage to the individual targets could be photographed easily enough, the problems of accurately assessing the results of bombing missions on industrial production were, as Lieutenant Colonel David MacIsaac has succinctly argued, another matter entirely.

> Suppose a decision is made to take out a plant producing ball bearings; suppose one hundred bombers are dispatched and succeed in utterly demolishing the plant. So far as the command and crews are concerned, the effectiveness of the mission is taken for granted to be 100 percent—the given target was attacked and destroyed. But suppose, also, that the ball bearing output of the destroyed plant is never missed by the enemy throughout the war—either because of huge stockpile or alternative sources of supply. In such a case, the *effectiveness* of the mission in speeding up victory *drops to zero* [emphasis added]; indeed, the question that arises, when one asks how the one hundred sorties might otherwise have been applied, whether or not the mission's effectiveness should be described as a negative (or minus) value.[36]

Throughout the late winter and spring of 1944, MacIsaac's hypothetical impediments to gauging accurately the impact of industrial bombing proved every bit as formidable for USSTAF generals and staff officers in practice as they appeared in theory. As in the fall of 1943, the story that emerges is one of subtle interplay between the expectations of prewar bombardment theory, gaps in information, and the enemy's unpredictability.

FRICTION IN 20TH CENTURY WARFARE

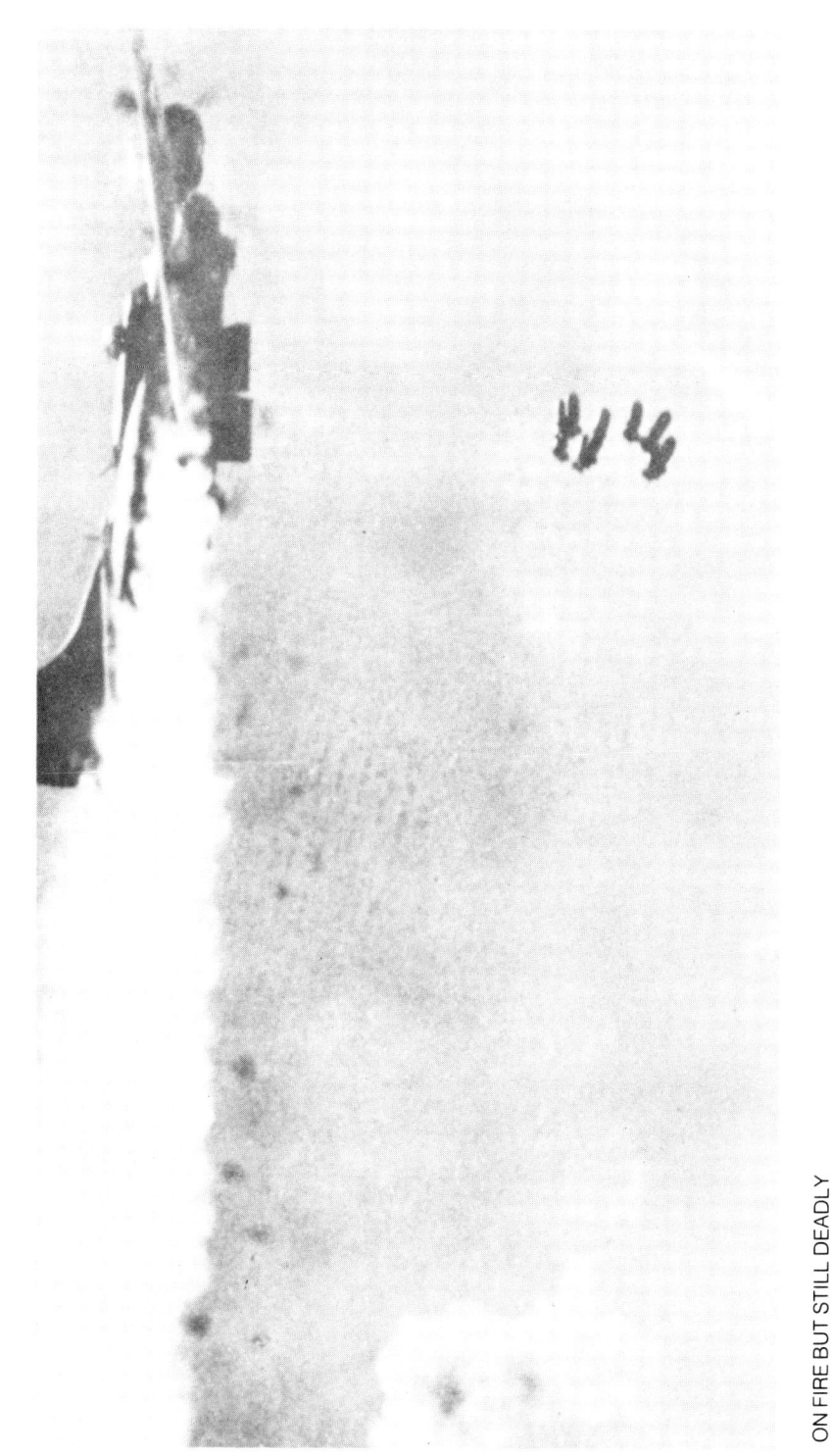

ON FIRE BUT STILL DEADLY
Although one wing of this B–17 Flying Fortress was afire, the plane's pilot managed to keep it in formation while the bombardier released his bombs over Berlin, Germany, on 22 March 1944. (US Air Force Photo)

FOUNDATIONS OF US AIR DOCTRINE

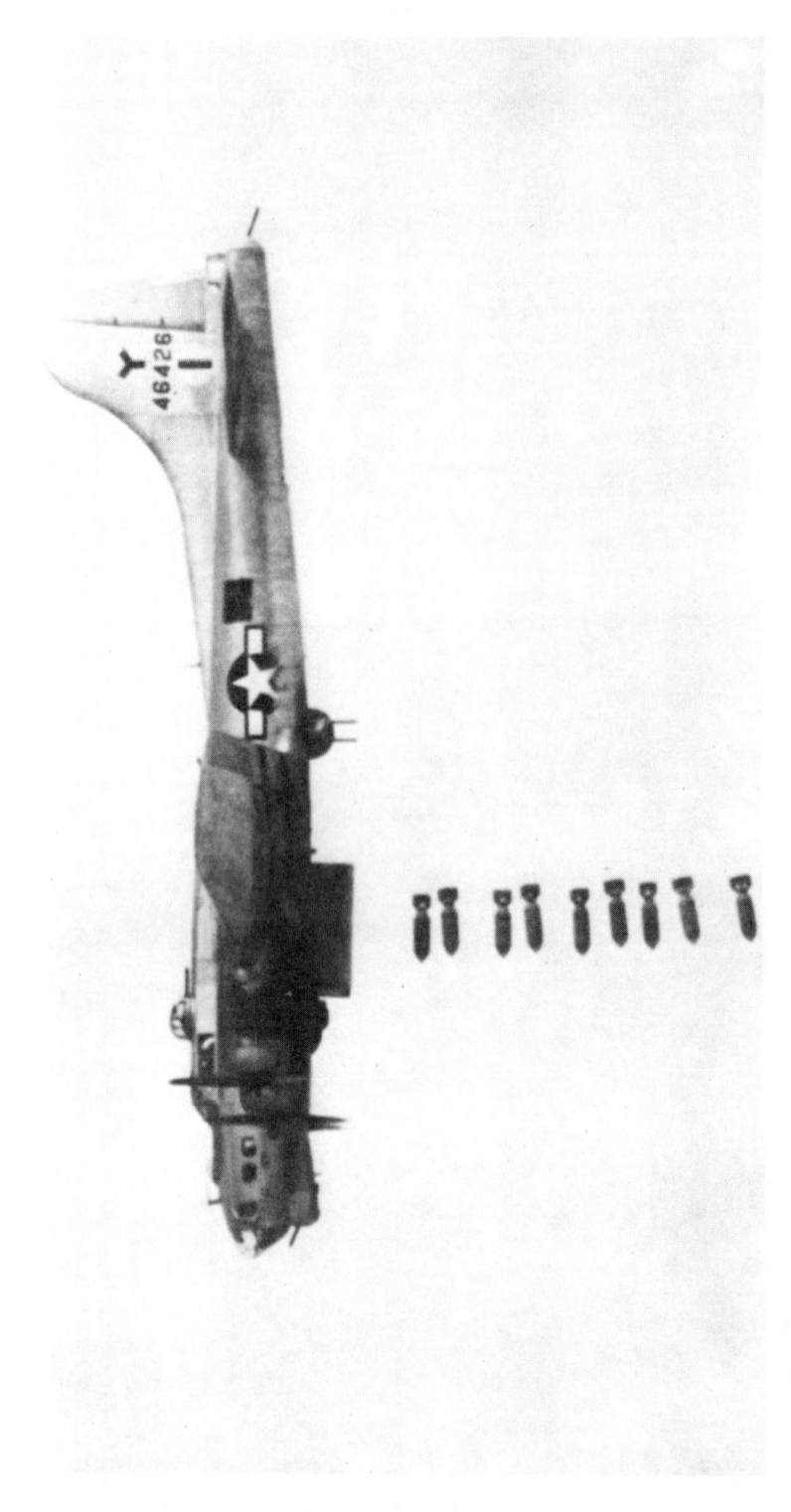

B-17 RELEASING A STRING OF BOMBS
One of the reasons why prewar Air Corps Tactical School tables for calculating the number of heavy bomber groups needed to have a 90-percent probability of imposing the required damage on a given target complex seldom applied during the Combined Bomber Offensive can be seen in this picture. In the face of German air defenses, the luxury of making the 8 or 10 passes over the target necessary to aim and release each bomb independently was rightly judged an unacceptable risk. (US Air Force Photo)

American air planners, like their British counterparts,[37] had expected from the beginning that a bomber offensive against Germany would "find a taut industrial fabric, striving to sustain a large Nazi war effort."[38] The Germans, however, did not fulfill the expectations of prewar Anglo-American bombardment theory. The outstanding feature of the German war effort, the Overall Economic Effects Division of the US Strategic Bombing Survey wrote in 1945, was

> the surprisingly low output of armaments in the first three years of the war—surprisingly low as measured not only by Germany's later achievement, but also by the general expectations of the time and by the level of production of her enemy, Britain. In aircraft, trucks, tanks, self-propelled guns, and several other types of armament, British production was greater than Germany's in 1940, 1941, and 1942.[39]

Thus, Allied efforts to quantify bombing effects were skewed from the outset by a natural presumption that German industry was working full tilt to support Hitler's war effort.

The tendency of this doctrinal basis to mislead US bomber commanders was, in turn, reinforced by another problem. Despite the increasing quality and volume of Allied intelligence production over the course of the war, crucial gaps remained. In the case of German fighter production—the intended victim of Big Week—Allied estimates proved wider of the mark after Big Week than they had been the previous fall.[40] Even the intelligence windfall afforded by "Ultra"[41] decryptions of high-grade German wireless traffic failed to give British and American bomber commanders the one thing they wanted most: a detailed picture of the actual effects of their efforts on the German war economy.

On top of this intelligence shortfall, German responses and countermeasures to the Combined Bomber Offensive piled further complications. After Albert Speer took over as *Reichminister* of armaments in February 1942, the German war economy displayed an amazing capacity to mitigate the effects of aerial bombardment. In the case of Big Week, investigation of German production records after the war revealed "the astonishing fact that, despite the staggering blows delivered by the Allies in February, aircraft acceptance figures for single-engine aircraft had risen rapidly until September 1944."[42]

General friction, therefore, plainly affected the Combined Bomber Offensive in early 1944. From Big Week to early summer of that year, the natural Allied expectation that the *Reich*'s economy would be fully mobilized at the outset of hostilities, gaps in Allied economic intelligence, and the phenomenal recuperability of Germany's armaments industry under Speer combined to shroud the economic impact of Anglo-American bombing in a more or less impenetrable fog.

March and April 1944: Friction as a Weapon

To this point we have looked at friction primarily as an impediment to one's own operations. But friction can also be a potent weapon. The enemy is constantly faced

FOUNDATIONS OF US AIR DOCTRINE

with his own frictions, and they can be used against him. A good example of one adversary capitalizing on the other's frictions is the two-month battle for control of the skies over central Germany that followed Big Week.

With Eighth Air Force's defeat in mid-October 1943, it was clear that unescorted heavy bombers could not attack major German industrial targets against determined fighter opposition without incurring unsupportable losses, and Allied escort fighters lacked the range to accompany the bombers to the more distant target complexes. The technical component of the solution to this problem lay in achieving greater escort fighter ranges. A first step in this direction had been taken as early as July 1943 when the P-47's radius of action from base was expanded from 230 to 340 miles through the use of a 75-gallon belly (or fuselage) tank.[43] But it was not until some months after the second Schweinfurt mission, when experiments with pairs of wing-mounted external drop tanks came to fruition, that real progress was achieved. More specifically, in February 1944 jettisonable wing tanks pushed the reach of Eighth Air Force P-47s and P-38s to what would prove to be their ultimate limits: 475 miles from base for the P-47 and 585 miles for the P-38.[44]

Nevertheless, even these distances were insufficient to cover US bombers all the way to the deepest CBO targets, and full exploitation of the range capabilities of American heavy bombers was not possible until the P-51B/C Mustang, which made its combat debut with Eighth Air Force in December 1943,[45] began to appear in numbers. While not as rugged as the P-47, the marriage of the sleek Mustang airframe with the Rolls-Royce Merlin engine gave the Allies a fighter whose air combat performance was superior in most respects to the main German interceptors, the Me-109 and FW-190.[46] More critically, the P-51B/C had a fuel consumption rate approximately half that of the P-47 or P-38, and once modified by the addition of an 85-gallon fuel tank in the fuselage (behind the pilot) and equipped with external wing tanks, it was able to escort bombers out to the phenomenal distance of 850 miles.[47] Thus, the Mustang evolved into a true long-range escort fighter, and by March 1944 P-51s were operating "in sufficient numbers to protect some of the Eighth's largest daylight bomber formations even over the most distant targets."[48]

With the technical means at hand to provide fighter escort to even the most distant German targets, USSTAF's daylight bomber campaign began to impose increasingly unmanageable attrition on the *Jagdgeschwaders* defending the *Reich*. But contrary to the longstanding hopes of American precision bombardment enthusiasts—as well as of General Eaker's CBO plan—the daylight bomber offensive did not, as we saw in the previous section, succeed in running the Germans out of airframes. Instead, the *Luftwaffe* began to run short of combat-capable aircrews. As Alfred B. Ferguson described the Germans' plight in the official Army Air Forces history:

> No matter how many aircraft were produced, they were of no possible use unless men were available to fly them. This appears to have been the weakest point in the entire German air situation. The bottleneck within the bottleneck was the training program. It has been discovered that . . . the German high command found itself in need of a substantially increased flow of pilot replacements in 1943. Pressure was consequently put on the fighter training schools to speed up their program. But the training of pilots requires aviation fuel; and Germany did not have enough

P-51 MUSTANGS IN CLOSE FORMATION

This flight of Merlin Mustangs was photographed going to or returning from an escort mission over German territory, probably sometime in late 1944. The 'B7' fuselage marking identifies these aircraft as belonging to the 374th Fighter Squadron (361st Fighter Group, Eighth Air Force). The two "straight back" Mustangs on the outsides of the formation are P-51B/Cs. (P-51Bs differed from Cs only in their place of manufacture in the United States.) The closest (B7-E) has the original Mustang canopy configuration; the farthest (B7-H) has been modified with the Spitfire's bulged Malcolm hood. The interior pair of Mustangs can be recognized as D models by their teardrop canopies. The P-51's phenomenal radius of action was largely the result of two factors: a low airframe drag (lower even than the Spitfire's) which permitted unusually low cruise power settings; and a large fuel capacity (achieved by the addition of an internal fuselage tank and two wing-mounted drop tanks). These models of the Merlin Mustang experienced a number of teething problems. Among the more serious were varying degrees of tail-heaviness and instability whenever the fuselage tank contained fuel, guns which jammed any time the pilot tried to fire while pulling more than 1.5–2 Gs, and an assortment of engine difficulties. (US Air Force Photo)

FOUNDATIONS OF US AIR DOCTRINE

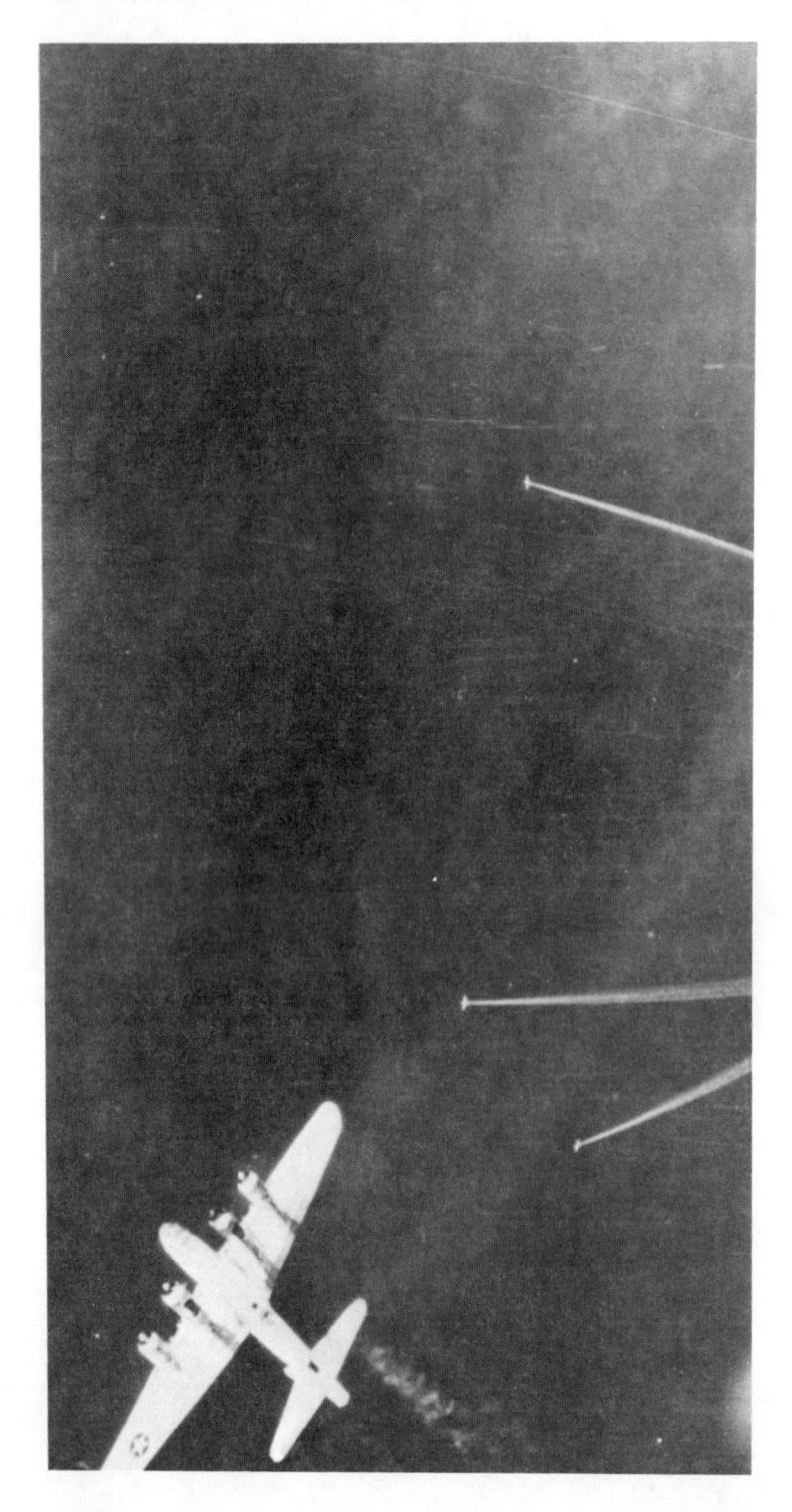

THE LONG REACH
This flight of four P-51s is flying high cover for Eighth Air Force heavy bombers en route to German targets. The flight is operating in two-ship elements. By having the elements fly criss-crossing paths, the faster fighters can maintain their position above the bomber stream, which by this stage of the war could be 80 or 90 miles in length. All the basic elements of the fluid-four patrol formation employed by American fighter pilots in the Korean and Vietnam Wars can be seen in this picture. (US Air Force Photo)

STRATEGIC AIR POWER, WINTER 1944–45
The Eighth Air Force B-17s in this picture were bound for Merseburg, Germany. The tail markings on the aircraft in the foreground identify it as belonging to the 95th Bombardment Group. By the time this mission was flown, the *Luftwaffe* was no longer able to contest American domination of the airspace over Nazi Germany. (US Air Force Photo)

FOUNDATIONS OF US AIR DOCTRINE

leeway in this respect to allow the schools to be prodigal in their gasoline consumption. In fact, it became difficult for the schools to obtain enough for a minimum program. They could, therefore, follow two alternative courses: either fall short of the required replacements or cut hours of training so that fuel allocations would be sufficient to produce the required number of pilots. They chose the latter policy, with the result that pilots entered combat increasingly ill-trained. Faced with thoroughly trained American and British pilots, these replacements fought at a disadvantage, which helps explain the increasing rate of attrition imposed on the GAF [German air force]. The consequent rise in the demand for replacements simply completed the vicious cycle.[49]

General der Jagdflieger Adolf Galland's wartime report to the *Reich* Air Ministry from the spring of 1944 provides firsthand confirmation, from the German perspective, of Ferguson's assessment.

Between January and April 1944 our daytime fighters lost over 1,000 pilots. They included our best squadron, *Gruppe* and *Geschwader* commanders. Each incursion of the enemy is costing us some fifty aircrew. The time has come when our weapon is in sight of collapse.[50]

In retrospect, the eventual collapse of Galland's weapon was not just a function of swelling American numbers. Equally important were two developments within the US Eighth Fighter Command regarding operational employment. The first concerned the bomber escort tactics employed by the American fighters.

Escort operations of Eighth Fighter Command were divided into two main phases. From 4 May 1943, when P-47s escorted Fortresses for the first time, through January 1944, fighters were tied closely to the bombers. They were *not* permitted to desert formations to pursue enemy aircraft. After January 1944, the doctrine of "ultimate pursuit of the enemy" was adopted and our fighters were allowed to follow the enemy until they destroyed him in the air or on the ground.[51]

Prior to this loosening of the escort fighters' ties to the bombers, Eighth Fighter Command had been extremely predictable. In most instances, *Luftwaffe* pilots had been able to count on encountering American fighters only at higher altitudes in the immediate vicinity of the B-17s and B-24s.[52] Now, at General James H. Doolittle's express direction to the head of Eighth Fighter Command, General William E. Kepner, these restrictions were gradually loosened.[53] After a fighter group had finished its escort duties, it was not only allowed but encouraged, fuel permitting, to descend the lower altitudes and seek out German fighters where they had previously been secure.

The other development that served to compound further the friction faced by the *Luftwaffe*'s *Jagdgeschwaders* in the West was the American decision to begin employing escort fighters in an air-to-ground strafing role.

The doctrine of "ultimate pursuit" of enemy fighters, initiated in January 1944, encouraged our fighters to attack enemy airfields, transportation, and other ground targets while returning to base. The success of these low-level operations promoted the planning in March 1944 of two full-scale offensives: Plans "Jackpot" and "Chattanooga Choo Choo". . . . Neither of these plans were fully exploited. Only when weather prevented bomber operations were the fighters free to execute them. On the few occasions when the plans could be put into effect, striking successes resulted.[54]

FRICTION IN 20TH CENTURY WARFARE

The encouragement—particularly to shoot up German airfields—offered by Eighth Fighter Command was subtle but effective: the establishment of a claims category for enemy aircraft destroyed on the ground[55] that would have equal standing with enemy aircraft downed in the air.[56] Colonel Hubert Zemke recorded Eighth Fighter Command's first kill credit in this new category on 11 February 1944.[57]

Since ground targets like *Luftwaffe* airfields were veritable flak traps,[58] this strategy proved a costly one. In the end, "the [Eighth] Air Force lost the cream of its [fighter] pilots" on strafing missions.[59] The Americans, however, were in a position to bear the attrition whereas the Germans were not. *Luftwaffe* daytime fighter tactics had long stressed avoiding combat with Allied fighters to concentrate on the American bombers.[60] But by March 1944, it was becoming harder and harder to avoid the growing numbers of Allied escort fighters, much less deal with the bombers.[61] In the air, the Germans' former sanctuary at the lower altitudes was gone; on the ground, their airfields were constantly at risk to unpredictable strafing attacks by marauding swarms of American fighters; and they no longer had any leeway left for regenerating a cadre of seasoned fighter leaders, or for building up a pilot reserve.[62]

From this stage on—and only from this stage on[63]—the wearing away of the *Luftwaffe*'s ability to control the skies over central Germany and occupied France became a matter of time. Increasingly, USSTAF bomber targets and mission routes were selected, as a matter of deliberate policy, to force the German air force into combat,[64] and, in contrast to the previous fall, USSTAF deep-escort fighters permitted these industrial attacks to be sustained. Although the direct contribution of American precision bombardment to the *Luftwaffe*'s destruction was probably modest through the spring of 1944,[65] the bombers did succeed in fixing the *Luftwaffe*'s day-fighter force, thereby exposing the German *Jagdgeschwaders* to destruction, primarily by American P–47s and P–51s.[66] The cumulative result of this combined action by USSTAF heavy bombers and escort fighters was to push their adversary's friction to levels with which even German ingenuity could not cope.

While we have considered friction both as an impedient and a weapon, the manifestations of *Friktion* within the daylight bomber offensive against the Third *Reich* have by no means been exhausted. In *The Air Plan that Defeated Hitler*, Hansell provides lengthy discussions of two others: errors in selecting industrial targets, particularly the failure to attack systematically German electric power;[67] and the many diversions of effort that caused bombardment resources to be employed against target systems not directly related to Germany's industrial fabric.[68] I believe, however, that enough evidence has been presented to support three judgments concerning general friction's overall role in the CBO.

First, from the time of the May 1943 Trident Conference, which approved Eaker's CBO plan, to the Allied landings at Normandy in June 1944, friction was central to the failures and successes of the American daylight bombing offensive. Eighth Air Force's bitter defeat in October 1943 was the explicit consequence of attempting to apply air power in rigid conformance with Air Corps Tactical School

FOUNDATIONS OF US AIR DOCTRINE

LIEUTENANT GENERAL JAMES H. DOOLITTLE
General Doolittle has recently written that his decision in early 1944, shortly after assuming command of Eighth Air Force, to turn the General Kepner's fighters loose to go hunting Jerries was the most important he made throughout World War II. (US Air Force Photo)

MAJOR GENERAL WILLIAM E. KEPNER
(US Air Force Photo)

IN THE AIR
Gun camera film from a 4th Fighter Group P–51 records the last moments of a Focke-Wulf 190 in March 1944. In the left frame, the American pilot has pulled lead. In the right, his bullets begin striking home around the wing root of the German fighter. The 4th Fighter Group, Eighth Air Force, flew its first mission with Mustangs on 28 February 1944; from 5 March through 24 April of that year, the group was credited with destroying 323 German aircraft (Fry and Ethell, *Escort to Berlin*, p. 52). (J. Romack via J. Ethell)

ON THE GROUND
The pilot of the P–47 in the foreground practically mows the lawn as he swoops in to strafe an unidentified German aircraft at a *Luftwaffe* airfield. (US Air Force Photo)

bombardment doctrine,[69] which is to say as if friction did not exist. Similarly, USSTAF's victory over the *Luftwaffe* in the spring of 1944 required not just an abundance of men and materiel but also the pragmatic success of airmen like Generals Carl T. Spaatz, Doolittle, and Kepner in finding ways to increase German frictions to unmanageable levels.

Second, the price in blood paid by American airmen during this period for failure and victory alike was unnecessarily high. In hindsight, the squandering of lives and planes in October 1943 needed to disabuse Eighth Air Force's leaders of the notion that bomber formations could be invulnerable was, on the whole, a self-inflicted wound. As for the eventual defeat of the *Luftwaffe*'s fighter arm the following spring, the use of bombers predominately to fix the German fighter force,[70] to say nothing of the costly strafing campaign unleashed by Eighth Fighter Command's claims category for enemy aircraft destroyed on the ground,[71] can only politely be described as extravagant.

Third and last, there appears to be precious little in the conduct of the daylight bomber offensive against Germany through June 1944 that vindicates the theory of precision, industrial bombardment developed at the Air Corps Tactical School. To insist otherwise is not merely to ignore the vast difference between real war and war on paper. It is to distort history. Hansell's insistence that with better judgment in selecting targets or less diversion of effort, the war in Europe could have been won by air power alone is, in the final analysis, a two-edged sword. On the one hand, it reveals how very close the American bomber commanders were by early 1944 to possessing the wherewithal to shatter Germany's economy from the air. In theory at least, USSTAF's bomber groups had the requisite destructive potential to do the job. On the other hand, the fact that USSTAF never quite managed to do so shows how powerful a force friction can be. To paraphrase Clausewitz, even the simplest thing is extremely difficult in war, and performance almost always falls far, far short of the ideal.

Epilogue in Korea: Railway Interdiction, August 1951–May 1952

The blindness to general friction so manifest among American airmen during the CBO did not end with Hiroshima and Nagasaki. As I suggested early in Chapter 5, the air power assumptions embedded in AWPD-1 continued to dominate Air Force doctrine long after service independence from the US Army in 1947.

Detailed confirmation of this point can be found in the ten-month interdiction campaign that the Air Force launched against North Korea's railway network in August 1951. The situation that had evolved by this stage of the conflict was one in which political negotiations had temporarily overtaken military operations. The Chinese Communist Forces (CCF) in Korea had planned a Fifth Phase Offensive as an end-of-the-war drive for the spring of 1951.[72] But by "rolling with the punches" and trading battered real estate for Chinese lives, the US Eighth Army managed to stop the CCF drives of late April and mid-May; in fact, the American counterstroke on the ground that immediately followed punished the Chinese as never before.[73] However,

> the Chinese wriggled out of this crisis by pretending a sudden interest in peace. Jacob Malik, the Soviet delegate to the United Nations, proposed truce talks and the Peiping radio hastily acquiesced. The United Nations could scarcely refuse to confer, and on July 10, 1951—a memorable date in the Korean conflict—UN and Communist delegates met at Kaesong.[74]

These talks produced a two-month pause in the fighting on the ground. It was during this lull that the railway interdiction campaign, initially designated "Operation Strangle,"[75] was planned and initiated.

The thinking behind this operation was no different from that evident in AWPD-1. There was, to begin with, considerable optimism about what air power could achieve. While the purpose of the ten-month rail interdiction program was later officially formulated as being merely to "interfere with and disrupt the enemy's lines of communication to such an extent that he will be unable to contain a determined offensive by friendly forces or be unable to mount a sustained offensive himself,"[76] Fifth Air Force planners in Seoul were sufficiently enthused at the outset to advertise that their program would force the Chinese ground forces to fall back to within about 100 miles of the Yalu River.[77]

Next, just as the heart of AWPD-1 lay in the identification of vital target systems, so too the crux of Operation Strangle lay in Fifth Air Force's determination that North Korea's rail transportation system was "of supreme importance to the Communists."[78] The considerations that directly underwrote this determination were two. First, from the Air Force's viewpoint, rail lines offered attractive targets. "Rail lines could not be hidden, nor could rail traffic be diverted to secondary routes or detours as could motor vehicles."[79] Second, Fifth Air Force planners came to believe that the alternative, motor transport, "would prove too costly for the Reds."[80]

These considerations rested, in turn, on the same sort of target-system analysis and engineering-style calculations on which AWPD-1 had been based.

> Eighth Army and Fifth Air Force intelligence officers in Seoul . . . recognized that the Communists had no major industry in North Korea capable of supporting their war effort, and, except for a few arms factories at Pyongyang and Kuni-ri, the Reds were compelled to bring their war supplies from Manchuria or Siberia. According to Eighth Army intelligence, the Reds had 60 divisions of various types in the battle zone south of a line drawn through Sariwon. The Eighth Army conservatively estimated that each enemy division could maintain itself in limited combat with 40 tons of supplies each day. Therefore, the Red logistical system had to transport 2,400 tons of supplies to the battleline each day. Having determined the amount of supplies the Reds required, Fifth Air Force officers examined the Red transportation system and found that it comprised motor and rail transport. In the front lines the Reds used human and animal bearers, but they depended upon trucks and trains for long hauls. The Russian-built trucks that the Communists possessed each carried approximately two tons, which meant that 1,200 trucks were required to haul a day's supplies to the Communist armies. The Eighth Army estimated that the round-trip time of a truck from Antung to the frontlines was ten days, and, to play safe, the Fifth Air Force figured the round-trip time at five days. According to the Fifth Air Force figure, the Reds would need 6,000 trucks to transport 2,400 tons of daily resupply from Antung to the battle

zone south of Sariwon. Each Korean boxcar had a load capacity of 20 tons, and thus only 120 boxcars could transport the Red daily supply requirement. . . . Because of its greater load-hauling capacity, the North Korean railway network was clearly the primary transportation capability of the Reds.[81]

In light of this analysis, Fifth Air Force planners then set about determining the best way to attack the North Korean railway system. For a variety of reasons, they concluded that direct destruction of railway track and roadbeds offered the most efficient approach; and based upon this determination, they computed the precise number of daily sorties available from Far East Air Forces and US Navy aerial assets that would be required to do the job.[82]

The thinking behind Operation Strangle involved a series of interconnected assumptions, and I think it will suffice to note that the collective risk inherent in them was not adequately taken into account by Fifth Air Force planners. In the event, Communist countermeasures to Strangle were able, by late December 1951, to break the attempted US aerial blockade of Pyongyang and win "the use of all key rail arteries."[83] Strangle's sequel in the spring of 1952, Operation Saturate, met much the same fate.

In retrospect, the official history of the Air Force in Korea concluded that although the comprehensive, ten-month railway-interdiction campaign had attained its limited purpose of hindering the Communist logistical effort, "the operation nevertheless disclosed certain regrettable failures in command, in planning, and in execution."[84] The planning defects in particular—underestimating the force structure needed to effect the desired degree of interdiction and failure to foresee the enemy's potential countermeasures[85]—document the same blindness to the cumulative dimension of general friction that bedeviled the CBO. In this sense there was no major change in the foundations of American air doctrine from the late 1930s through the early 1950s. Indeed my personal experience during 100 missions in the F–4 over North Vietnam, as well as that of other Air Force aviators who flew combat there, strongly suggests that the mindset of AWPD–1 continues to dominate Air Force thinking to this day, despite the fact that the nuclear missile age has been upon us for two decades.

PART 2

Friction in the Missile Age

There has been a systematic overestimation of the importance of the so-called "fog of war"—the inevitable uncertainties, misinformation, disorganization, or even breakdown of organized units—that must be expected to influence central war operations.[86]

Herman Kahn

> The overwhelming odds are that when and if the crisis comes, the man occupying the seat of power in the United States will exercise at least the caution of a John F. Kennedy during the Cuban missile crisis, who by his brother's intimate account was appalled by the possibility that any precipitous use of physical power by the United States would unleash nuclear holocaust.[87]
>
> Bernard Brodie

The thrust of Brodie's 1978 paper, "The Development of Nuclear Strategy," was to review some of the rumination and writing on nuclear strategy and the nature of deterrence that had followed the publication of *The Absolute Weapon* in 1946.[88] A number of provocative theses emerged from this critical review.

(1) Contrary to the implication of Albert Wohlstetter's well-known article "The Delicate Balance of Terror," the nuclear balance between the United States and the Soviet Union never has been, or ever could be, "delicate."[89]

(2) Mr. Paul Nitze's idea that the Soviet political leadership might attempt a surprise nuclear attack against the land-based portion of the US retaliatory force on the esoteric calculation that the American president could be counted on to quit the fight rather than to retaliate presumes a willingness to take risks, if not foolishness, on the part of the Soviets that is, literally, beyond belief.[90]

(3) The Schlesinger-Lambeth proposal that, in an extremely tense crisis, any useful purpose is likely to be served by firing off strategic nuclear weapons, however limited in number, is so divorced from how human beings actually behave in such circumstances as to fit Raymond Aron's definition of strategic fiction analogous to science fiction.[91]

In considering whether friction might be as important in the missile age as it was during World War II, it is not so much the explicit content of these observations as their underlying rationale that is of interest. As we will see, frictional considerations underlie much of what Brodie had to say in "The Development of Nuclear Strategy."

The Not-So-Delicate Balance of Terror

Turning first to the stability issue broached in "The Delicate Balance of Terror," the stated aim of Wohlstetter's 1959 article was to debunk the popular view that the possession of even a relatively small number of nuclear weapons and delivery vehicles would effortlessly, or necessarily, suffice to deter nuclear war. Characterizing deterrence as being able to strike back in spite of an enemy attack,[92] Wohlstetter's case for the precarious nature of the US-USSR nuclear balance hinged on enumerating the successive hurdles that American bombers would encounter in (1) surviving a Soviet first-strike, (2) receiving valid launch and execution orders, (3) reaching the Soviet Union, (4) penetrating active USSR air defenses, and (5) destroying the target despite the Soviet Union's dispersal, hardening, and civil defense measures. In light of these hurdles, Wohlstetter offered the following assessment:

> Deterrence is a matter of comparative risks. The balance is not automatic. First, since thermonuclear weapons give an enormous advantage to the aggressor, it takes great ingenuity and realism at any given level of nuclear technology to devise a stable equilibrium. And second, this technology itself is changing with fantastic speed. Deterrence will require urgent and continuing effort.[93]

It turns out that this assessment was motivated by more than just a desire to correct popular misconceptions about deterrence. According to Brodie, "The Delicate Balance of Terror" was also inspired by Wohlstetter's frustration with the US Air Force. After more than a year's work, Wohlstetter's project group at the Rand Corporation had concluded that the best means of protecting American bombers from a Soviet surprise attack "was a slightly-below-ground shelter for each aircraft."[94] But the Air Force had vehemently rejected this solution in favor of the Douhetan notion of striking at the enemy before he could get off the ground. Thus, "The Delicate Balance of Terror" was a public appeal aimed at pressuring the Air Force into paying more attention to Rand's recommendations.

In the end, events overtook Wohlstetter's concern about sheltering bombers. His article appeared "on the eve of the coming of the ICBM [intercontinental ballistic missile], which lent itself to being put underground without controversy, and not far behind was the Polaris submarine."[95] So despite the strong theoretical reasons for sheltering bombers, the issue was rendered far less pressing by the emergence of land- and sea-based intercontinental ballistic missiles.

How did Brodie view this indecisive outcome from the vantage point of the late 1970s? His initial comments in "The Development of Nuclear Strategy" appear quite unremarkable coming from the author of *The Absolute Weapon* and *Strategy in the Missile Age*.

> The Air Force still has no shelters for these bombers and does not contemplate any.... In fact, on the often-mentioned grounds that they can be sent off early because they are recallable, our bombers are frequently projected as virtually a non-vulnerable retaliatory force. Well, perhaps they are, if one knows how to read and respond to the various types of ambiguous warning. The problem is not only not to send them off . . . late but also not to send them off too early.[96]

By and large, the thinking in this passage is that of the speculative theorist. The final quip, especially, is vintage Brodie and shows little change from *Strategy in the Missile Age*.[97]

Against this backdrop, Brodie's next remarks should have come as a shock to anyone familiar with his previous writings. Having more or less reiterated the theoretical soundness of Wohlstetter's concern over sheltering bombers, he immediately added:

> However, I do support fully the belief implicit in the Air Force position that some kind of political warning will always be available. Attack out of the blue, which is to say without a condition of crisis, is one of those worst-case fantasies that we have to cope with as a starting point for our security planning, but there are very good reasons why it has never happened historically, at least in modern times, and for comparable reasons I regard it as so improbable for a nuclear age as to approach virtual certainty that it will not happen, which is to say it is not a possibility worth spending much money on.
>
> For similar reasons, I must add before leaving the Wohlstetter article that I could never accept the implications of his title—that the balance between the Soviet Union and the United States ever has been or ever could be "delicate." My reasons have to do mostly with human inhibitions against taking monumental risks or doing things which are universally detested, except under motivations far more compelling than those suggested by Wohlstetter in his article. This point is more relevant today than ever before because of the numbers and variety of American forces that an enemy would need to have a high certitude of destroying in one fell swoop.[98]

What I would stress is the extent to which these mostly sensible comments regarding the stability of the US-USSR nuclear balance represent a definite break with Brodie's writings on deterrence through the late 1950s. The third of the three conclusions that Brodie had, by 1959, elevated to the status of a basic principle of action for the United States in the thermonuclear era was the prospect that deterrence could fail, and the theoretical basis for this conclusion in the text of *Strategy in the Missile Age* indicates that there was considerable congruence between Brodie's views on nuclear stability during the 1950s and Wohlstetter's. For instance, Brodie had asserted at one point: "The typical citizen simply does not believe that there is any chance of a total war occurring. In that respect, he is plainly wrong."[99] And even earlier in *Strategy in the Missile Age*, he had given the following explication of the first of two basic principles about defense in general and warning in particular:

> A conspicuous inability or unreadiness to defend our retaliatory force must tend to provoke the opponent to destroy it; in other words, it tempts him to an aggression he might not otherwise contemplate. How can he permit our SAC to live and constantly threaten his existence, if he believes he can destroy it with impunity?[100]

It seems fair to say, then, that the Brodie of *Strategy in the Missile Age* felt that the nuclear balance was delicate. Certainly, it was the delicacy of the balance that he emphasized in his theoretical writings through 1959, not its stability.

By comparison, Brodie's 1977 reflections on Wohlstetter's article display a markedly different viewpoint. Unexpectedly, we now find Brodie insisting that the balance of terror neither was, nor ever could be, delicate. His reasons, moreover, have little to do with speculative abstractions about nuclear options. Instead, we find him resting his case on the inhibitions of ordinary human beings against taking monumental risks or universally detested actions without compelling motivations.

The Emergence of Friction in Brodie's Thought

I emphasize the role of frictional considerations in "The Development of Nuclear Strategy" because it also formed the basis of his brusk dismissal, somewhat later in the article, of the supposed vulnerability of the US retaliatory force to a partially disarming, surprise Soviet attack.

> Mr. Paul Nitze . . . offers us a scenario in which the Soviet Union delivers a surprise attack which does not, to be sure, eliminate more than a portion of our retaliatory forces but which leaves us so inferior that the President, whoever he is at the time, elects to quit the fight before making any reply in kind. Thus, the Soviet Union succeeds in making that otherwise elusive first-strike-with-impunity! An interesting thought, but it would take an exceedingly venturesome and also foolish Soviet leader to *bank* on the President's not retaliating. Even Mr. Nitze is not really sure; he only says he *believes* the President would not.[101]

Again, the break with *Strategy in the Missile Age* is sharp. Whereas in 1959 Brodie had emphasized that *any* unreadiness to defend our retaliatory nuclear forces would tend to tempt the Soviets to undertake aggressions they might not otherwise contemplate, by 1977 he no longer appeared greatly bothered by possibilities as remote as the elusive first-strike-with-impunity. Such distant contingencies had, he conceded, a certain intellectual fascination. But with over 9,000 strategic warheads in the US arsenal, a partially disarming first-strike seemed far too daring psychologically to warrant being taken seriously.

In this same vein, the powerful psychological inhibitions that national decision makers would surely experience, even in contemplating limited nuclear gambits, were also the source of Brodie's difficulties in "The Development of Nuclear Strategy" with the Schlesinger-Lambeth policy of selective nuclear options. As explained by Benjamin S. Lambeth in 1976, the objective of this revised American targeting policy was to enhance "US deterrence credibility not only against a full-scale Soviet attack on the CONUS [continental United States] but at all levels of the nuclear spectrum, both against the CONUS and in possible local theaters of engagement."[102] In other words, the immediate aim was to supplement the last resort, massive response schemes of the basic SIOP (Single Integrated Operational Plan) "with both a range of preplanned 'limited nuclear options' (LNOs) and the necessary real-time retargeting capabilities and command and control support to permit the NCA [National Command Authorities] to improvise strike options tailored to the unique demands of the situation *during* a crisis."[103]

A variety of concerns prompted this policy. There was the natural desire to discourage the Soviets from attempting to reap political gains by threatening nuclear use. But even more fundamental was the hope of being able to provide the American president with additional targeting choices that might terminate conflict before large-scale damage to cities had occurred during any confrontation involving actual nuclear operations.[104] To paraphrase (then) Secretary of Defense James R. Schlesinger, limited nuclear options offered "a means of carrying out the *least miserable* option in a situation where *all* options would be painful, yet where some (such as indiscriminately unleashing of the full SIOP) would be far more painful than necessary."[105]

From a Clausewitzian perspective, the truly revealing elements in Lambeth's 1976 *Selective Nuclear Options in American Strategic Policy* are his few examples. To cite his most detailed example of a limited nuclear option:

> Let us postulate a European theater war in which things are going badly for NATO and the US NCA decides to raise the stakes by launching a demonstrative nuclear attack on a Soviet rear-area support facility in the Western portion of the Soviet ZI [Zone of the Interior]. Let us further assume that the President would prefer to use only a single delivery vehicle so as to leave no room for Soviet doubt that the operation was consciously being limited. At first glance, an ICBM would appear to be the obvious weapon for such an assignment. Yet it could also be dangerous because being launched directly from CONUS, it might give the Soviets the unintended impression that the United States had embarked on full-fledged intercontinental war. In such a situation, the President might instead wish to use an aircraft delivery system, such as a forward-deployed FB-111 rotated from its main operating base in the United States and launched out of England. Such an alternate might appear particularly attractive because the FB-111 could perhaps be perceived by the adversary as being somewhat more consonant with the notion of "extended theater war" than an ICBM or SLBM. On the other hand, the FB-111 would have to confront a fully alerted and undegraded Soviet air defense network, and the US NCA would accordingly have to ask whether a single aircraft could successfully penetrate the assigned target. If it turned out that multiple sorties of aircraft using nuclear SRAM [short range attack missile] attacks en route for defense suppression would have to be dispatched to assure a high-confidence FB-111 strike, the *image* of the operation in Soviet eyes might begin to look altogether different from what the US NCA intended, notwithstanding the limited and discriminating *objective* of the mission. Given such a dilemma, what sort of choice would the President make? The answer is by no means clear. There can be no mistaking the considerable operational and political difficulties he would have to confront.[106]

For the Brodie of "The Development of Nuclear Strategy," an even more basic question about such scenarios was their psychological plausibility. In the midst of a US-USSR crisis, would any sane American leader want to experiment with nuclear weapons, however selectively? Lambeth's own example suggests that such experimentation probably would be the last thing an American president would try. The operational frictions involved in any such demonstration are too great and the consequences of error or miscalculation too appalling.[107]

The Cuban Missile Crisis

The one historical instance of such a situation, the Cuban missile crisis, appears to confirm this conclusion. As Brodie pointed out in 1978, President Kennedy showed no eagerness on that occasion to experiment with nuclear weapons. Chilled by intelligence estimates that the Soviet missiles being readied in Cuba would, if launched, kill 80 million Americans within minutes,[108] Kennedy and his close advisers saw themselves engaged in making decisions that, if wrong, "could mean the destruction of the human race."[109] The President, as reported by his brother, was particularly sensitive to the importance of understanding the full implications of every step: "It isn't the first step that concerns me," John Kennedy said in discussing the proposed air strike, "but both sides escalating to the fourth and fifth step—and we don't go to the sixth because there is no one around to do so."[110]

The profound risks and uncertainties perceived by Kennedy and his advisers during the Cuban missile crisis are, of course, what Brodie seized upon in "The Development of Nuclear Strategy" to condemn the whole idea of limited nuclear options.

> Where Lambeth argues that the Schlesinger proposals introduced flexibility into an area of thinking hitherto marked by extreme rigidity, and that it introduces also strategy (in the form of choice) where no possibility of strategy existed before, he is simply playing with words. The rigidity lies in the situation, not in the thinking. The difference between war and no war is great enough, but that between strategic thermonuclear war and war as we have known it in the past is certain to be greater still. Any rigidity which keeps us from entering the new horrors or from nibbling at it in the hopes that a nibble will clearly be seen as such by the other side, is a salutary rigidity. And we need not worry whether the choices the President is obliged to make during extremely tense situations fill out anyone's definition of strategy. The important thing is that they be wise choices under the circumstances.[111]

Brodie's assessment is a ringing condemnation of theory unrestrained by practical realities if there ever was one, and the essential basis of his criticism is, once again, friction. Even in Clausewitz's time, the commander's responsibility to make life-or-death choices for hundreds or thousands of people imposed a terrible burden. In the age of thermonuclear weapons, that frictional burden, far from being erased by technology, has been horrifically multiplied.

This thought suggests a further insight about general friction: It is probably not going to go away. As long as people make war for political ends and are subject to the violence implicit in any use of military means, the very structure of human cognition argues that friction will continue to be the fundamental atmosphere of war. Technological innovations can affect the ways in which friction manifests itself. But if thermonuclear weapons have failed to vanquish general friction, I can see little reason to suppose that future changes in weaponry will do so.

NOTES

CHAPTER 6

1. Paul R. Schratz, "Clausewitz and the Naval Strategist," *Shipmate*, June 1980, p. 6.
2. Thomas A. Fabyanic, "Strategic Analysis and MX Deployment," *Strategic Review*, Fall 1982, p. 30.
3. Hansell, *The Air Plan that Defeated Hitler*, p. 136.
4. Hansell, *The Air Plan that Defeated Hitler*, p. 193.
5. Fabyanic, "Strategic Analysis and MX Deployment," p. 31.
6. Hansell, *The Air Plan that Defeated Hitler*, p. 75.
7. During World War II, American airmen continued to imbue the cause of air power, especially industrial bombardment, with the flavor of a holy crusade. As two of the official historians of the US Army Air Forces during that conflict later wrote, the USAAF "was guided by the sense of a special mission to perform" (Alfred Goldberg and Albert F. Simpson, "Final Reorganization," *The Army Air Forces in World War II*, Vol. 2, p. 735). A powerful, but I think accurate, evocation of this sense of a special mission can be found in Beirne Lay and Sy Bartlett's 1948 novel *Twelve O'Clock High!* Beirne Lay was one of the original seven officers who deployed to England in February 1942 with General Eaker; he later saw combat with the 100th Bombardment Group and commanded a B-24 unit (Roger A. Freeman, *The Mighty Eighth: Units, Men and Machines (A History of the US 8th Army Air Force)* (Garden City, New York: Doubleday, 1970), pp. 4 and 141). However, to appreciate the price in blood paid by American aircrews to further the cause of strategic air power, one should also read Bendiner's *The Fall of Fortresses*.
8. von Clausewitz, p. 78. Clausewitz entitled this subsection of Chapter 1, Book One, of *On War* 'Modifications in Practice.'
9. von Clausewitz, pp. 78–80.
10. To cite two instances among dozens of Clausewitz's rejection of calculations and formulas: "absolute, so-called mathematical factors never find a firm basis in military calculations. From the very start, there is an interplay of possibilities, probabilities, good luck and bad that weaves its way throughout the length and breadth of the tapestry. In the whole range of human activities, war most closely resembles a game of cards" (von Clausewitz, p. 86); "in the conduct of war, perception cannot be governed by laws . . . no prescriptive formulation universal enough to deserve the name of law [meaning the relationship between things and their effects] can be applied to the constant change and diversity of the phenomena of war" (pp. 151 and 152).
11. Hansell, *The Air Plan that Defeated Hitler*, p. 121. Clausewitz explicitly described weather as a chance factor in war. "This tremendous friction, which cannot, as in mechanics, be reduced to a few points, is everywhere in contact with chance, and brings about effects that cannot be measured, just because they are largely due to chance. One, for example, is the weather" (von Clausewitz, p. 120).
12. US Army Air Forces leaders in the European theater during World War II were often wrong in their estimates of the enemy situation, and their evaluations of the damage inflicted on German targets were frequently exaggerated (Craven and Cate, *The Army Air Forces in World War II*, Vol. 2, p. x).
13. Secretary, Office of the Combined Chiefs of Staff, *Trident Conference: May 1943, Papers and Minutes of Meetings* (Washington, DC: 1943), National Archives Record Group 218, p. 14. The rationale for making the *Luftwaffe* an intermediate objective of the CBO was as follows: "The German

fighter force is taking a toll of our forces both by day and by night, not only in terms of combat losses but more especially in terms of tactical effectiveness. If the German fighters are materially increased in number, it is quite conceivable that they could make our daylight bombing unprofitable and perhaps our night bombing too. Conversely, if the German fighter force is partially neutralized, our own effectiveness will be vastly improved'' (p. 13).

14. Alfred B. Ferguson, ''POINTBLANK,'' *The Army Air Forces in World War II*, Vol. 2, p. 666; also see Joe L. Norris, *The Combined Bomber Offensive: 1 January to 6 June 1944 (Short Title: AAFRH-22)* (Washington, DC: Headquarters Army Air Forces, April 1947), p. 100. While the need to defeat the German air force in Western Europe initially grew out of the internal logic of the CBO itself, this task took on even greater importance as Allied commanders began to contemplate landings in France and Italy. ''It is a conceded fact,'' General Arnold told the commanders of the Eighth and Fifteen Air Forces on 27 December 1943, ''that Overlord and Anvil will not be possible unless the German air force is destroyed. Therefore, my personal message to you—this is a MUST—is to, *'Destroy the Enemy Air Force wherever you find them, in the air, on the ground and in the factories'* '' (Futrell, *Ideas, Concepts, Doctrine: A History of Basic Thinking in the United States Air Force 1907–1964*, p. 78).

15. Ira C. Eaker to Joint Chiefs of Staff (JCS), 29 April 1943, *Minutes of Meeting: Presentation of Combined Bomber Offensive Plan to the JCS*, National Archives Record Group 218, CCS 334, 71st–86th Meetings, p. 9 (A31833). At this point, Eaker was clearly convinced that escort fighters would not be crucial to the eventual success of the long-range bomber offensive. Instead he saw them as an interim measure that would only be necessary until Eighth Air Force had acquired enough operational airframes to attack in strength. Three hundred heavy bombers (100 for diversions and 200 for the main attack) constituted the minimum unescorted force size deemed sufficient to penetrate German fighter defenses and to carry out worthwhile destruction of deep targets without unacceptable losses (p. 6 (A31830)). Note, too, that during the execution of the CBO, as opposed to its planning, a portion of the daylight heavy bomber effort was allocated to direct bombardment of *Luftwaffe* airfields. But although airfield bombardment eventually accounted for around 10 percent of Eighth Air Force's wartime bomb tonnage (Hansell, *The Air Plan that Defeated Hitler*, pp. 279–80), this target system was not systematically attacked. For example, from 20 February through 30 April 1944, the period during which the *Luftwaffe* lost the battle for control of the *Reich's* skies, only 14 of the 38 fields against which Eighth's heavies mounted saturation bombing raids were in Germany (Freeman, *Mighty Eighth War Diary*, pp. 183–234). Further, Eighth Air Force's own account of its tactical development does not even mention airfield bombardment in discussing the reasons for the German air force's defeat in the first half of 1944 (William E. Kepner, *Eighth Air Force Tactical Development: August 1942–May 1945* (England: Eighth Air Force and Army Air Forces Evaluation Board, European Theater of Operations, July 1945), pp. 76–77), and the Army Air Forces' classified history of this period attributes the *Luftwaffe*'s decline to Allied ''attacks on the aircraft industry combined with the campaign to knock the GAF out of the air'' (Norris, p. 208). Thus, there seems good reason to think that sporadic airfields bombing by the command's B–17s and B–24s did not play any great role in defeating the German fighter arm prior to the Normandy invasion.

16. Ferguson, *The Army Air Forces in World War II*, Vol. 2, p. 705.
17. Craven and Cate, *The Army Air Forces in World War II*, Vol. 2, p. xii.
18. Kepner, *Eighth Air Force Tactical Development: August 1942–May 1945*, p. 100.
19. Kepner, *Eighth Air Force Tactical Development: August 1942–May 1945*, p. 86.
20. Freeman, *The Mighty Eighth: Units, Men, and Machines*, p. 74.
21. Major Edgar F. Woodard, HQ US STRATEGIC AIR FORCES IN EUROPE statistical data, September 1945, file 570.677A, Albert F. Simpson Historical Research Center, Maxwell AFB, Alabama. These data sheets were originally transmitted under a HQ US STRATEGIC AIR FORCES IN EUROPE ''carrier sheet'' with a CONFIDENTIAL classification. The table below, which was extracted from them, summarizes Allied claims from daylight bombing missions in October 1943. Woodward's package was prepared for the express purpose of comparing Allied claims with actual German losses. The judgment of Colonel Lewis P. Powell, to whom Woodard sent the data, was that at least through 1943, British and American claims had been ''substantially in excess of actual German combat losses'' (Ibid).

ALLIED CLAIMS IN THE EUROPEAN THEATER OF OPERATIONS, OCTOBER 1943			
	BOMBER Crew Claims		FIGHTER Claims	
Date	Destroyed +Probable	Damaged	Destroyed +Probable	Damaged
4 Oct 43	112	47	25	3
8 Oct 43	201	81	24	14
9 Oct 43	156	63	–	–
10 Oct 43	204	55	30	10
14 Oct 43	215	88	16	7
TOTALS for October 1943	888	334	95	34

22. Murray, *Strategy for Defeat: The Luftwaffe 1933–1945*, p. 225.

23. "Fighter claims," Eighth Air Force tacticians stated in July 1945, "are not subject to nearly as much error as bomber claims. Claim-evaluators have movie [or gun camera] films of the fights to aid them. There may be some factor of error in fighter claims, but it is believed that fighter claims generally are close to the truth" (Kepner, *Eighth Air Force Tactical Development: August 1942–May 1945*, p. 100). Eighth's fighters were using gun cameras in July 1943 ("German Fighters Destroyed in Air, as Shown by Gun Camera Films Taken from P–47s," *IMPACT: The Army Air Forces' Confidential Picture History of World War II* (New York: James Parton, 1980), Book 2, pp. 10–11; this article, along with selected gun-camera photos, appeared in the October 1943 issue of IMPACT).

24. For the Schweinfurt mission of 14 October 1943, the bomber crews' initial tally was 288 German fighters destroyed in action (Freeman, *The Mighty Eighth: Units, Men, and Machines*, p. 79). While this figure was reduced to 186, even the reassessed tally exceeded the losses reflected in German Air Ministry records—31 aircraft destroyed and another 12 written off as unrepairable—by a factor of 4.33 (Ferguson, *The Army Air Forces in World War II*, Vol. 2, p. 704; Murray, *Strategy for Defeat: The Luftwaffe 1933–1945*, p. 225).

25. Murray, *Strategy for Defeat: The Luftwaffe 1933–1945*, p. 225.

26. Freeman, *Mighty Eighth War Diary*, pp. 123–26.

27. Murray, *Strategy for Defeat: The Luftwaffe 1933–1945*, Table XLIX on p. 234.

28. Murray, *Strategy for Defeat: The Luftwaffe 1933–1945*, p. 226.

29. Murray, *Strategy for Defeat: The Luftwaffe 1933–1945*, p. 170. At the time of this letter, Eaker's senior officers were absolutely convinced that 300 bombers could "attack any target in Germany with less than 4 percent losses" (Ibid.). Six months later, Eaker presented much the same view to the US Joint Chiefs of Staff during his presentation of the CBO Plan in Washington DC (Eaker, p. 6 (A31830)).

30. Ferguson, *The Army Air Forces in World War II*, Vol. 2, p. 699. The 1st Bombardment Division dispatched 149 B–17s to Schweinfurt and the 3rd put up 142; in addition, a small force of B–24s from the 2nd Bombardment Division flew what turned out to be a fruitless diversionary mission (Ibid.).

31. Freeman, *The Mighty Eighth: Units, Men, and Machines*, p. 79. The Schweinfurt mission of 14 October 1943 witnessed the first large-scale use of standoff rockets coordinated with other fighter tactics (Ferguson, *The Army Air Forces in World War II*, Vol. 2, p. 699). For a firsthand account of this mission, see Elmer Bendiner, *The Fall of Fortresses* (New York: G.P. Putnam's Sons, 1980), pp. 213–25.

32. Arthur B. Ferguson, "Big Week" in Wesley F. Craven and James L. Cate, *The Army Air Forces in World War II*, Vol. 3, Europe: *ARGUMENT to V-E Day, January 1944 to May 1945* (Chicago: University of Chicago Press, 1951), pp. 33 and 35.

33. USSTAF (originally abbreviated USSAFE) effectively came into being as the overall headquarters for the American daylight bomber effort in early January 1944 (Freeman, *The Mighty Eighth: Units, Men, and Machines*, p. 104). USSTAF's heavy bomber elements were Eighth Air Force in England and

the Fifteenth in Italy (Craven and Cate, *The Army Air Forces in World War II*, Vol. 3, p. xi). Along with the creation of USSTAF, Generals Spaatz and Doolittle were brought from North Africa to take over USSTAF and Eighth Air Force, respectively, while General Eaker was given the newly created Mediterranean Allied Air Forces (Murray, *Strategy for Defeat: The Luftwaffe 1933–1945*, p. 236).

34. Murray, *Strategy for Defeat: The Luftwaffe 1933–1945*, p. 237.

35. Ferguson, *The Army Air Forces in World War II*, Vol. 3, p. 43. During Big Week, Eighth Air Force contributed 3,300 sorties and the Fifteenth 500 (Ibid.). Though USSTAF targets included German "aero-engines, ball bearings, transportation, and other industries," the heaviest dosages of bombs were against "airframe assembly and components factories" (Norris, p. 110).

36. MacIsaac, *Strategic Bombing in World War Two: The Story of the United States Strategic Bombing Survey*, pp. 161–2.

37. Hastings, *Bomber Command*, p. 223.

38. Hansell, *The Air Plan that Defeated Hitler*, p. 197.

39. J. Kenneth Galbraith et al., *The Effects of Strategic Bombing on the German War Economy* (Washington, DC: US Government Printing Office, 31 October 1945), p. 6. "Hitler had confidently planned on a short war of conquest and he envisioned no need for complete industrial mobilization. Even after the setback on the Russian Front in the winter of 1941–42, which prompted greatly increased production, much of the German economy continued to function on a one shift per day basis and, unlike England and the United States, few women were used in industry" (Hansell, *The Air Plan that Defeated Hitler*, pp. 197–98).

40. While Allied estimates of German fighter production were reasonably accurate throughout 1943, following Big Week they increasingly became, in the words of the official Army Air Forces history, "grossly optimistic" (Ferguson, *The Army Air Forces in World War II*, Vol. 3, p. 45). "The average monthly production of German single-engine fighters during the last half of 1943 was 851, as against Allied estimates of 645. For the first half of 1944, on the other hand, actual production reached a monthly average of 1,581, whereas Allied intelligence estimated only 655. Allied estimates were even further off in dealing with the antifriction-bearing industry" (Ibid.). The USSTAF judgment that Big Week dealt the German aircraft industry a blow "from which it never fully recovered" is, therefore, hard to support (Norris, p. 107a). But in light of USSTAF's bomber losses during Big Week—156 heavies from Eighth Air Force and 95 from Fifteenth (Ibid., pp. 110–11)—the American assessment is certainly understandable.

41. 'Ultra' was a codeword which British Intelligence introduced in June 1941 to identify decrypts of German naval Enigma wireless traffic (high-grade signals intelligence) for the purpose of transmission to selected Flag Officers by means of a totally secure, one-time cypher (F. H. Hinsley, *British Intelligence in the Second World War* (London: Her Majesty's Stationery Office, 1979), Vol. 1, footnote on p. 139 and p. 346). By 1943, the British Ultra decryption effort at Bletchley Park had become a major industry, employing some 6,000 people in "unbuttoning" around 2,000 Enigma-enciphered German wireless signals a day (Anthony Cave Brown, *Bodyguard of Lies* (New York: Harper and Row, 1975), p. 253). During the decisive struggle for air superiority over the *Reich* that followed Big Week, Ultra greatly aided Allied air commanders in keeping pressure on the *Luftwaffe* where it hurt most by revealing the effectiveness of USSTAF tactics and the severity of the German air force's difficulties (Murray, *Strategy for Defeat: The Luftwaffe 1933–1945*, p. 244). But even Ultra failed to provide much insight into either bomb damage against specific targets or the overall effects bombardment was exerting on the German fighter industry.

42. Ferguson, *The Army Air Forces in World War II*, Vol. 3, p. 60. Under Speer's management, the *Reich*'s aviation industry delivered over 25,000 single-engine fighters during 1944 (Ibid.).

43. Kepner, *Eighth Air Force Tactical Development: August 1942–May 1945*, p. 96. July 1943 marked the advent of the first practical external drop tanks in Eighth Fighter Command.

44. Kepner, *Eighth Air Force Tactical Development: August 1942–May 1945*, p. 96.

45. Ferguson, *The Army Air Forces in World War II*, Vol. 3, p. 49.

46. Freeman, *The Mighty Eighth: Units, Men, and Machines*, p. 120. At altitudes up to 28,000 feet, the P-51B (or C) "was 50 mph faster than the FW-190A, increasing to 70 mph above that height. It had a similar lead on the Me-109G being 30 mph faster at 15,000 feet and increasing to 50 mph by 30,000

feet. The Me-109G had better accleration in the initial stages of a dive but the Mustang could overhaul it if the 109 pilot was foolish enough to prolong the dive: there were no problems in out-diving the FW-190. In dogfights it could easily out-turn the Messerschmitt and usually had the edge on the Focke-Wulf. The latter had a much better rate of roll though the P-51B was on a par with the Me-109G in this respect. Rate of climb was also superior to most models of these German fighters that were met in battle at this time [early 1944]'' (Ibid.). This summary appears to have been based on tactical trials at RAF Wittering in early 1944 during which a new Mustang III (P-51B/C) was flown against the FW-109A and Me-109G (Jeffrey Ethell, *Mustang: A Documentary History of the P-51* (London: Jane's, 1981), pp. 58 and 60-61). The Mustang's solid performance in air combat was an important factor in the willingness of American pilots to stick with the airplane despite its considerable teething problems (Ethell, pp. 62-65).

47. In March 1944 it was demonstrated that the P-51 with two 75-gallon wing tanks could provide escort for bombers to a point approximately 650 miles from base; with two 108-gallon tanks, this distance was extended to 850 miles (Ferguson, *The Army Air Forces in World War II*, Vol. 3, p. 49).

48. Ferguson, *The Army Air Forces in World War II*, Vol. 3, p. 49. For example, on the mission to Berlin of 8 March 1944, four groups of P-51s, numbering 174 fighters, supported the bombers "on the last leg of the penetration flight, throughout the target area, and for considerable distance on the withdrawal'' (p. 52).

49. Ferguson, *The Army Air Forces in World War II*, Vol. 3, p. 62.

50. Hans Dieter Berenbrok (Cajus Bekker pseudonym), *The Luftwaffe War Diaries*, trans. Frank Zeigler (Garden City, New York: Doubleday, 1968), p. 522. More recent research has put *Luftwaffe* fighter crew losses for February and March 1944 at 945 (Murray, *Strategy for Defeat: The Luftwaffe 1933-1945*, Table LIII on p. 240).

51. Kepner, *Eighth Air Force Tactical Development: August 1942-May 1945*, p. 50.

52. Freeman, *The Mighty Eighth: Units, Men, and Machines*, p. 119. Even as late as November 1943, the conventional wisdom within units like the Eighth Air Force's 4th Fighter Group was that the P-47 was not a match for the Me-109 or FW-190 below 19,000 feet (John T. Godfrey, *The Look of Eagles* (New York: Random House, 1958), p. 76).

53. General Doolittle recently authored the following account of his decision to unleash the Eighth Air Force's fighters soon after assuming command from General Eaker in early 1944. "Even though we were soon mounting large missions, we were still sustaining serious losses to Jerry fighters. Something had to be done, and it was on a visit to Bill Kepner that I made my most important decision of World War II. Bill Kepner was a typically aggressive fighter pilot, and he was chafing under the restrictions being placed on his fighters' freedom of action in their prevailing role of escorts to the bombers. My eye was caught by a prominent sign in his office at Fighter Command: THE FIRST DUTY OF THE EIGHTH FIGHTERS IS TO BRING THE BOMBERS BACK ALIVE. 'Who dreamed that one up, Bill?' I asked. 'The sign was here when I arrived,' he answered. 'Take it down,' I said, 'and put up another one: THE FIRST DUTY OF THE EIGHTH AIR FORCE FIGHTERS IS TO DESTROY GERMAN FIGHTERS.' As the message sank in, tears sprang to his eyes. 'You're authorizing me to take the offensive?' he asked. 'I'm *directing* you to,' I said. 'We'll still provide reasonable fighter escort for the bombers, but the bulk of your fighters will go hunting for Jerries. Flush them out in the air and beat them up on the way home. Your first priority is to take the offensive.' Kepner was on the phone almost before I could get out of his office. And the fighter pilots rose to the occasion. I never had cause to regret the decision'' (James H. Doolittle with Beirne Lay, Jr., "Daylight Precision Bombing'' in *IMPACT: The Army Air Forces' Confidential Picture History of World War II*, Book 6, p. xv).

54. Kepner, *Eighth Air Force Tactical Development: August 1942- May 1945*, p. 56.

55. Freeman, *The Mighty Eighth: Units, Men, and Machines*, p. 121. As Deighton has poignantly suggested in his fictional portrait of an American P-51 group during the winter of 1943-44, Eighth's decision to award credit for German aircraft destroyed on the ground was an offer that the more successful American fighter pilots could not easily refuse; the very spirit that had made these men successful in air combat tended to drive them to take risks strafing German airfields that, in the absence of the new claims category, few of them would have voluntarily embraced (Len Deighton, *Goodbye, Mickey Mouse* (New York: Knopf, 1982), pp. 131-32).

56. Freeman, *Mighty Eighth War Diary*, p. 259.

57. Freeman, *The Mighty Eighth: Units, Men, and Machines*, p. 121.

58. Without a doubt, strafing German airfields was a risky business. As Godfrey observed: "Skill was not necessary and often blind luck was the principal factor in a successful strafing. The 20 mm and 40 mm fire of the Germans who were protecting their airdromes was deadly" (Godfrey, p. 113). Bledsoe, based on extensive strafing experience in the European theater from 9 June through 3 October 1944, has expressed much the same opinion: "Strafing an enemy airdrome was by far the most dangerous of all combat missions. The bases were well protected by antiaircraft" (Marvin Bledsoe, *Thunderbolt: Memoirs of a World War II Fighter Pilot* (New York: Van Nostrand-Reinholt, 1982), p. 102). In fact, strafing proved so much more dangerous than bomber escort that in late September 1944, Eighth Air Force headquarters calculated "that at the going rate of loss, fighter pilots had one chance in a hundred of living to finish a 300-hour tour" (Bledsoe, p. 250).

59. Godfrey, p. 113. The 4th Fighter Group's Ralph K. Hofer (15 air-to-air victories) "turned out to be the only major Eighth Air Force ace to be lost in aerial combat during the war. Everyone else went down while attacking things on the ground" (Garry L. Fry and Jeffrey L. Ethell, *Escort to Berlin* (New York: Arco, 1980), p. 73).

60. Ferguson, *The Army Air Forces in World War II*, Vol. 2, p. 702; also Vol. 3, pp. 37–38.

61. As the table below illustrates, the build-up of Eighth Air Force's strength during the first six months of 1944 was truly relentless.

SELECTED EIGHTH AIR FORCE AIRCRAFT AND AIRCREW STRENGTHS*		AIRCRAFT Fully Operational	AIRCREWS Combat Effective
HEAVY BOMBER	Dec 1943	752	723
	Jun 1944	2,123	1,855
DAY FIGHTER	Dec 1943	565	565
	Jun 1944	906	885

*Murray, *Strategy for Defeat: The Luftwaffe 1933–1945*, p. 234.

62. Murray, *Strategy for Defeat: The Luftwaffe 1933–1945*, pp. 244–45 and 254–55.

63. As Peter Vigor has correctly noted in the context of Soviet thinking about "deep battle" with conventional means only, the view that modern war is essentially a function of economics, and that the victor will be one who possesses the greater economic potential, is true only if *"the war continues long enough for that greater potential to be realized"* (Peter H. Vigor, *Soviet Blitzkrieg Theory* (New York: St Martin's Press, 1983), p. 2).

64. Ferguson, *The Army Air Forces in World War II*, Vol. 3, pp. 47–48. "Beginning in March [1944], the Eighth Air Force discontinued efforts to evade enemy fighters in its operations. To accomplish our mission," the command's tacticians reasoned, "we must not only bomb the aircraft factories, but also force enemy fighters into the air. We now sought to provoke enemy fighter reaction" (Kepner, *Eighth Air Force Tactical Development: August 1942–May 1945*, pp. 76–77).

65. "It is of vital significance that, of all the tonnage of bombs dropped on Germany, only 17 percent fell prior to January 1, 1944, and only 28 percent prior to July 1, 1944. Not until the war in the air had been won and the landings in the Mediterranean and France successfully accomplished were the heavy bombers free to exploit the victory in the air and attack in full force the centers of oil production, the centers of transport, and the other sustaining sources of military strength within the heart of Germany" (Franklin D'Olier et al., *The United States Strategic Bombing Survey: Over-All Report (European War)* (Washington, DC: US Government Printing Office, 30 September 1945), p. 10).

66. Regarding the relative contribution of the various types of American fighters to the *Luftwaffe*'s defeat in 1944, General Kepner observed in May of 1944 that "by far the large proportion of our escort fighters to date have been P–47 Thunderbolts and their share of the 2321 enemy planes destroyed by this Command in combat, with 1496 probably destroyed and damaged, is in ratio to their numbers. If it can be said that the P–38's struck the *Luftwaffe* in its vitals and the P–51's are giving it the coup de grace, it was

the Thunderbolt that broke its back" (William E. Kepner, *The Long Reach: Deep Fighter Escort Tactics* (England: Eighth Fighter Command, 29 May 1944), p. 3). As for the relative contribution of USSTAF heavy bombers and escort fighters to the attrition of the *Luftwaffe*'s fighter force from Big Week to the end of April 1944, examination of Eighth Air Force kill-claims data from this period suggests that the escort fighters did the majority of the killing. From 20 February through 30 April 1944, the initially allowed claims of enemy aircraft destroyed by Eighth's escort fighters were nearly double those of its heavy bomber crews (just under 900 for the heavy bombers versus nearly 1,100 in the air and over 600 on the ground for the fighters) (Freeman, *Mighty Eighth War Diary*, pp. 183-234). In all likelihood, however, the bombers' share is even smaller than the allowed-claims figures indicate. *Luftwaffe* summary statistics for 1944 reveal that, at best, "the US strategic air forces shot down half the number of enemy airplanes they thought they had" (John E. Fagg, "Mission Accomplished" in *The Army Air Forces in World War II*, Vol. 3, pp. 802-3). So if US fighter claims are assumed to have been fairly close to the truth, then Eighth's heavy bombers probably did not destroy as many as 300 German aircraft in the air from 20 February through 30 April 1944. Nevertheless, even accepting this figure, it is still not possible to quantify precisely how much more productive Eighth's fighters were in the overall destruction of German fighters than the heavy bombers. Since Eighth's heavies mounted over 40 saturation bombing raids against *Luftwaffe* airfields in France and Germany during this period, the bombers too must have destroyed some aircraft on the ground. But because no aggregate figures on how many are extant, all that can be concluded is that the escort fighters, besides allowing the bombing to be sustained, were three to four times more productive than the heavies *in the air*. Note, though, that Eighth's own tacticians appear to have felt that the *Schwerpunkt* of the daylight bomber campaign in the months preceding the Normandy invasion was in the air. "The enemy fighter force," they wrote, "included one item which would be virtually impossible to replace within the limited time before the invasion was scheduled—experienced pilots. Aircraft can be produced in a matter of weeks, but a pilot requires a year and a half for adequate training. Also the supply of high-grade pilot material was limited, and battle experience was lost when a veteran was replaced by a trainee. Hence attacks on fighters in the air were far more valuable than on aircraft on the ground" (Kepner, *Eighth Air Force Tactical Development: August 1942-May 1945*, p. 76).

67. In March 1943, the Air Staff's Committee of Operations Analysts demoted German electric power, which had been given first priority in AWPD-1 and fourth in AWPD-42, to thirteenth (Hansell, *The Air Plan that Defeated Hitler*, pp. 154 and 158). This action led eventually to the virtual elimination of electric power from the CBO (pp. 259-62). Hansell has since argued that destruction of this vital link was well within USSTAF's capability no later than mid-1944: "Based upon *actual* average bombing experience in combat and actual average size of targets, it is evident that collapse of the electric power system was well within the capacity of the air forces actually available in the spring and early summer of 1944, over and above the *initial* catastrophic attacks on oil" (p. 262). The details of Hansell's after-the-fact assessment of the feasibility and likely consequences of having attacked German electric power can be found in Appendix III (titled 'The German Electric Power Complex as a Target System') of *The Air Plan that Defeated Hitler* (pp. 286-97).

68. According to Hansell's figures, American heavy bombers expended some 378,780 tons of bombs in the European theater on "non-CBO" targets (Hansell, *The Air Plan that Defeated Hitler*, p. 279). This total for diverted, non-CBO tonnage does not include any bombs dropped by the 9th, 12th, and 1st Tactical Air Forces, or the 385,710 tons delivered by the Eighth and Fifteenth Air Forces in support of the Normandy invasion and in attacking German transportation systems (land and water) (pp. 279-80). Total tonnage for Eighth and Fifteenth Air Forces over the course of World War II was 1,005,091 tons (p. 279).

69. AWPD-1 in particular explicitly implied that pursuit airplanes would only be required to defend American bomber bases *(Graphic Presentation and a Brief: A-WPD/1, Munitions Requirements of the Army Air Forces to Defeat Our Potential Enemies)*.

70. For the period 20 February to 30 April 1944, Eighth Air Force lost 820 B-17s and B-24s on operational missions; associated heavy bomber crews losses included 455 killed in action and over 8,100 missing in action (Freeman, *Mighty Eighth War Diary*, pp. 183-234). By comparison, Eighth Fighter Command's losses on bomber escort, fighter sweep, and strafing missions during this period totalled slightly over 400 aircraft (Ibid.).

71. A precondition for the Normandy invasion was, of course, overwhelming air superiority over France, and Allied air leaders rightly had few qualms prior to 6 June 1944 about sacrificing fighters in impromptu strafing attacks on German airfields to meet this precondition. Later, however, the high costs of fighter strafing became harder to justify, and by January 1945, impromptu strafing was forbidden "because the fighter losses were not worth the few targets available" (Kepner, *Eighth Air Force Tactical Development: August 1942–May 1945*, p. 56).

72. Montross, p. 986.

73. Montross, p. 987.

74. Montross, p. 988.

75. Futrell, *The United States Air Force in Korea 1950–1953*, p. 407. The original "Operation Strangle" occurred during World War II. (For an exhaustive account of the original "Strangle," see F. W. Sallagar, *Operation "STRANGLE" (Italy, Spring 1944): A Case Study of Tactical Air Interdiction* (Santa Monica: Rand, February 1972), Rand report R–851–PR.) The second Operation Strangle, launched during the final week of May 1951 in support of the US Eighth Army's counterstroke, was a road interdiction effort focused between Chinese Communist frontlines in Korea and Communist railheads around the 39th parallel (Futrell, p. 403). Air Force enthusiasm over the prospects of the August 1951 railway interdiction campaign led Fifth Air Force in Seoul to adopt this same code name (pp. 407–08). By Air Force reckoning, this third Operation Strangle ended by mid-December 1951 (p. 413). Its successor, Operation Saturate, was put into effect on 3 March 1952; Saturate was planned to provide round-the-clock concentration of the available railway interdiction assets against short segments of railway tracks in North Korea (p. 416).

76. Futrell, *The United States Air Force in Korea 1950–1953*, pp. 435–36.

77. Futrell, *The United States Air Force in Korea 1950–1953*, p. 407.

78. Futrell, *The United States Air Force in Korea 1950–1953*, p. 405.

79. Futrell, *The United States Air Force in Korea 1950–1953*, p. 405.

80. Futrell, *The United States Air Force in Korea 1950–1953*, p. 407.

81. Futrell, *The United States Air Force in Korea 1950–1953*, pp. 403 and 404.

82. Futrell, *The United States Air Force in Korea 1950–1953*, p. 406.

83. Futrell, *The United States Air Force in Korea 1950–1953*, p. 413. By December 1951, the World War II problem of measuring the effects of air attack had resurfaced. At a Fifth Air Force planning conference in Seoul on 12 December 1951, the candid admission was made that "although the enemy had made no large-scale attack, we don't know whether it is the result of interdiction or whether he never intended to attack" (Ibid.).

84. Futrell, *The United States Air Force in Korea 1950–1953*, p. 436.

85. Futrell, *The United States Air Force in Korea 1950–1953*, pp. 436-37.

86. Herman Kahn, *On Escalation: Metaphors and Scenarios* (Washington and New York: Praeger, 1965), p. 211. Kahn followed this statement with an explicit argument to the effect that if the commander or decision maker knows the starting conditions of a nuclear war, he can run the campaign for at least a few days even though completely cut off "from all information external to his own organization and forces, and perhaps even from much of that" (pp. 211–12). How? By "playing" both sides hypothetically by "dead reckoning" in much the same way that a pilot, knowing his starting point, and the times and distances for subsequent legs of the flight, can determine his position by mathematical calculation (Ibid.).

87. Brodie, "The Development of Nuclear Strategy," p. 81.

88. This article was based on an address Brodie gave at the last Plenary Session of the National Conference, Inter-University Seminar on the Armed Forces and Society, University of Chicago. David MacIsaac, who attended the conference, recalls that it was held in October 1977.

89. Brodie, "The Development of Nuclear Strategy," p. 69.

90. Brodie, "The Development of Nuclear Strategy," pp. 73–74.

91. Brodie, "The Development of Nuclear Strategy," p. 82. Aron's observation that much of the strategic literature written in the United States after Hiroshima resembled fiction was provoked by Herman Kahn's 1965 *On Escalation: Metaphors and Scenarios*. As Aron later explained, "At the beginning of his book on escalation, Herman Kahn quotes a phrase from one of my books which

expressed the following idea: there is no deterrent in a general or abstract sense, it is a case of knowing *who* one can deter *from what, in what circumstances, by what means* (by threats or organizing defence). This perfectly ordinary and apparently innocent statement is the result of integrating the doctrine of the diplomatic use of nuclear arms within the general doctrine of strategy (or of total diplomacy) between states. Herman Kahn quotes this phrase and immediately adds that he does not study specific historical problems of the kind that confront statesmen. He imagines, invents, and describes with minuteness bordering on unreality, dozens of situations of conflict reduced to simplified schemes, and the decisions that suit these situations. Failing science fiction, what other name but strategic fiction could one give to this form of literature" (Raymond Aron, "Modern Strategic Thought," trans. J. E. Gabriel, *Problems of Modern Strategy*, (New York: Praeger, 1970), pp. 30–31).

92. Albert Wohlstetter, "The Delicate Balance of Terror," *Foreign Affairs*, January 1959, p. 213.

93. Wohlstetter, p. 222.

94. Brodie, "The Development of Nuclear Strategy," p. 68.

95. Brodie, "The Development of Nuclear Strategy," p. 68.

96. Brodie, "The Development of Nuclear Strategy," p. 68.

97. In *Strategy in the Missile Age*, Brodie strongly supported the sheltering of bombers. For example, in the final chapter he stated that the "conclusion seems inescapable that a bomber should be brought together with a strong shelter, because it is hardly worth buying without one" (Brodie, *Strategy in the Missile Age*, p. 395). For other variations on this theme in *Strategy in the Missile Age*, see pages 183, 219, and 283.

98. Brodie, "The Development of Nuclear Strategy," pp. 68–69. The motivations for a Russian nuclear attack offered by Wohlstetter in 1959 were as follows: "What can be said, then, as to whether general war is unlikely? Would not a general thermonuclear war mean 'extinction' for the aggressor as well as the defender? 'Extinction' is a state that badly needs analysis. Russian casualties in World War II were more than 20,000,000. Yet Russia recovered extremely well from this catastrophe. There are several quite plausible circumstances in the future when the Russians might be quite confident of being able to limit damage to considerably less than this number—if they make sensible strategic choices and we do not. On the other hand, the risks of not striking might at some juncture appear very great to the Soviets, involving, for example, disastrous defeat in peripheral war, loss of key satellites with danger of revolt spreading—possibly to Russia itself—or fear of attack by ourselves. Then, striking first, by surprise, would be the sensible choice for them, and from their point of view the smaller risk" (Wohlstetter, p. 222).

99. Brodie, *Strategy in the Missile Age*, p. 213. Strictly interpreted, Brodie's wording overstates his case. Presumably all he really meant was that too many people had lightly concluded that there was *hardly* any likelihood of nuclear war (p. 274).

100. Brodie, *Strategy in the Missile Age*, p. 185. The principle that this passage reinforced was that "it is absolutely essential to defend our retaliatory force, or a substantial portion of it" (Ibid.).

101. Brodie, "The Development of Nuclear Strategy," pp. 73–74.

102. Benjamin S. Lambeth, *Selective Nuclear Options in American and Soviet Strategic Policy* (Santa Monica: Rand Report R–2034–DDRE, December 1976), p. 24.

103. Lambeth, *Selective Nuclear Options in American and Soviet Strategic Policy*, p. 12.

104. Lambeth, *Selective Nuclear Options in American and Soviet Strategic Policy*, pp. 24–25 and 56. While the United States has always had the theoretical capability to execute a range of "limited" strategic attacks, from the very large (McNamara's counterforce second-strike) to the quite small (Schlesinger's proposed attack on Soviet oil refineries), much of the hardware needed to make more controlled strikes feasible has only been deployed since the mid-seventies (Friedberg, "A History of the US Strategic 'Doctrine'—1945 to 1980," p. 62).

105. Lambeth, *Selective Nuclear Options in American and Soviet Strategic Policy*, p. 23. As Secretary Schlesinger said in his Fiscal Year 1976 Defense Department posture statement, "Even if there is only a small probability that limited response options would deter an attack or bring a nuclear war to a rapid conclusion without large-scale damage to cities, it is a probability which, for the sake of our citizens, we should not foreclose" (p. 56).

106. Lambeth, *Selective Nuclear Options in American and Soviet Strategic Policy*, pp. 31-32.

107. If the point of limited nuclear options is to avert, not provoke, all-out nuclear war, then it is truly difficult to envisage concrete situations in which the risks of something going wrong would not appear prohibitive to the US president. Or, if the risks of things going awry are driven tolerably low—for instance, by insisting upon being able to abort the strike up until the very last minute—then the likelihood of successful penetration to the target by a lone FB-111 or B-52 tends to become too low to make the enterprise worthwhile.

108. Robert F. Kennedy, *Thirteen Days: A Memoir of the Cuban Missile Crisis* (New York: Norton, 1969), pp. 13-14. As Allison has rightly said, however, "Deaths of this magnitude would have occurred only in the worst case" (Allison, note 1 on p. 278).

109. Kennedy, p. 22. According to (then) Special Counsel Theodore Sorenson, who was one of the fifteen principal members of the National Security Council's Executive Committee (ExCom) during the Cuban missile crisis, the President estimated the odds on nuclear war as "between one out of three and even" (Allison, pp. 1 and 57). Reportedly, though, the major US government postmortem of the crisis, written by Walt Rostow and Paul Nitze in February 1963, concluded that President Kennedy and his advisors had placed too much stress on the danger of nuclear war (Allison, p. 62).

110. Kennedy, p. 76. Regarding the escalatory potential of the Cuban missile crisis, the pivotal question is why the Soviets ultimately chose to withdraw their missiles. It is Allison's judgment that "Khrushchev withdrew the Soviet missiles not because of the implicit threat of 'further action,' but because of the *explicit* threat of air strike or invasion on Tuesday [30 October 1962]—unless he served immediate notice that the missiles would be withdrawn" (Allison, p. 65). One piece of evidence cited by Allison in support of this interpretation is the testimony of Secretary of Defense Robert McNamara before the House Committee on Appropriations in February 1963. "We had," McNamara stated, "a force of several hundred thousand men ready to invade Cuba. . . . Khrushchev knew without any question whatsoever that he faced the full military power of the United States, including its nuclear weapons . . . *and that is the reason, and the only reason, why he withdrew those weapons* [Allison's emphasis]" (Ibid.).

111. Brodie, "The Development of Nuclear Strategy," p. 82.

CHAPTER 7

TOWARD A LESS MECHANISTIC IMAGE OF WAR

I have too often seen the tide of battle turn around the high action of a few unhelped men to believe that the final problem of the battlefield can ever be solved by the machine.[1]

S. L. A. Marshall, 1947

As a result of our military experience and our strong national faith in technical solutions to problems, Americans have concluded that technology offers a particularly cheap, humane method of waging war. Under the influence of this conclusion, our nation has developed an unbalanced attitude toward war in which we attach exaggerated significance to technology at the expense of military skills and human sacrifice, which traditionally have played prominent roles in warfare.[2]

Lieutenant Colonel Donald R. Baucom, 1981

War is fundamentally a human phenomenon, a matter of emotions, aspirations, exertion, and suffering. Though concrete physical and statistical factors obviously play a role in determining conflict's outcome, war ultimately comes down to a contest of knowledge, intelligence, willpower, and human endurance.[3]

Lieutenant Colonel John F. Guilmartin, 1982

From Mitchell's *Winged Defense* through Brodie's *Strategy in the Missile Age*, mainstream US air power theorists largely overlooked friction, which is to say the collective factors that distinguish real war from war on paper. Yet it is still possible to wonder how serious this omission truly has been. Are we dealing with a minor oversight that can be filled in, or has the basic conceptual framework of US air power doctrine—meaning its implicit image of war's nature—somehow been fundamentally wrong? Further, if the omission has been and remains serious, then might Clausewitz's notion of general friction be of use in delineating a direction in which a more adequate, more complete theory of the air weapon could be developed?

These questions loosely outline the subjects I will address in this concluding section. Although I do not, and cannot, guarantee final answers to any of them, I believe it is vital to make the attempt. Trying to answer them is tantamount to starting to work out broad criteria or conditions that any comprehensive theory of war in general, and of aerial warfare in particular, must meet if it is to account for such things as chance, danger, the enemy's unpredictability, and the intractable uncertainties in the information upon which combatants must act. It is also to renew, after a century and a half of neglect, the essential task of Clausewitz's *On War:* the construction of an overarching theory of war.

US Air Doctrine and Laplacian Determinism

How concerned should we be over the propensity of US airmen since Mitchell to approach war as a vast engineering project whose essential processes are as precisely calculable as the tensile strength requirements of a dam or bridge? On the one hand, the failure of even nuclear weapons to diminish the importance of general friction argues that so mechanistic a view of war cannot be entirely satisfactory. On the other, if the error is largely one of omission, can we not somehow fill in the gaps?

It is my view that the basic mistake in traditional US air doctrine is too deeply rooted, too elemental to be repaired by any amount of *ad hoc* backfilling. The strongest evidence for this conclusion comes from developments in physics and mathematics that have seldom been connected with war or politics.[4]

That American airmen have tended to be overzealous in their enthusiasm for pat formulas and engineering-type calculations seems hard to deny. Witness the stubborn adherence of Eighth Air Force leaders to the doctrine that 300 unescorted B-17s could be self-defending—particularly during the roughly two months in 1943 that spanned Eighth's first and second missions to the ball bearing plants at Schweinfurt. Or, to raise a more recent (but not unrelated) example, consider the US defense establishment's lengthy search for a secure MX-missile basing scheme during an era in which the "historical trend of warfare clearly has been away from survivability and toward vulnerability—not only for weapons systems but for population and industrial bases as well."[5] Nevertheless, simply pointing out this predilection toward rigid formulas and quantification does not penetrate to the heart of what has been wrong with US air doctrine. I would argue that shibboleths like the Air Corps Tactical School's doctrine of bomber invulnerability can be traced to a far deeper mistake: tacit acceptance of the deterministic *Weltanschauung* (literally, manner of looking at the world) adopted by physicists in the century following Isaac Newton's death.

What was the *Weltanschauung* that evolved from the final (1726) edition of Isaac Newton's *Mathematical Principles of Natural Philosophy?*[6] In the hands of Newton's successors, the driving paradigm[7] became the idea of the universe as a mechanical clockwork. Based upon the universal force of gravity and three laws of motion, Newton had been able to calculate precise values for observed phenomena ranging from the behavior of falling bodies near the surface of the earth to the moon's orbit about the earth, the motion of the earth and the five planets around the sun, the flattening of planets like Jupiter along their polar axes, and the rise and fall of the earth's tides.[8] During the century following Newton's death in 1727, mathematicians and natural scientists, culminating with Pierre Simon de Laplace (1749–1827), expanded Newton's original synthesis into an all-embracing world view. Among other things, by showing that every secular variation in the solar system then known to science, including the changing speeds of Jupiter and Saturn, was cyclic, Laplace established that the solar system was stable and, hence, needed no divine maintenance.[9] His work led, therefore, to a view of the universe as a Newtonian world machine whose behavior was completely and inexorably determined by physical laws.[10]

What does this Laplacian paradigm have in common with mainstream US air doctrine? Simply answered, American airmen, like Newton's successors, embraced Laplacian determinism in its most mechanistic sense. Possibly the most conspicuous example of this fact is the plan for the CBO from the United Kingdom. The immediate objective of its authors was to transform the Casablanca Directive (CCS 166/I/D from the Combined Chiefs of Staff to Air Marshal Arthur Harris and General Eaker) into realistic orders for Bomber Command and Eighth Air Force.[11] The detailed planning was begun in March 1943 under the direction of (then) Brigadier General Haywood Hansell,[12] and the resulting plan, christened POINTBLANK, was approved by the Combined Chiefs of Staff in May 1943.[13] The essential train of logic articulated in this document (see appendix) can be distilled to five basic points.

(1) Study of the German military and industrial system by US and British experts has produced "complete agreement" on six economic target systems, comprising 76 *precision targets,* whose destruction would "fatally weaken the capacity of the German people for armed resistance."

(2) Based on Eighth Air Force experience during 12 missions in early 1943, the *desired degree of destruction* against such targets can be achieved throughout a 1,000-foot radius circle around the aim point by 100 bombers.

(3) This *"yardstick" of 1,000-foot radius circles of destruction* (each requiring 100 bombers) can be used to *compute* the bomber force required to destroy the critical 76 industrial targets in Germany.

(4) Assuming complementary attacks by British bombers at night, a four-phase buildup culminating in *2,702 American heavy bombers* by March 31, 1944, *will reduce* German submarine construction by 89 percent, fighter production by 43 percent, bomber production by 65 percent, ball bearing output by 76 percent, synthetic rubber capacity by 50 percent, *disastrously disrupt* German supplies of finished oil products, and *eliminate* a large portion of German military vehicle production.

(5) This same force buildup to 2,702 American bombers will also suffice to *arrest German fighter* strength in Western Europe and, eventually, cause it to decline precipitously.[14]

The underlying approach to aerial warfare presumed here is unmistakably deterministic, uncompromisingly Laplacian. Not only are the CBO plan's predictions concerning bombing effects offered with the quantitative precision of a physical science, they are expressly portrayed as effects that *will occur* if the requisite bombing forces are made available.[15]

This stark (and probably unwitting) commitment to Laplacian determinacy cannot be dismissed as some special quirk of the CBO plan. The evidence of Chapter 6 demonstrates that, through the time of the Normandy landings, American conduct of the daylight portion of the Combined Bomber Offensive was every bit as mechanistic as Eaker's plan.

Nor do I see much room for supposing that the private image of aerial warfare held by airmen like Hansell and Eaker was less deterministic than that suggested by the planning documents they endorsed and their conduct of heavy bomber operations. General Hansell has stated unequivocally that the thinking behind the original US strategic air plan, AWDP-1, was *mechanistic* in the specific sense of not getting involved in the action-reaction typical of combat between land armies.[16] Together with the role that this mindset subsequently played in Eighth Air Force's costly defeat during the second week of October 1943, his characterization appears to confirm beyond reasonable doubt that the image of war held by US precision bomber advocates was deeply mechanistic through the fall of 1943.

Nor, once again, is it possible to argue that American air power theorists later renounced Laplacian determinism. We need look no further than the general acceptance within the American defense community of the impending vulnerability of US land-based ICBMs to a first strike by Soviet SS-18s and SS-19s to recognize that the infatuation with formulas and calculations so manifest in the CBO plan continues to characterize mainstream American thinking about the air weapon.[17]

How serious, then, was (and is) the blindness to general friction evident in US air doctrine? As I have labored to establish throughout this study, war is so unruly a phenomenon that total knowledge of its processes is seldom possible even long after the fact, much less at the time. Thus, to the extent that combat experience in this century has reaffirmed Clausewitz's view that no other human activity is so continuously or universally bound up with chance and uncertainty as war,[18] I can only conclude that the implicit presumption of US aviators and air power theorists that warfare can be treated as an exhaustively determinant phenomenon was fundamentally mistaken. While the conduct of war clearly involves engineering, it cannot be reduced to engineering.

Cartesian Hypotheses, Uncertainty, Undecidability

Over and above the evidence of the battlefield, there is a more compelling argument for concluding that the elemental error in mainstream US air doctrine is not an easily reparable omission. The comprehensive certainty that American precision bombardment advocates sought in aerial warfare was not attainable, it turns out, even in physics. As Isaac Newton realized full well in private, an irreducible kernel of uncertainty lay at the center of his world system.

> Newton had indeed exposed and rejected certain hypotheses as detrimental; he knew how to tolerate others as being at least harmless; and he, like everyone else, knew how to put to use those that are verifiable or falsifiable. But the fact is that Newton also found one class of hypotheses to be impossible to avoid in his pursuit of natural philosophy—a class that shared with Cartesian hypotheses the characteristic of being *neither demonstrable from the phenomena nor following from them by an argument based on induction* [emphasis added].[19]

Significantly, physics since Newton has not been able to eradicate such "Cartesian" hypotheses. Albert Einstein, for example, later made expressly non-Newtonian assumptions about space and time when he rejected "absolutely stationary space" and the attachment of any absolute significance to the concept of simultaneity.[20] But while the assumptions about space and time of Einstein's special theory of relativity permitted a degree of unification between mechanics and electrodynamics that Newton's physics did not, they remained to the same degree Cartesian (that is, not strictly demonstrable from any empirical phenomena).[21]

As it turns out, the limitation on the method of empirical science evident in the failure of physicists from Newton through Einstein to purge Cartesian hypotheses from their theories is but the tip of the iceberg. Advances in physics since special relativity, particularly Werner Heisenberg's discovery that particles like the electron "yield only limited information,"[22] have served to broaden, not diminish, the limits of human knowing. As Jacob Bronowski has so eloquently said concerning the limits to human knowledge discovered by quantum physics:

> One aim of the physical sciences has been to give an exact picture of the material world. One achievement of physics in the twentieth century has been to prove that that aim is unattainable. . . . There is no absolute knowledge. And those who claim it, whether they are scientists or dogmatists, open the door to tragedy. All information is imperfect. We have to treat it with humility. That is the human condition, and that is what quantum physics says. I mean that literally.[23]

Similar limits have also emerged in that most exact and certain of all the sciences: mathematics. Two famous instances in the very foundations of mathematics are Alonzo Church's discovery that no mechanical routine exists for deciding the validity of arbitrary inferences in predicate (or quantificational) logic,[24] and Kurt Goedel's 1931 proof that any formal axiom system strong enough for the arithmetic of natural numbers will always contain undecidable propositions, meaning arithmetical truths that can be neither proved nor disproved within the system of arithmetic.[25] Granted, a strict interpretation would be that these limiting theorems only apply to the formal methods (or languages) of symbolic logic. But as Howard DeLong has noted, *"There do not appear to be any other means."*[26] Insofar as we rely upon language for expression, there is no "entirely nonpoetic and nonfictional account of the universe in general."[27]

What do these seemingly esoteric findings in physics and mathematical logic imply about the omission of friction in traditional US air doctrine? On the presumption that absolutely determinant knowledge was attainable, American army and air force aviators sought, and often claimed, absolute knowledge within the realm of aerial warfare. This presumption is the very essence of the percentages of destruction confidently detailed in Eaker's CBO plan, of Eighth Air Force's rigid adherence to the doctrine of bomber invulnerability, and of the infatuation of most missile-age theorists since Brodie with various canonical US-USSR nuclear exchange calculations. We have, however, seen evidence from fields of inquiry as independent of one another as pure mathematics and atomic physics that argues that such exhaustively determinant knowledge was never possible, not even in the "exact" sciences. And if we cannot aspire to such certainty in physics or mathematics, then it would surely seem ill-advised to seek or profess absolute knowledge in our theories of war.

This conclusion, I hasten to add, should not be taken to mean that the methods of the engineer have no place in the conduct of war. All that can be engineered should be. My point is that success in war as a whole cannot be reliably engineered.[28]

The Human Cost of War

Given the high value that Americans have long placed on individual human life, this conclusion may seem a bitter pill to swallow. Because combat decisions are often matters of life and death, the unavoidable frictions of actual combat imply that those who lead and command can never be confident, much less certain, that lives will not be inadvertently wasted as a result of their actions—a realization that brings us face to face with the inherent tragedy of war.

This realization further underscores the gravity of the omission of friction in US thinking about the air weapon. If we truly value human life, then the American tendency to conceive of war principally as a resource allocation problem that can be precisely engineered with formulas and calculations has, on the evidence, been tragically misguided. To suggest otherwise is to ignore the enormity of the gap between Mitchell's brave hope that the airplane offered a cheap, humane alternative to the unmitigated slaughter of the First World War and the carnage that the Combined Bomber Offensive inflicted on opposing airmen (to say nothing of the destruction wrought on the cities of Germany).

My own inclination, therefore, is to insist that the bedrock error in traditional US air doctrine—the assumption that war's essential processes can be precisely and exhaustively determined—is beyond redemption. Thinking about conflict in the United States would be better served by shifting toward a less mechanistic vision of war's underlying processes.

Of course, to be consistent with my own evidence, I must acknowledge that this proposition cannot be grounded on airtight proofs. The proposal that future US air doctrine be based on a less mechanistic view of war is tantamount to proposing a paradigm shift, and choices between competing paradigms cannot, by their very nature, be strictly matters of unambiguous evidence and indisputable arguments therefrom. As the philosopher Thomas Kuhn has rightly said concerning the problem of resolving paradigm debates in the natural sciences: "All historically significant theories have agreed with the facts, *but only more or less* [emphasis added]."[29] Thus, I cannot even hope to offer absolutely compelling reasons for my conclusion that we would be better served by a different paradigm from the deterministic, engineering mindset that, historically, has dominated US Army and Air Force experience with the air weapon.

Combat Psychology as Context

Yet to say that "in matters of theory-choice, the force of logic and observation cannot in principle be compelling is neither to discard logic and observation nor to suggest that there are not good reasons for favoring one theory over another."[30] It remains worthwhile to ask: What kinds of considerations would support the adoption of a less mechanistic *Weltanschauung* by US airmen? The remainder of this chapter will attempt to answer this question by developing two general lines of argument for preferring a less mechanistic image of conflict.

The first line of argument I shall offer amounts to insisting that to embrace a less mechanistic view of war as a whole is to place the phenomena of combat in their proper context, meaning the psychology of combatants. This idea arises from a simple, but elementary question: What prompts men in battle, against every instinct of self-preservation, to risk death and fight rather than to flee or hide? As a combat historian for the US Army during World War II, S.L.A. Marshall was afforded the unprecedented opportunity to conduct post-combat mass interviews of some 400 American infantry companies in the Central Pacific and European theaters.[31] Based in large measure on these interviews, Marshall concluded that the individual soldier is mainly motivated to fight by a sense of psychological unity with the members of his primary combat group.

> I hold it to be one of the simplest truths of war that the thing which enables an infantry soldier to keep going with his weapons is the near presence or the presumed presence of a comrade. The warmth which derives from human companionship is as essential to his employment of the arms with which he fights as is the finger with which he pulls a trigger or the eye with which he aligns his sights. . . . So it is far more than a question of the soldier's need of physical support from other men. He must have at least some feeling of spiritual unity with them if he is to do an efficient job of moving and fighting. Should he lack this feeling for any reason . . . he will become a castaway in the middle of a battle and as incapable of effective offensive action as if he were stranded somewhere without weapons.

> This is a basic principle in the elementary psychology of the infantry soldier. Though I have personally investigated several hundred of the heroic exploits by single individuals in the past war . . . I have yet to find the episode which is at odds with it.[32]

The immediacy and scope of Marshall's wartime experiences certainly seem sufficient for his conclusion that infantrymen are sustained primarily by psychological bonds with their fellows, not by their weapons alone. Moreover, this point can be extended to forms of combat as seemingly individualistic and highly dependent upon technology as air-to-air engagements between jet fighters armed with state-of-the-art missiles.[33]

Why, though, should combatant psychology be singled out as the proper context for theorizing about war in general? Consider the various types of factors that can shape or drive combat outcomes. Without making any pretense at being exhaustive, we might plausibly list:

(1) The various intangible human factors—including combatant psychology, the morale of military units, and the will of a nation's political leadership—that generally defy quantification.

(2) Physical factors such as the size of opposing forces, their composition, and the performance characteristics of their weaponry.

(3) Spatial or geometrical relationships between opposing forces over time.

(4) Terrain.

(5) Logistical factors.[34]

The fruitful question to raise about these various factors concerns, as Lieutenant Colonel John F. Guilmartin has pointed out, the speed with which they change over time relative to one another. Guilmartin's answer, which I take to be sound in its broad thrust, is as follows:

> If the technological realities of the battlefield change rapidly across history and the political and social realities of war change with comparable and, at times, greater speed, then the geographical and topographical circumstances affecting the timing and nature of battle change at a more deliberate pace and the ultimate physiological limitations of the combatant change hardly at all. Within this frame of reference, changes in the psychology of combat plainly lie toward the slow end of the spectrum of temporal change.[35]

The substantive implication for military theory here is that combatant psychology constitutes the most stable, most timeless dimension of war. While the political goals of a particular conflict, weapons technologies, and, above all else, the tactics appropriate against a given adversary on a given day can all change virtually overnight, "combat is combat and a combatant is a combatant."[36] Despite the appearance of thermonuclear weapons and intercontinental delivery vehicles, the outcomes of battles still hinge, often as not, on the vision, determination and courage of a comparatively small percentage of the combatants involved. Consequently, to choose anything except combatant psychology as the basic context for the theory or practice of war is to build upon sand.

Again, my intent is not to imply that the concrete and statistical aspects of war should be either ignored or approached other than from the standpoint of the engineer. Rather, it is to insist that even though many of the elements that contribute to victory can (and must) be engineered, the "engineerable" parts do not generally comprise the whole.

While this point may, by now, seem obvious, there are reasons for returning to it. As recently as the Vietnam War, the presumption that overall victory could be engineered remained deeply entrenched in the American way of war. Witness the conversation that Colonel Harry G. Summers, Jr., had in Hanoi during April of 1975:

> "You know you never defeated us on the battlefield," said the American colonel [Summers]. The North Vietnamese colonel pondered this remark a moment. "That may be so," he replied, "but it is also irrelevant."[37]

In other words, how could the army in Vietnam have succeeded so well, tactically and logistically, in everything that it set out to do, and yet have lost the war? Colonel Summers' answer in *On Strategy: The Vietnam War in Context* is that US decision makers failed to address the question of "how" to use military means to achieve political goals. And he is surely on target in identifying as errors in strategy such beliefs as the assumption that the quantitative methods of peacetime systems analysis could be extended to the battlefields of Southeast Asia, or that repeated tactical successes against the Viet Cong and the North Vietnamese army would necessarily add up to strategic victory for the United States.[38] I would merely note that common to these strategy errors is the very same view of war as a deterministic or engineering enterprise that drove the planning and conduct of the Combined Bomber Offensive.[39]

The other reason for coming back to the profound gap that exists in actual practice between victory and the elements of war that can be engineered is the tremendous theoretical appeal of deterministic paradigms. Even S. L. A. Marshall was once seduced by the idea that victory could be reduced to the mathematical problem of assembling more men and machines at the key point than the enemy, although, to his lasting credit, he later changed his mind in the face of experience.

> In my collected thinking about my experiences with battle troops, there is one lasting impression which stands above all others. As a student of military history, my readings between the wars had made me overrespectful of the factor of the preponderance of force in warfare. I came to believe that battles and campaigns were almost invariably won according to which side was in a position to apply the greatest weight at the decisive point. This is perhaps a relative truth. But once one falls in love with this idea, it is only a short step to a wholly materialistic concept of the balancing of power and the making of military decision. Success becomes a purely mathematical problem of counting men and machines and what is required to supply them. I know now that that is not true . . . the great victories of the United States have pivoted on the acts of courage and intelligence of a very few individuals. The time always comes in battle when the decisions of statesmen and of generals can no longer effect the issue and when it is not within the power of our national wealth to change the balance decisively. Victory is never achieved prior to that point; it can be won only after the battle has been delivered into the hands of men who move in imminent danger of death.[40]

I have argued in this section that mainstream US air doctrine would be improved by the adoption of a less deterministic image of war. I did so on the grounds that something as patently unamenable to quantification and engineering as combatant psychology appears to be the enduring context for military success in the broadest sense. However, I must admit that disabusing ourselves of the tendency to assume that victory can be engineered will not be easy. The persistence of this mechanistic mindset in US military thinking as late as the Vietnam War, as well as its deep theoretical appeal to a society that places the highest value on individual human life, both suggest that any attempt to move away from our prevailing image of war would encounter tremendous institutional and psychological resistance.

I cannot offer any easy way to cut through such resistance. Nevertheless, there are two further points that may help to round out the argument I have mounted in favor of striving to do so. First, the idea of making combatant psychology the principal context for our thinking about war as a whole is not academic hair-splitting. If seriously pursued, it would have concrete, far-reaching consequences for the American military. To provide some feel for all that a more combatant-oriented perspective might entail, I want to direct the reader's attention to the introductory portion of the German *Truppenfuehrung* (literally, "Troop Leading"), or field service regulations, which appeared in 1933 and remained in effect through 1945:[41]

> 1. The conduct of war is an art, depending upon free, creative activity, scientifically grounded. It makes the highest demands on the personality.
>
> 2. The conduct of war is based on continuous development. New means of warfare call forth ever-changing employment. Their use must be anticipated, their influence must be correctly estimated and quickly utilized.
>
> 3. Situations in war are of unlimited variety. They change often and suddenly and only rarely are from the first discernible. Incalculable elements are often of great influence. The independent will of the enemy is pitted against ours. Friction and mistakes are of every day occurrence.
>
> 4. The teaching of the conduct of war cannot be concentrated exhaustively in regulations. The principles so enunciated must be employed dependent upon the situation.
> Simplicity of conduct, logically carried through, will most surely obtain the objective.
>
> 5. War is the severest test of spiritual and bodily strength. In war, character outweighs intellect. Many stand forth on the field of battle who in peace would remain unnoticed.
>
> 6. Armies as well as lesser units demand leaders of good judgment, clear thinking and far seeing, leaders with independence and decisive resolution, leaders with perseverance and energy, leaders not emotionally moved by the varying fortunes of war, leaders with a high sense of responsibility.
>
> 7. The officer is a leader and a teacher. Besides his knowledge of men and his sense of justice, he must be distinguished by his superior knowledge and experience, his earnestness, high self-control and high courage. . . .
>
> 10. In spite of technique, the worth of man is the decisive factor. Its significance is increased in group combat.

> The emptiness of the battlefield demands independently thinking and acting fighters, who, considering each situation, are dominated by the conviction, boldly and decisively to act, and determined to arrive at success.
>
> Being accustomed to physical accomplishments, lack of consideration for self, willpower, self-confidence, and courage qualify a man to master the most difficult situations.
>
> 11. The worth of leaders and men determines the battle worth *[Kampfkraft]* of the troops, which is supplemented by the possession, care and maintenance of arms and equipment.
>
> Superior battle worth can equalize numerical inferiority. The higher the battle worth, the more vigorous and versatile can war be executed.
>
> Superior leadership and superior troop battle readiness are reliable portents of victory.
>
> 12. The leaders must live with their troops, participate in their dangers, their wants, their joys, their sorrows. Only in this way can they estimate the battle worth and the requirements of the troops.
>
> Man is not responsible for himself alone, but also for his comrades. He who can do more, who has greater capacity of accomplishment must instruct the inexperienced and weaker. . . .
>
> 15. From the youngest soldier on up the employment of every spiritual and bodily power is demanded to the utmost. Only in such conduct is the full power of accomplishment of the troops achieved. So do men develop and maintain their courage and powers of decision in hours of stress and carry forward with them to greater deeds their weaker comrades.
>
> The first demand in war is decisive action. Everyone, the highest commander and the most junior soldier, must be aware that omissions and neglects incriminate him more severely than the mistake of choice of means.[42]

What I would underscore is that the relentless focus in these paragraphs on combatant psychology—on steeling soldiers and commanders at every echelon to withstand the terrible dangers, stresses, and uncertainties of actual combat—has largely been missing from basic American doctrinal writings on war. For example, from the standpoint of having been in effect during World War II, the comparable American document to the *Wehrmacht*'s (German Army's) 1933 *Truppenfuehrung* is the US Army's *Field Service Regulations: Operations (FM 100–5)* of 22 May 1941. But as the historian Martin van Creveld has observed:

> Though entire sentences [in the US manual] were clearly lifted straight from the German Regulations, the overall effect is subtly different and, indeed, indicative of a dissimilar conception of the nature of war. . . . From Clausewitz, the German Army took over the idea that war is the clash of independent wills and consequently dominated by friction. In the US Army's manual by contrast, the enemy is not mentioned except as a factor that may disrupt one's own pattern of activity. . . .[43]

Since I have yet to discover any instance of a US Army or Air Force basic doctrinal manual with an emphasis on the psychology of combatants comparable to the 1933 *Truppenfuehrung*'s, I can only conclude that for contemporary American doctrine to embrace a less mechanistic mindset would necessitate substantive and far-reaching changes in our whole approach to war.

The other point to be made is simply that Colonel John R. Boyd's historical investigations appear to offer the conceptual wherewithal needed to progress in this direction. Generalizing from his experience with fighter-versus-fighter combat,[44]

Boyd has argued that the fundamental cognitive problem of conflict—from the most elementary one-on-one tactical interactions to the broadest problems of national strategy—is that of repeatedly cycling through four successive stages:

(1) OBSERVATION: sensing what is taking place in the battle environment.

(2) ORIENTATION: constructing images or impressions of unfolding events.

(3) DECISION: choosing a course of action appropriate to the situation.

(4) ACTION: implementing that course of action against the adversary.[45]

If correct, the very scope of Boyd's generalization strongly corroborates my argument that the psychology of combat *is* the proper context for everything from designing weapons and planning force structures to actual employment on the battlefield.[46] Further, Boyd's notion of Observation-Orientation-Decision-Action cycles offers a carefully wrought conceptual framework for exploring and elaborating war's proper context.

Some Consequences of Embracing a More Organic Image of War

The second line of argument I want to develop in favor of moving away from the mechanistic mindset that has dominated US air doctrine arises from asking: Would such a change help us to cope with the total phenomenon of war more effectively? The broad answer I would offer is, yes. If friction truly constitutes the fundamental atmosphere of war, then a strongly deterministic *Weltanschauung* cannot help but neglect the uncertainties, chance occurrences, dangers, demands for exertion, and other frictions of actual conflict. In contrast, a more organic image, meaning one grounded on the psychology of battle and the pervasive reality of general friction, should encompass both the calculable and noncalculable aspects of war's underlying processes more completely.

One way of fleshing out this bare skeleton of an argument is to consider the relative utility of a more organic perspective. Is a less mechanistic paradigm likely to be more useful in revealing the lessons of past military experience? Would it offer better guidelines for what our military organizations ought to be emphasizing in the present? And might it produce more fruitful exemplars for the conduct of future operations? All three of these questions can, I believe, be given affirmative answers.

Learning from History

Regarding the lessons of history, I would simply offer the first part of Chapter 6 as evidence that a more organic view of war can facilitate better understanding of past combat experience. Since 1945, most discussions of the British-American air campaign against Nazi Germany have ultimately revolved around questions such as: *Precisely* how much did the efforts of Allied airmen contribute to victory?[47] And in light of the great cost of the air campaign "in men, material, and effort,"[48] was Allied air power *decisive*?[49] Such questions, however, with their implicit demand for a precise accounting of a demonstrably nondeterministic enterprise, seem unlikely to lead anywhere, and recurring attempts over four decades to answer them "decisively" have made little progress.[50] By comparison, examining the air campaign—particularly the daylight bombardment effort during late 1943 and early 1944—from the standpoint of move and countermove between intelligent adversaries not only reveals the central role of friction in war—both as an impediment and as a weapon—but enables us to transcend unproductive feuding about the decisiveness of the bomber offensive and get on with the important job of learning from our own past.

Nurturing Military Genius

Concerning the question of a more balanced and effective approach to the organizing, equipping, and training of US combat forces in the present, I would argue basically that we need to begin moving toward greater emphasis on nurturing warriors in addition to the necessary managers, planners, engineers, and technicians.[51] The problem is that if victory cannot be mechanized, then how can we best prepare ourselves to cope with friction in the broad sense of the incalculable uncertainties that form the atmosphere of war? The solution I would propose is the same one Clausewitz outlined over 150 years ago: Do everything necessary to select for, encourage, and support military genius. If combatants are to emerge unscathed from the relentless struggle with the unforeseen imposed by battle, Clausewitz wrote,

> two qualities are indispensable: *first, an intellect that, even in the darkest hour, retains some glimmerings of the inner light which leads to truth; and second, the courage to follow this faint light wherever it may lead.* The first of these qualities is described by the French term, *coup d'oeil;* the second is *determination.*[52]

From a pragmatic standpoint, this suggestion leads immediately to another question: How do you cultivate military genius? In a rigorously deterministic sense, the answer is that the question has no answer: Formulas for mechanically cranking out true military geniuses are no more likely to exist than deterministic recipes for engineering victory. Yet we need not give up. In terms of rough empirical approximations close enough to get the job done, practical methods for cultivating, even institutionalizing, the harmonious balance of qualities that the World War II *Truppenfuehrung* termed *character* have been known (at least in some quarters) since the early days of the German General Staff Academy.[53]

Consider the case of the *Wehrmacht* during World War II. By virtually every imaginable standard, from qualities as elusive as reputation to measures as exact as the ability to inflict casualties at higher rates than the enemy, the German armies of 1939–45 consistently outfought the far more numerous Allied armies that eventually defeated them. In 1943–44 the German combat effectiveness superiority over the Western Allies (Americans and British) was in the order of 20–30 percent. On a man-for-man basis, the German ground soldiers consistently inflicted casualties at about a 50-percent higher rate than they incurred from the opposing British and American troops under all circumstances. This was true when they were attacking and when they were defending, when they had a local numerical superiority and when, as was usually the case, they were outnumbered, when they had air superiority and when they did not, when they won and when they lost.[54]

More importantly, the kinds of things that underwrote this German superiority in fighting power *(Kampfkraft)*[55] are not mysterious. During the years preceding World War II, the German Army, acting on the conviction that leadership was a paramount prerequisite for its officers, "took very great pains to determine its presence."[56] Drawing upon the research at the *Wehrmacht*'s "psychological laboratory" under J. B. Riefert and, later, Max Simoneit, young men who had been put forward as officer-candidates by their regiments were screened explicitly for Clausewitz's harmonious balance of *coup d'oeil* and determination.[57] Concurrently, despite extensive use of psychological screening, the Germans were careful to leave ultimate decisions about officer selection "in the hands of the very men who were later to train the cadets and lead them into battle"[58]—an approach that has been adopted by at least one other highly successful military organization: the Israeli Air Force.[59]

Along with persistent German efforts (however imperfect[60]) to select for military genius went a willingness to accept certain inefficiencies to sustain the fighting power of combat units. For instance, the Germans' belief that unit cohesion depended heavily on the troops sharing a common background led to *Wehrmacht* divisions and smaller units being formed on a national basis (Prussian, Bavarian, Wurtembergian, etc.), even though this practice meant that frontline units could not be continuously maintained at full strength.[61] Further, in sharp contrast to the focus of the US Army's World War II rotation system on equalizing the burden of combat duty (as measured by time in theater), the German Army's replacement system concentrated on restoring and preserving *Kampfkraft*.[62] Accordingly, replacement training battalions in Germany had one or more "parent" divisions in the frontlines, and combat units were often allowed to request by name as officer-replacements men who had previously served in those same units as NCOs (noncommissioned officers). Also, prior to committing new troops to battle, German combat divisions strove to provide enough training in the parent unit's field replacement battalions to ensure that "the replacements would reach the front already knowing both each other and their commanders, and forming part of a well-integrated team."[63] Finally, the *Wehrmacht*, like the *Luftwaffe*, "systematically and consistently sent its best men forward to the front, consciously and deliberately weakening the rear."[64] In fact, until almost the end of the war, the Germans refused to lower the standards of their middle-level leadership: "Better no officer than a bad officer" would be a legitimate characterization of how the Germans viewed the requirements of officership.[65]

From the Clausewitzian standpoint of viewing war as a clash of independent wills dominated by friction, therefore, I would argue that the kinds of practices that lay at the core of superior German fighting power throughout World War II are little more than military common sense. If, as Clausewitz maintained, military genius founded on battle experience is the most effective antidote to the incalculable frictions of real war, then it seems baseless to object to Clausewitz's antidote on the grounds that we do not know exactly how to quantify this quality today. True, there almost surely are no infallible formulas for producing a Clausewitz, a von Manstein, or a Jimmy Doolittle. But in a generic sense, the basic kinds of pragmatic techniques used by the Germans, and more recently by the Israelis,[66] seem clear enough to anyone willing to look.

Of course, the priorities of the World War II *Wehrmacht* were not those of the US Army Air Forces (just as they are not those of the US Air Force today). Whereas the Germans were persuaded that individual character, not intelligence or efficiency, was the key to withstanding the stresses of combat,[67] the American view of war as a vast engineering project naturally gave priority to the explicit and quantifiable. Given the American propensity to formulate warfighting in the most explicit, quantifiable manner possible, the German willingness to operate on the basis of *implicit* knowledge offers a particularly germane illustration of the concrete differences in priorities that flowed from their divergent images of war.

Take treatment of Clausewitz at the *Kriegsakademie* between the two world wars. The Clausewitzian perspective that German line and general staff officers so frequently exhibited, in their writings as well as in their actions on the battlefield,[68] are strong confirmation of Marine Captain C. A. Leader's thesis that the most significant accomplishment of the *Kriegsakademie* was to imbue the *Wehrmacht*'s officer corps with a workable synthesis of Clausewitzian theory and practice.[69] Yet it turns out that even at the *Kriegsakademie*, Clausewitz's bulky masterpiece *Vom Krieg* was neither explicitly read nor studied.[70] Rather, the German system actualized Clausewitz's injunction to "end the absurd difference between theory and practice"[71] by nurturing the implicit ability of talented leaders in cohesive combat organizations to grasp the essentials of battlefield situations despite the pervasive presence of friction.[72]

What I would infer from the Germans' consistently superior tactical performance on the battlefields of World War II, consequently, is that a more implicit approach can work. On balance, in fact, it seems fair to say that the Germans' more implicit and organic approach left them better prepared to adapt to the tactical extremities of that conflict than were any of their adversaries.

Exemplars for Future Wars: Friction as a Weapon and Entropy

Can a more organic view of war produce better exemplars for the conduct of future operations? It seems hard to believe that greater attention to the psychology of combat and war's dominance by friction could produce worse exemplars than we have had in the past. The purest expression of the deterministic mode of thought that dominated the Army Air Forces during World War II was not the defeat of the German *Jagdgeschwaders* in Western Europe prior to the Allied landings at Normandy. It was Eighth Air Force's ill-conceived attempts, the preceding fall, to rely on sheer mass and the supposed invincibility of American bombers to overcome whatever operational frictions the daylight bombing offensive might encounter.

Still, the question remains: If a more Clausewitzian image of war is accepted, can it lead to better patterns for the conduct of future operations than we have had in the past? The concrete exemplar I would offer is the proposition that, in combat, actions taken to drive up the adversary's friction are as vital to success as those taken to minimize your own.

Innocuous as this statement may sound, it does yield a practical exemplar for future operations. All we need to do is link general friction with uncertainty in information and information loss, in turn, with entropy in physics.

The first step is to notice that every component of general friction identified by Clausewitz can be related to uncertainty in information. Unforeseeable occurrences and uncertainties in the data upon which action in war must be based are explicitly about information being either unavailable, distorted, ambiguous, or otherwise unreliable. As for the dangers and demands for exertion so manifest in war, they can be understood as impediments that inhibit combatants from using what information is available to orient themselves on the battlefield.

The other linkage we need can be found in Claude Shannon's work on the mathematical theory of communication. In 1948, Shannon was able to show that even in the simplest case of communication (discrete, noiseless systems),[73] the only equation that satisfies all the conditions necessary for describing the rate at which "information"[74] is produced has the same form as entropy (energy unavailable to do useful work) in statistical mechanics,[75] which is to say that entropy can be understood as a measure of the "lack of information about the structure of a system."[76]

Since statistical mechanics is a mathematical interpretation of classical thermodynamics,[77] general friction in war can be linked with the concept of entropy in the only important area of physics since Newton whose range of applicability has broadened steadily with the passage of time, rather than being increasingly constrained by limits.[78] How does this connection illuminate the idea that it is as important to attack the adversary's friction as it is to keep your own within manageable limits? While the second law of thermodynamics states that the entropy (or lost information) of an *isolated* system never diminishes, a conspicuous characteristic of all living organisms is a robust capacity to diminish their own entropy at the expense of the surrounding environment. Thus, what my prospective schema[79] for future operations emphasizes about war is the limit inherent in concentrating too narrowly upon the "well-oiled" functioning of your own military "machine." Even near-perfect efficiency regarding frictions internal to your own forces is no guarantor of victory if your operational schemes and patterns of employment are, as Eighth Air Force's were in the fall of 1943, divorced from the combat actions of the enemy and war's inherent unpredictability. Blind luck aside, operational patterns that fail to place the psychology of combat and war's unavoidable dominance by friction firmly at the center of things are unlikely to prepare combatants to take advantage of the enemy's frictions.

Summing Up

The thrust of this final chapter has been to advance the best possible case for supplanting the mechanistic image of war that has so long captivated US airmen with a more organic outlook. I would again reiterate, however, that absolutely compelling arguments for or against a more Clausewitzian paradigm are probably not possible: You can be "darned sure," but never 100 percent certain.

Nonetheless, to deny the possibility of certain knowledge in military affairs is not to deny the possibility of producing good reasons for preferring a more organic image of war, and we have hardly come up empty-handed. As a minimum, the arguments presented in this study surely justify the conclusion that whoever hopes to use military means to achieve political ends must take friction, particularly its cumulative or collective aspects, into account. Moreover, I think we have seen some awfully good reasons for doubting whether deterministic approaches could ever be expected to cope adequately with friction. As for how we choose to characterize alternative approaches to those of the engineer, it may matter little in the end whether Clausewitz's concept (general friction), Heisenberg's (uncertainty), Goedel's (undecidability), or Rudolf Clausius' (entropy) is used. At an operational level, it may not even be necessary to have an explicit conceptualization of the things that distinguish real war from war on paper. The point is that real war is profoundly different; and if we intend to win rather than lose, we must be able to master *Friktion im Kriege*—both as an inescapable impediment to activity and as a potent weapon.

NOTES

CHAPTER 7

1. Marshall, *Men Against Fire: The Problem of Battle Command in Future War*, p. 209.
2. Donald R. Baucom, "Technological War: Reality and the American Myth," *Air University Review*, September–October 1981, p. 57.
3. John F. Guilmartin, Jr., "Military Experience, the Military Historian, and the Reality of Battle" (address at the Shelby C. Davis Center for Historical Studies, Princeton University, 8 October 1982), p.4.
4. Instances of the developments I have in mind are Goedel's incompleteness theorems in mathematical logic, Heisenberg's uncertainty principle in quantum physics, and the second law of thermodynamics. So far as I know, John R. Boyd's unpublished 1976 paper, "Destruction and Creation," is the first serious attempt to bring such things to bear on the general problems of conflict and war.
5. Fabyanic, "Strategic Analysis and MX Deployment," p. 32.
6. Isaac Newton's great unifying work, the *Mathematical Principles of Natural Philosophy*, first appeared in 1687; a second edition followed in 1713, and a third in 1726.
7. In a 1969 postscript to the original 1962 edition of *The Structure of Scientific Revolutions*, Thomas Kuhn delineated two basic senses of the term 'paradigm.' "On the one hand, it stands for the entire constellation of beliefs, values, techniques, and so on shared by the members of a given community. On the other, it denotes one sort of element in that constellation, the concrete puzzle-solutions which, employed as models or examples, can replace explicit rules as a basis for the solution of the remaining puzzles of normal science" (Thomas S. Kuhn, *The Structure of Scientific Revolutions* (Chicago: University of Chicago Press, rev. ed., 1970), p. 175). My use of 'paradigm' in reference to the idea of the universe as a deterministic clockwork involves both senses of the term. As examples of the puzzle-solutions that might be elements in the constellation of beliefs comprising a "global" paradigm, Kuhn cites such propositions as: heat is the kinetic energy of the constituent parts of bodies, and the molecules of gas behave like tiny elastic billiard balls in random motion (p. 184). Insofar as these propositions can be plausibly subsumed under the notion of a deterministic universe, my use of 'paradigm' in discussing the worldview of Newton's successors is "global." But because the idea of the universe as a clockwork mechanism is, at most, a shorthand model for the entire constellation of beliefs that made up the "global" world view of Newton's immediate successors, it also acts like a concrete puzzle-solution within a global paradigm. I mention these problems of definition because the paradigm that has been the focus of this essay—the idea that war is an engineering science commensurate with pat formulas and exact calculations—exhibits this same ambiguity. You can plausibly subsume under a mechanistic image of war beliefs such as: aerial strategy is simply a matter of choosing targets; and a well-planned and well-conducted bombardment attack, once launched, cannot be stopped. But the notion of war as an engineering science also acts like a concrete puzzle-solution when viewed as a shorthand model for the entire constellation of beliefs that have comprised mainstream US air doctrine.
8. Sir Isaac Newton, *Mathematical Principles of Natural Philosophy*, trans. Andrew Motte in *The Great Books of the Western World*, ed. Robert M. Hutchins (Chicago: Encyclopedia Britannica, 1952), Vol. 34, pp. 276–84, 286–88, and 296–99. Newton's discovery of universal gravitation, like all his great thought, was conceived at his mother's house in Woolsthorpe during the plague years of 1665 and 1666. There, as Newton himself later said, "I deduced that the forces which keep the planets in their orbs must be reciprocally as the squares of their distances from the centres about which they revolve; and thereby

compared the force requisite to keep the moon in her orb with the force of gravity at the surface of the earth; and found them answer pretty nearly" (Bronowski, p. 223). In other words, Newton at once tested his gravitational theory by *calculating* the period of the moon and got a first rough answer close to the true value, about 27 1/4 days (Bronowski, pp. 222–23).

9. R. Harré, "Pierre Simon de Laplace," *The Encyclopedia of Philosophy,* ed. Paul Edwards (New York: MacMillan and the Free Press, 1967), Vol. 4, p. 392.

10. Dudley Shapere, "Isaac Newton," *The Encyclopedia of Philosophy,* Vol. 5, p. 491.

11. Hastings, *Bomber Command,* pp. 184–85; for the CBO plan's statement of the tasking from the Casablanca conference, see Appendix, pp. 135–6.

12. Hansell, *The Air Plan that Defeated Hitler,* p. 157.

13. *Trident Conference: May 1943, Papers and Meetings of Minutes,* p. 398.

14. Eaker, pp. 2–3 (A31826–27), 5–7 (A31829–31), and 10 (A31834). Eaker's presentation on this occasion consisted mainly of a verbatim reading of the CBO plan.

15. According to Hastings, Eaker went so far at one point as to assert that the percentages of destruction indicated in the CBO plan were conservative and could "be absolutely relied upon" (Hastings, p. 185).

16. Major General Haywood S. Hansell, Jr., telephone conversation with author, 10 December 1981.

17. Zeiberg's 1980 formulation of the "nuclear arithmetic" underlying America's dawning ICBM vulnerability went as follows: "Our Minuteman and Titan ICBM forces, which are based in hardened, reinforced concrete silos, will soon lose their ability to survive a nuclear attack. This danger results from the improved accuracy of a newly deployed generation of Soviet ICBMs. The warheads on these missiles are large enough and accurate enough to destroy any fixed target in the United States. They will be deployed in large numbers and will allow the Soviets to shoot two warheads at each of our ICBM silos" (Seymour L. Zeiberg, "M-X: The Full Perspective," *Defense 80,* September 1980, p. 3). Of course, even a modest attempt to think through the immense difficulties and uncertainties that the Soviets would face in actually executing such a strike tends to make the theoretical vulnerability of US land-based ICBMs appear somewhat less troubling. As Lambeth has recently noted, this much-heralded American vulnerability probably impresses US defense analysts more than it does the Soviets: "If Soviet decision makers derive any comfort at all from this impending US liability, it probably stems more from US expressions of anxiety over it than from any independent technical evaluations of their own counterforce capabilities" (Benjamin S. Lambeth, "Uncertainties for the Soviet War Planner," *International Security,* Winter 1982/1983, p. 151).

18. von Clausewitz, p. 85.

19. Gerald Holton, *Thematic Origins of Scientific Thought: Kepler to Einstein* (Cambridge, Massachusetts: Harvard University Press, 1973), p. 51. Obvious examples of "Cartesian" hypotheses in Newton's *Mathematical Principles of Natural Philosophy* would be his assumptions about space and time: Absolute, mathematical time, he asserted, "flows equably and without relation to anything external"; and absolute space "remains always similar and immovable" (Newton, p. 8).

20. Albert Einstein, "On the Electrodynamics of Moving Bodies," trans. W. Perret and G. B. Jeffrey in H. A. Lorentz et al., *The Principle of Relativity: A Collection of Original Memoirs on the Special and General Theory of Relativity* (New York: Dover, 1923), pp. 37–38 and 42.

21. As Einstein remarked late in life: "A theory can be tested by experience, but there is no way from experience to the setting up of a theory. Equations of such complexity as are the equations of the gravitational field can be found only through the discovery of a logically simple mathematical condition which determines the equations completely or [at least] almost completely" (Albert Einstein, "Autobiographical Notes" in *Albert Einstein: Philosopher-Scientist,* ed. Paul A. Schilpp (La Salle, Illinois: Open Court, 1949), p. 89).

22. Heisenberg's principle of uncertainty (or indeterminacy) states that the "information that the electron carries is limited in its totality. That is, for instance, its speed *and* its position fit *together* in such a way that they are confined by the tolerance of the quantum" (Bronowski, p. 365); or, somewhat more precisely, "h [Planck's constant, 6.62×10^{-27} erg sec] *represents an absolute limit to the simultaneous measurement of co-ordinate and momentum,* a limit which in the most favorable case we may get down to, but which we can never get beneath" (Max Born, *Atomic Physics* (New York: Hafner, 7th ed., 1962),

trans. John Dougall, p. 101). I would simply note that the similarity between indeterminacy in quantum physics and friction in war appears to be more than mere coincidence.

23. Bronowski, p. 352. Briefly summarized, Bronowski's argument against the possibility of absolute knowledge starts by characterizing the method of the artist as being that of a blind woman attempting to describe a man's face through her sense of touch. A portrait painter, for example, "does not so much fix the face as explore it . . . each line that is added strengthens the picture but never makes it final" (Ibid.). He then goes on to demonstrate that the electromagnetic spectrum of information available to physics is subject to the same lack of ultimate precision as the artist painting a man's face, which is to say that the method of the artist is also the method of science (pp. 353–55). Heisenberg's uncertainty principle is presented as a precise formulation of the idea that the information carried by the electron is limited in its totality.

24. Richard C. Jeffrey, *Formal Logic: Its Scope and Limits* (New York: McGraw-Hill, 1967), p. 196. In more technical terms, Church's theorem states that there is no algorithm (or mechanical procedure) that will always determine, in a finite number of steps, whether any predicate logic proposition (or formula) is a logical truth; equivalently, first-order predicate logic is *undecidable*. Of course, at least one mechanical procedure for testing predicate formulas is known to exist: Jeffrey's so-called "tree" method (pp. 63–79 and 111–16). Should you apply the tree method to a formula that happens to be a predicate-logic truth, then the procedure is guaranteed to tell you so in a finite number of steps. But if you apply Jeffrey's "tree" rules to nontruths, there are two possibilities: the procedure may identify the formula in question as a nontruth in a finite number of steps; or it may go on forever, thus giving no answer one way or the other. The logical structure of the sentence 'Someone does not love everyone' illustrates the second possibility. While just one narcissistic individual suffices to show that it cannot be a logical truth, the Jeffrey "tree" is infinite (pp. 142–44).

25. Formally, the generalized version of Goedel's "first incompleteness theorem" says that any axiom system rich enough to support Peano arithmetic is *incomplete* in the sense of being rich enough to permit the construction of a sentence which, when properly interpreted, asserts its own unprovability *within the system* and, hence, its own truth (Kurt Goedel, "On Formally Undecidable Propositions" in *From Frege to Goedel: A Source Book in Mathematical Logic, 1879–1931*, ed. Jean van Heijenoort (Cambridge, Massachusetts: Harvard University Press, 1967), pp. 598–99). The existence of such *undecidable* propositions destroys "the cozy relationship between truth and provability which we attempt to achieve in a formal system—namely that the set of true sentences [under any interpretation that makes the axioms all true] and the set of provable sentences be identical" (Howard DeLong, *A Profile of Mathematical Logic* (Menlo Park, California: Addison-Wesley, 1970), pp. 161–62).

26. DeLong, p. 193.

27. DeLong, p. 227.

28. Regarding possible recipes for winning a modern war during its initial period (that is, before the enemy has had time to mobilize, concentrate, and deploy his forces), Vigor has written: "Another lesson that we should learn from history concerning the waging of *Blitzkriegs* is that an accurate forecast of loss rates is never possible. . . . The conclusion to be drawn from this particular lesson is that the numbers of men and weapons and equipment that should be made available for the intended *Blitzkrieg* must be far higher than those theoretically arrived at during the preliminary planning sessions. Listen to the figures that your planner gives you, and immediately double them. Double them again for safety's sake, and add 20 percent for luck. . . . This approach is likely to prove fruitful" (Vigor, p. 95).

29. Kuhn, *The Structure of Scientific Revolutions*, p. 147. Paradigm shifts are not, in the final analysis, small matters. Consider, for example, Max Planck's sad observation that "a new scientific truth does not triumph by convincing its opponents and making them see the light, but rather because its opponents eventually die, and a new generation grows up that is familiar with it" (p. 151).

30. Thomas S. Kuhn, "Reflections on My Critics," *Criticism and the Growth of Knowledge*, ed. Imre Lakatos and Alan Musgrave (London: Cambridge University Press, 1970), p. 234.

31. Marshall, *Men Against Fire: The Problem of Battle Command in Future War*, p. 53.

32. Marshall, *Men Against Fire: The Problem of Battle Command in Future War*, pp. 42–43. Without question, the most shocking result of Marshall's investigations during World War II was the discovery that even within well-trained, campaign-seasoned American infantry units, no more than 25 percent of

the men actually persisted in firing their weapons at the enemy during combat actions (p. 50). What made this revelation so surprising was that not one of the battalion, company, and platoon commanders involved in Marshall's interviews had previously "made the slightest effort to determine how many of his men had actually engaged the enemy with a weapon" (p. 53). Yet there were many who, on first being asked about how many of their men had fired, made the automatic reply: "I believe that every man used a weapon at one time or another" (p. 54). Note, too, that the pattern of only a small percentage of individuals within combat units producing most of the results has by no means been limited to the infantry. For example, the Korean War ace Frederick Blesse (10 kills) concluded, based on his experience in MiG Alley, that a fighter squadron commander would be fortunate to have more than three pilots in his unit who possessed "those things necessary to be exceptional leaders and produce more than an occasional kill or two" (Frederick C. Blesse, "No Guts No Glory (A Reprint)," *USAF Fighter Weapons Review*, Spring 1973, p. 26). And more recently, Thomas J. Horner has deployed a range of evidence to support the likelihood that most of the US Army's "current tank crews will not be truly effective in combat. A few will be real *killers* and account for the bulk of the enemy tanks destroyed by our tanks; most will be *fillers*, simply maneuvering with the rest of the tanks and trying not to be destroyed themselves; and a number will be *fodder*, certain to be defeated within their first few encounters with the enemy" (Thomas J. Horner, "Killers, Fillers, and Fodder," *PARAMETERS, Journal of the US Army War College*, September 1982, p. 29).

33. Since the earliest days of air combat in 1915, when Oswald Boelcke and Max Immelmann first began flying together as a team because of their shared concern about the unseen adversary attacking from behind, the driving force in the evolution of air-to-air tactics has been the quest for effective schemes of mutual support given the fire and maneuver characteristics of current fighter aircraft (Barry D. Watts, "Fire, Movement and Tactics," *TOPGUN Journal*, Winter 1979/80, pp. 11–20).

34. My list of the factors that drive battle outcomes follows Clausewitz's summary of the strategic elements that affect the use of engagements for the purpose of war (von Clausewitz, p. 183). This list tacitly presumes the influence of other factors, notably human physiological limitations, the purpose of the conflict, the social-political realities affecting each side, and, of course, friction.

35. Guilmartin, pp. 7–8.

36. Guilmartin, p. 7.

37. Harry G. Summers, Jr., *On Strategy: The Vietnam War in Context* (Carlisle Barracks, Pennsylvania: US Army War College, 1981), p. 1.

38. Summers, pp. 31–32 and 57. Summers' Clausewitzian notion of strategy presumes that civilian and military decision makers engaged in war will develop coherent political and military objectives, a condition that was not met in the case of US involvement in Vietnam. For example, after 1964 the US Army tended to respond "mainly to Hanoi's simulated insurgency rather than to its real but controlled aggression," and "American political aims were never clear during the entire course of the war" (pp. 55–56 and 62).

39. Up until early 1966, Secretary of Defense Robert S. McNamara, who had more or less run the American effort in Vietnam to that point, viewed the war "almost exclusively in quantitative terms, calculating that the United States could win simply by committing its superior resources effectively" (Stanley Karnow, *Vietnam: A History* (New York: The Viking Press, 1983), p. 498).

40. Marshall, *Men Against Fire: The Problem of Battle Command in Future War*, pp. 207–8.

41. Martin van Creveld, *Fighting Power: German Military Performance, 1914–1945* (Potomac, Maryland: Canby and Luttwak Associates, December 1980), note on p. 30. This study was subsequently published by Greenwood Press in 1982.

42. General Ludwig Beck, *Truppenfuehrung (Troop Leading): German Field Service Regulations*, Part I, trans. US Army, Report No. 14,507, 18 March 1936, pp. 1–2. The psychological premise of the *Truppenfuehrung*'s introduction is clearly that, more often than not, men will fail under the intense pressures of actual combat. S. L. A. Marshall's discovery that no more than 25 percent of the World War II US infantrymen he surveyed immediately after engagements with the enemy had persisted in firing their weapons certainly supports this presumption.

43. van Creveld, pp. 36–37. Textual comparison of the two manuals readily confirms van Creveld's assessment. Most striking is the fact that the 1941 version of *FM [Field Manual] 100-5* omitted entirely

the introduction that provided the overarching context for the German regulations; instead, the US manual began with a series of definitions (War Department, *Field Service Regulations: Operations (FM 100–5)* (Washington, DC: US Government Printing Office, 1941), pp. 1–4).

44. For a brief account of Boyd's contributions to air combat tactics, see Watts, p. 9. Boyd's major work in this field is his *Aerial Attack Study* (Nellis AFB, Nevada: USAF Fighter Weapons School Document 50–10–6C, 1960).

45. A given cycle in this open-ended process is Boyd's so-called "OODA Loop." Price has characterized the OODA Loop concept as Lonergan's "cognitional theory writ large" (James R. Price, *Patterns of Conflict and Complex Technology* (Briefing, 5 March 1982), p. 17). As explained in Boyd's *Patterns of Conflict* briefing, his essential schema for combat is to "Observe, Orient, Decide and Act more inconspicuously, more quickly, and with more irregularity" than the opponent; or, put another way, the problem of combat is to "operate inside [the] adversary's Observation-Orientation-Decision-Action loops" (John R. Boyd, *Patterns of Conflict* (Briefing, April 1982), p. 122). Boyd himself has gone on to suggest that orientation, which inevitably draws upon far more of the individual's makeup and past than direct observations in an isolated OODA cycle, is the most important part of the process (John R. Boyd, *Organic Design for Command and Control* (Briefing, 11 March 1982), pp. 14–15).

46. Those inclined to resist the suggestion that Boyd's schema can be extended as far as I have implied should consider this question: In war, would you really prefer to be more conspicuous, more predictable, and slower than your adversaries?

47. Fagg, *The Army Air Forces in World War II*, Vol. 3, p. 785.

48. D'Olier, *The United States Strategic Bombing Survey: Over-All Report (European War)*, p. 108.

49. The conclusion of the official Army Air Forces history as of 1951 was that "allied air power had been *decisive* in the war *in Western Europe* [emphasis added]" (Fagg, *The Army Air Forces in World War II*, Vol. 3, p. 791). Three aspects of this judgment warrant comment. First, Fagg's wording carefully avoids the issue of weighing the Anglo-American contribution in Western Europe against that of the Soviets in the East. Second, his text is unequivocal in stating that of all the accomplishments of the British and American air forces in the West, "the attainment of air superiority was the most significant, for it made possible the invasions of the continent and gave the heavy bombers their opportunity to wreck the industries of the Reich" (p. 792). Third, Fagg's overall assessment is, on virtually all counts, identical to that rendered by the US Strategic Bombing Survey. To quote the summary report on the European air war, "Allied air power was decisive in the war in Western Europe. Hindsight inevitably suggests that it might have been employed differently in some respects. Nevertheless, it was decisive. In the air, its victory was complete; at sea, its contribution, combined with naval power, brought an end to the enemy's greatest naval threat—the U-boat; on land, it helped turn the tide overwhelmingly in favor of Allied ground forces. Its power and superiority made possible the success of the invasion. It brought the economy which sustained the enemy's armed forces to virtual collapse, although the full effects of this collapse had not reached the enemy's frontlines when they were overrun by Allied forces. It brought home to the German people the full impact of modern war with all its horror and suffering" (D'Olier, *The Unites States Strategic Bombing Survey: Over-All Report (European War)*, p. 107).

50. Although the US Strategic Bombing Survey and the official Army Air Forces history both called the Anglo-American air effort in Western Europe "decisive," they also skirted the issue of how much the Soviets contributed to final victory (see note 49 above). While I would argue that the demand for a quantitatively precise accounting of the importance of one causal strand among many is misguided, even the most casual glance at the magnitude and scale of the war on the Eastern Front surely suggests that the Soviet contribution to Nazi Germany's defeat cannot be so easily dismissed. "The Soviet-German war of 1941–1945 involved more men, guns, and more casualties and was fought over a more extended battlefront than any other war in history. The Soviet-German frontline stretched for 4,500 kilometers at the outbreak of war and was increased some 6,000 kilometers in the fall of 1942, when the Wehrmacht came close to overrunning the Caucasus. Even in January 1945, not long before the war ended, when the Germans were pulling back in almost all areas, the front was still 2,000 kilometers long. In comparison, the front in Western Europe in 1945 was 400 kilometers. Even the combined frontage upon which Western forces fought, in North Africa, Sicily, Italy, and southern France, was not nearly so extensive as that on which Soviet troops were engaged, and the numbers of Germans whom the Soviets faced were

also significantly greater" (Trevor N. Dupuy, *Great Battles on the Eastern Front: The Soviet–German War, 1941–1945* (Indianapolis/New York: Bobbs-Merrill, 1982), p. 1). Such facts notwithstanding, to this day most US and British assessments of the air effort in Western Europe have tended to ignore the Soviet contribution in the East. For example, Hansell's clearest reference to the Soviet contribution was to insist that Anglo-American bombing of German oil resources "played a vital part in making possible Russian victories in the East" (Hansell, *The Air Plan that Defeated Hitler*, p. 225). But Hansell's position here seems hard to defend historically: Among other things, the first major attack on Germany's petroleum industry, the August 1943 raid against the Rumanian refineries at Ploesti, occurred the month after the flower of the German *Panzer* elite was decimated in the Kursk salient by the Soviets (David Downing, *The Devil's Virtuosos: German Generals at War 1940–45* (New York: Saint Martin's Press, 1977), pp. 166–78).

51. "The United States," as Baucom has pointed out, "produces legions of managers, engineers, technicians, and bureaucrats. In time of war, we could draft ample numbers of people in all of these specialties; we could mobilize whole transportation companies and data-processing firms. But where will our soldiers come from if not from the armed forces?" (Baucom, p. 65.)

52. von Clausewitz, p. 102. Clausewitz explained *coup d'oeil* as "the quick recognition of a truth that the mind would ordinarily miss or would perceive only after study and reflection" (Ibid.). A more contemporary German figure of speech is *Fingerspitzengefuehl* (literally fingertip feel, but usually translated as instinct, intuition, or flair). Closely related to *coup d'oeil* and determination, according to Clausewitz, is presence of mind in the sense of an increased capacity to respond quickly to the unexpected (pp. 103–4).

53. The German Academy for Young Officers was reconstituted under Scharnhorst's direct supervision in 1810 and, shortly afterwards, the new school was renamed the Military School for Officers; in 1859, it became known as the *Kriegsakademie* or War Academy (Trevor N. Dupuy, *A Genius for War: The German Army and General Staff, 1807–1945* (Englewood Cliffs, New Jersey: Prentice-Hall, 1977), p. 30). Over the 135 years of its existence, this institution "educated what is collectively probably the single most talented group of military officers in modern military history" (C. A. Leader, "The Kriegsakadamie [sic]: Synthesizer of Clausewitzian Theory and Practice," unpublished draft, 30 July 1982, p. 1).

54. Dupuy, *A Genius for War: The German Army and General Staff, 1807–1945*, pp. 253–54. The Germans' superiority in fighting power was even more pronounced on the Russian Front: "German combat effectiveness superiority over the Russians in the early days of the war was close to 200 percent; this means that, on average, one German division was at least a match for three Russian divisions of comparable size and firepower, and that under favorable circumstance of defense, one German division theoretically could—and often did—hold off as many as seven comparable Russian divisions. In 1944 this superiority was still nearly 100 percent and the average German frontline soldier inflicted 7.78 Russian casualties for each German lost" (p. 254). The statistical data upon which Dupuy based his assessments of German fighting power during World War II can be found in Appendix E (pages 336–43) of *A Genius for War*.

55. *Kampfkraft* is one of those key terms used in German military writings that "have no English equivalent and are indeed untranslatable" (van Creveld, p. 189).

56. van Creveld, p. 157.

57. van Creveld, pp. 76–79. At the *Wehrmacht*'s psychological laboratory, "willpower and the inclination towards an outdoor life; technical competence and a warlike nature (manifested, among other things, by rebelliousness at school; to have repeated a class or two was accordingly taken as a point in favor); the capacity to represent and the ability to lead; these, and not cerebral excellence per se, were presumed to be the prime qualities needed in an officer" (p. 155). In the Israeli Army, officer selection, training, and promotion all appear to be based on values and methods very similar to those pursued by Riefert and Simoneit. "The officer in the IDF is neither first a gentleman nor a technical manager. His claim to leadership and position rests in his ability to demonstrate that he is the first soldier in the unit, the best of the bred." (Major Richard A. Gabriel and Colonel Reuven Gal, "The IDF Officer: Linchpin in Unit Cohesion," *Army*, January 1984, p. 43.)

58. van Creveld, pp. 157–58.

59. As of the early 1970s, Israeli screening of aircrew candidates was largely "based on intense psychological testing on the ground, personally observed by instructor pilots as well as psychologists. Cadets in groups are assigned physical problems—such as getting everyone across a small stream within a certain time limit—using only the materials at hand. Instructors can thus determine at first hand which ones possess qualities of leadership and innovation" (J. A. Cook as cited in Edward W. Youngling et al., *Feasibility Study to Predict Combat Effectiveness for Selected Military Roles: Fighter Pilot Effectiveness* (St Louis, Missouri: McDonnell Douglas, 29 April 1977), MDC E1634, p. 3–80). Moreover, after successful completion of basic and advanced pilot training, the Israeli practice in the early 1970s was to assign all fighter pilots to the A–4 for at least 18 months, with subsequent matriculation into air-to-air units being based on individual success during a small number of flights against two or three of the very best air-to-air combat pilots in Israel (pp. 3-82 and 3-83). .

60. "Though the identification of 'character' and the prediction of its future development were enormously difficult tasks that must sometimes have led to errors (not to mention the influence of political considerations which, prior to 1933, denied 'character' not merely to anybody tinged slightly red but also to scions of the 'wrong' families), it cannot be denied that the Germans tried hard and, in doing so, pioneered methods that are in use in many armies" (van Creveld, p. 158).

61. van Creveld, pp. 51–52 and 87. In fairness, the US Army's recently adopted COHORT (Cohesion, Operational Readiness, and Training) system aims at increasing unit cohesion by emphasizing shared training experiences and personnel stability at the company level *(The New Manning System: Unit Replacement/Regimental System* (Washington, DC: Department of the Army, 15 October 1982), DA Circular 600–82-2, p. 2–1).

62. van Creveld, p. 104.

63. van Creveld, pp. 88–89. This pattern of going to extraordinary lengths to preserve the cohesion of combat units was equally evident in the *Luftwaffe*. "Units were not left in the frontline for interminable periods of time, with replacements arriving one or two at a time. Rather, when units had been badly shattered by heavy losses, they were pulled out of the line to be physically rebuilt with new crews and new aircraft. The Germans were thus *able to renew the bonds between those who would fly and fight together and who would depend on each other for survival*" [emphasis added]. (Murray, *Strategy for Defeat: The Luftwaffe, 1933–1945*, p. 318).

64. van Creveld, p. 188. By comparison, the US Army during World War II tended to concentrate its lower quality recruits in the ground combat arms (p. 82).

65. Murray, *Strategy for Defeat: The Luftwaffe, 1933–1945*, p. 318.

66. Israeli military directives for combat leaders in the mid-1960s reflected an orientation remarkably similar to that of the *Wehrmacht*'s World War II *Truppenfuehrung*. Consider, for example, these standing Israeli instructions: "[1] When your orders have not gotten through, assume what they must be. [2] When in doubt, strike. . . . [6] The battle will never go as you planned it. Improvise. [7] Surprise is your most important weapon. [8] Risk, risk, risk" (S. L. A. Marshall, *Swift Sword: The Historical Record of Israel's Victory, June 1967* (New York: American Heritage, 1967), p. 133). For a more recent and systematic account of the Israeli approach to leadership, see Gabriel and Gal's "The IDF Officer: Linchpin in Unit Cohesion" in the January 1984 issue of *Army*.

67. As *General die Infantrie* Guenther Blumentritt wrote in a 1952 essay on the role of character in war: "Knowledge is important: efficiency even more so. But character and personality are the most important. Knowledge can easily fail and can, in fact, be the cause of failure. Not intelligence but character is the unfailing factor. Only character is reliable in tough situations and a dependable companion in combat" (Leader, p. 42).

68. Leader offers von Manstein's *Lost Victories*, Foertsch's three basic rules for conducting training, and Rommel's operational style as evidence of the assimilation of Clausewitz by the German officer corps (Leader, pp. 24–26). As further evidence, I would mention Hermann Balck's insistence that the World War II *Wehrmacht* "lived off a century-long tradition, which is that in a critical situation the subordinate with an understanding of the overall situation can act or react responsibly" *(Generals Balck and von Mellenthin on Tactics: Implications for NATO Military Doctrine* (McLean, Virginia: BDM Corporation, 19 December 1980), BDW/W–81–077–TR, p. 19). This tradition of Balck's appears aimed at one thing: overcoming friction. It is also instructive to compare these words of Balck's with those in

paragraph 10 of the introduction to the German *Truppenfuehrung* (see pages 114–15); the former were spoken in 1980 while the latter were written no later than 1933.

69. "The role of the Kriegsakadamie was to take the objective science of Clausewitzian theory and synthesize it into the subjective form of military skills possessed by the students. There was no role on the General Staff for soldiers who were pure theorists" (Leader, p. 23).

70. Blumentritt, who wrote extensively on pre-World War II German military education after the war was over, has stated that "neither at the officer candidate [level] nor at the three-year Kriegsakadamie did we have anything detailed concerning Clausewitz's philosophy of war" (Leader, p. 22). In fact, he went so far to say that by the eve of World War II, *On War* had at most been read by possibly 100 officers of the German Army and been understood by 50 (Ibid.).

71. von Clausewitz, p. 142.

72. By way of documenting how thoroughly Clausewitzian the *Kriegsakademie*'s approach to war was, I would offer the following passage from the concluding chapter to Book One of *On War*. "We have identified danger, physical exertion, intelligence, and friction as the elements that coalesce to form the atmosphere of war, and turn it into a medium that impedes activity. In their restrictive effects they can be grouped into a single concept of general friction. Is there any lubricant that will reduce this abrasion? Only one, and a commander and his army will not always have it readily available: combat experience. . . . In war the experienced soldier reacts rather in the same way as the human eye does in the dark: the pupil expands to admit what little light there is, discerning objects by degrees, and finally seeing them distinctly. By contrast, the novice is plunged into the deepest night. No general can accustom an army to war. Peacetime maneuvers are a feeble substitute for the real thing; but even they can give an army an advantage over others whose training is confined to routine, mechanical drill. To plan maneuvers so that some of the elements of friction are involved, which will train officers' judgment, common sense, and resolution is far more worthwhile than inexperienced people might think. It is immensely important that no soldier, whatever his rank, should wait for war to expose him to those aspects of active service that amaze and confuse him when he first comes across them. If he has met them even once before, they will begin to be familiar to him" (von Clausewitz, p. 122).

73. Telegraphy, where the message is a sequence of letters and the signal a sequence of dots, dashes and spaces, is an example of a discrete communication system; radio and television, by contrast, typify continuous systems (Claude E. Shannon and Warren Weaver, *The Mathematical Theory of Communication* (Urbana, Illinois: University of Illinois Press, 1980), pp. 34–5).

74. For Shannon, the word 'information' has a technical definition that is almost opposite to its usual sense. Not only did Shannon view the meaning of words in messages as irrelevant to the engineering aspects of communicating them, but he formally defined information as a measure of one's freedom of choice when selecting a message (Shannon and Weaver, pp. 8–9 and 31). Thus, information in Shannon's technical usage has "a special meaning that measures freedom of choice and hence uncertainty as to what choice has been made" (p. 19).

75. Shannon and Weaver, pp. 12–13 and 48–51.

76. G. J. Withrow, "Entropy," *The Encyclopedia of Philosophy*, Vol. 2, p. 528.

77. "By the middle of the 19th century it was clear that two distinct principles were involved in the theory of heat. On the one hand, in any closed system—any system theoretically isolated from the rest of the universe—the total quantity of energy is constant. . . . This law of conservation of energy (First Law of Thermodynamics) therefore asserts the invariance of the total *quantity* of energy in a system that is not interacting with its surroundings. On the other hand, the Second Law of Thermodynamics concerns the *quality* of this energy, that is, the amount of energy available in the system for doing useful work. It determines the direction in which thermodynamic processes occur and expresses the fact that, although energy can never be lost, it may become unavailable for doing mechanical work. This law, as formulated by Rudolf Clausius and William Thomson (later Lord Kevin), was a refinement and generalization of the hypothesis that heat cannot, of itself, pass from a colder to a hotter body" (Withrow, p. 526). In 1854 Clausius restated the second law of the thermodynamics in terms of entropy (from the Greek for 'a transformation'), asserting that the entropy of an isolated system never diminishes (Ibid.). However, because the thermodynamic concept of entropy did not represent anything that could be readily apprehended by the senses or grasped intuitively, in the second half of the 19th century physicists such as

Ludwig Boltzmann sought a mechanical interpretation. Boltzmann's statistical interpretation of the second law was that "any closed system tends toward an equilibrium state or maximum probability, which is associated with equalization of temperature, pressure, and so forth"; in other words, the law signifies that ordered arrangements tend to degenerate into disordered ones (p. 527).

78. According to Weaver, as early as 1874 Ludwig Boltzmann observed in some of his work on statistical mechanics that entropy is related to "missing information" inasmuch as entropy has to do with "the number of alternatives which remain possible after all microscopically observable information concerning it has been recorded" (Shannon and Weaver, p. 3). Leo Szilard extended Boltzmann's idea to information in physics in 1925, and John von Neumann treated information in quantum mechanics and particle physics in 1932 (Ibid.).

79. By 'schema' I simply mean a pattern requiring intelligent application in each and every situation.

APPENDIX

General Eaker's Presentation of the Combined Bomber Offensive Plan to the Joint Chiefs of Staff

This appendix reproduces the record copy (number 22 of 22) of the meeting of the US Joint Chiefs of Staff at which Major General Ira C. Eaker presented the plan for the Combined Bomber Offensive from the United Kingdom. Originally classified SECRET, this document is available in the US National Archives (Washington, DC, Archives Record Group 218, CSS 334, 71st–86th Meetings, pages A31823–A31838). Except for correcting obvious misspellings and punctuation errors, the text has been reprinted verbatim from the JCS records.

Joint Chiefs of Staff

Minutes of Meeting Held in Room 100-A, The Combined Chiefs of Staff Building, on THURSDAY, April 29, 1943, at 1400

Present

Admiral W. D. Leahy, USN
General G. C. Marshall, USA

Admiral E. J. King, USN
General H. H. Arnold, USA

Secretariat

Brigadier General J. R. Deane, USA
Captain F. B. Royal, USN

Additional Officers Present

Lieutenant General S. D. Embick, USA
Lieutenant General J. W. Stilwell, USA
Lieutenant General J. T. McNarney, USA
Brigadier General O. A. Anderson, USA
Captain C. R. Brown, USN

Vice Admiral R. Willson, USN
Vice Admiral R. S. Edwards, USN
Major General I. C. Eaker, USA
Rear Admiral C. M. Cooke, Jr., USN
Rear Admiral B. H. Bieri, USN
Brigadier General T. J. Hanley, USA
Brigadier General J. E. Hull, USA
Brigadier General A. C. Wedemeyer, USA
Colonel C. P. Cabell, USA
Colonel E. O'Donnell, USA
Colonel S. E. Anderson, USA
Colonel W. R. Wolfinbarger, USA
Colonel J. E. Smart, USA
Colonel Henry Berliner, USA
Colonel C. B. Bubb, USA
Commander V. D. Long, USN
Lieutenant A. Peter, USN
Mr. B. L. Webster

1. PLAN FOR COMBINED BOMBER OFFENSIVE FROM THE UNITED KINGDOM (JCS 277)

ADMIRAL LEAHY called the meeting to order, and Major General M. S. Fairchild introduced General Eaker who gave the following presentation on the above subject:

Introduction

Gentlemen:

This is a copy of a report recently completed by the Committee of Operations Analysts in the United States, and submitted to the Commanding General, European Theater of Operations for further analysis, and for recommendations. (Copy of large folder "Report of Committee of Operations Analysts" was shown.)

The Committee of Operations Analysts consists of some of the most highly qualified economic and industrial experts available in the United States, and they have made use of the best sources of information both in the United States and in Great Britain including:

> The Board of Economic Warfare
> The Office of Strategic Services
> The Ministry of Economic Warfare
> The Air Ministry
> War Department G-2, and the
> War Production Board

The report of the Operations Analysts comprises a detailed study of the vulnerability to air attack of the German economic, industrial and military structures. After careful examination, research and analysis, it lists nineteen systems of objectives which are suitable to air attack.

The report has been examined by the Target Analysts of the Air Ministry in London as well as our own Target Analysts in the Eighth Air Force.

The result is the complete agreement on the high priority objectives which are suitable for air attack.

Having agreed upon the *suitability* of the objectives, there remains the problem of determining the *feasibility*, from the tactical point of view, of destroying them; the selection of a limited number of them which would accomplish the mission assigned the bomber forces operating from the U.K.; and the determining of the size and composition of the force required.

To meet this latter problem (determination of the *feasibility* of carrying out the tactical operations), a Joint Board—including members of the RAF as well as the Eighth Air Force—was appointed. The Board was given the two-fold task:

a. To make a careful study of the Report of Operations Analysts on industrial targets in Germany.

b. To determine the Air Force required progressively and effectively to attack with sufficient force to accomplish the destruction and neutralization of the most vital industrial targets.

The Board was headed by Commanders with combat operational experience in this theater, who approached the problem in the knowledge that they might have to carry out the plan which they recommended. Other members of the Board comprised target analysts who have been working on this problem ever since the Eighth Air Force arrived in this theater. They worked in continuous collaboration with experienced bombardment personnel of the RAF.

The report submitted by this Board has been subject to the most careful examination by the Chief of the Air Staff, Royal Air Force, and the Air Officer, Commanding in Chief, British Bomber Command as well as the Commanding General, European Theater of Operations. In its present form it has their unqualified indorsement.

Because the wording of the report has been so carefully examined by those RAF Commanders and has received their complete agreement, I should like to read to you verbatim the salient parts of the report.

The Combined Bomber Offensive From the UK

1. The Mission

The mission of the U.S. and British Bomber Forces, as prescribed by the Combined Chiefs of Staff at Casablanca, is as follows:

To conduct a joint U.S.-British air offensive to accomplish the "progressive destruction and dislocation of the German military, industrial and economic system, and the undermining of the morale of the German people to a point where their capacity for armed resistance is fatally weakened." This is constructed as meaning "so weakened as to permit initiation of final combined operations on the Continent."

2. The Principal Objectives

A thorough study of those elements of the German military, industrial, and economic system which appeared to be profitable as bombing objectives was made by a group of Operations Analysts consisting of eminent U.S. experts. The Report of the Operations Analysts concludes that:

> The destruction and continued neutralization of some sixty (60) targets would gravely impair and might paralyze the Western Axis war effort. There are several combinations of targets from among the industries studied which might achieve this result.

Examination of this report shows complete agreement by U.S. and British experts. From the systems proposed by the Operations Analysts, six systems, comprising *seventy-six (76) precision targets* have been selected. These targets are located within the tactical radius of action of the two air forces, and their destruction is directed against the three major elements of the German military machine: its submarine fleet, its air force, and its ground forces, and certain industries vital to their support.

The six systems are:

    Submarine construction yards and bases.
    German aircraft industry.
    Ball Bearings.
    Oil.
    Synthetic rubber and tires.
    Military transport vehicles.

Concentration of effort against these systems will have the following effect. The percent of destruction is as indicated by the Operations Analysts.

Submarine Construction Yards and Bases.

Destruction of the submarine building yards selected will reduce present submarine construction by eighty-nine percent (89%). Attack of submarine bases will affect the submarine effort at sea. If it is found that successful results can be achieved, these attacks should continue whenever conditions are favorable for as long and as often as is necessary.

German Aircraft Industry.

Depletion of the German air force will fatally weaken German capacity to resist our air and surface operations. Complete domination of the air is essential for our ultimate decisive effort. Destruction of forty-three percent (43%) of the German fighter capacity and sixty-five percent (65%) of the German bomber capacity is provided for in this Plan, and will produce the effect required.

Ball Bearings.

The critical condition of the ball bearing industry in Germany is startling. The concentration of that industry renders it outstandingly vulnerable to air attack. Seventy-six percent (76%) of the ball bearing production can be eliminated by destruction of the targets selected. This will have immediate and critical repercussions on the production of tanks, airplanes, artillery, diesel engines—in fact, upon nearly all the special weapons of modern war.

Oil.

The quantities of petroleum and synthetic oil products now available to the Germans are barely adequate to supply the life blood which is vital to the German war machine. The oil situation is made more critical by failure of the Germans to secure and retain the Russian supplies. If the Ploesti refineries, which process thirty-five percent (35%) of current refined oil products available to the Axis, are destroyed, and the synthetic oil plants in Germany which process an additional thirteen percent (13%) are also destroyed, the resulting distribution will have a disastrous effect upon the supply of finished oil products available to the Axis.

Synthetic Rubber and Tires.

These products are vital to all phases of German military strength on land and in the air. Provision is made for destruction of fifty percent (50%) of the synthetic rubber capacity and nearly all of the tire production. This destruction will have a crippling effect.

Military Transport Vehicles.

Seven (7) plants produce a large proportion of the military transport and armored vehicles. The precise proportion is unknown. Loss of these plants will strike directly at the German military strength. *The cumulative effect of the destruction of the targets comprising the systems just listed will "fatally weaken" the capacity of the German people for armed resistance.*

The selection of these objectives is confirmed by the fact that the systems about which the Germans are most sensitive, and about which they have concentrated their defenses such as ballons, camouflage, anti-aircraft, searchlights, decoys and smoke are:

    Aircraft Factories.
    Submarine Construction Yards.
    Ball Bearings.
    Oil.

3. Intermediate Objective

The Germans, recognizing the vulnerability of their vital industries, are rapidly increasing the strength of their fighter defenses. The German fighter strength in Western Europe is being augmented. *If the growth of the German fighter strength is not arrested quickly, it may become literally impossible to carry out the destruction planned and thus to create the conditions necessary for ultimate decisive action by our combined forces on the Continent.*

Hence the successful prosecution of the air offensive against the principal objective is dependent upon a prior (or simultaneous) offensive against the German fighter strength.

(See Chart A.*) To carry out the Eighth Air Force's part of this combined bomber offensive, it will be necessary to attack precision targets deep in German territory in daylight. The principal obstacle to this is the growing strength of the German air force. The growth of this fighter force has become so pronounced as to warrant a brief review of this development.

This upper curve shows what has been happening to the German air force in the past nine (9) months. As you will see, the bomber strength has been sharply reduced from 1,760 bombers to 1,450 in operational units. The fighters, on the other hand, increased from 1,690 to 1,710. They suffered a reduction in strength doubtless caused by the intense operations in Russia and the Mediterranean as well as in the Western Front, but those losses have been made good at the expense of the bombers. That same trend is reflected in the lower curve, which shows production was maintained fairly constantly for about five (5) months and then increased so that fighter production has risen from 720 to 810 per month. Over a longer period of time, from the entrance of the U.S. into the war until the present time, the trend has been even more pronounced. German fighter strength has increased by forty-four

---

*Copies of the charts and maps shown during General Eaker's presentation have not survived in the National Archives collection.

percent (44%) in that period in spite of the heavy losses. (See Chart B.) This chart shows the margin of production over average monthly wastage in German fighters. Of course, the monthly wastage has not been constant over the past seven (7) months, as shown on the chart, but the average for that period has been fairly accurately determined as 655 fighters per month. The production rate as of last February showed 810 fighters per month. The average increase in production over the six (6) month period indicated a monthly surplus of production over average wastage of 108 airplanes. If this trend simply continues in its present ratio, it is well within the capacity of the Germans to produce enough fighter airplanes over and above wastage to provide a strength of 3,000 fighters by this time next year. (See Chart A.) This is, of course, a capability and not necessarily a German intention, although current German development points very strongly in that direction. The increase in fighter strength is not reflected in this curve covering the past eight (8) months; however, during that period the Germans diverted a great many fighter type airplanes into fighter bombers and fighter reconnaissance airplanes. The wastage rate was very high in those units and that probably accounts for the temporary decline in German fighter strength; however, in the last three (3) months it has shown a sharp uprise.

(See Chart C.) The disposition of German fighters is also significant. The top line shows the number of fighters on the Western Front. Since we entered the war, that strength has nearly doubled. It has risen from 420 to 830. This in spite of the heavy drains on the Russian and Mediterranean fronts. When we entered the war, only thirty-six percent (36%) of German fighters were concentrated on the Western Front; today, fifty percent (50%) of all fighters available to the German air force are concentrated in opposition to our principal bombing effort from the U.K. The German fighter force is taking a toll of our forces both by day and by night, not only in terms of combat losses but more especially in terms of reduced tactical effectiveness. If the German fighters are materially increased in number it is quite conceivable that they could make our daylight bombing unprofitable and perhaps our night bombing too. On the other hand, if the German fighter force is partially neutralized our effectiveness will be vastly improved.

For this reason German fighter strength must be considered as an *intermediate* objective second to none in priority.

4. Integrated Royal Air Force—U.S. Army Air Forces Offensive

The combined efforts of the entire U.S. and British bomber forces can produce the results required to achieve the mission prescribed for this Theater. Fortunately, the capabilities of the two forces are entirely complementary.

The tremendous and ever-increasing striking power of the RAF bombing is designed to *so* destroy German material facilities as to undermine the willingness and ability of the German worker to continue the war. Because of this, there is great flexibility in the ability of the RAF to direct its material destruction against those objectives which are closely related to the U.S. bombing effort, which is directed toward the destruction of specific essential industrial targets. It is considered that the most effective results from strategic bombing will be obtained by directing the combined day and night effort of the U.S. and British bomber forces to all-out attacks against targets which are mutually complementary in undermining a limited number of selected objective systems. All-out attacks imply precision bombing of related targets by day and night where tactical conditions permit, and area bombing by night against the cities associated with these targets. The timing of the related day and night attacks will be determined by tactical consideration.

This plan does not attempt to prescribe the major effort of the RAF Bomber Command. It simply recognizes the fact that when precision targets are bombed by the Eighth Air Force in daylight, the effort should be complemented and completed by RAF bombing attacks against the surrounding industrial area at night. Fortunately, the industrial areas to be attacked are in most cases identical with the industrial areas which the British Bomber Command has selected for mass destruction anyway. They include Hamburg, Bremen, Hanover, Berlin, Leipzig, Wilhelmshaven, Bremershire, Cologne, Stuttgart, and many other principal cities. They also, of course, include smaller towns whose principal significance is coupled with the precision targets prescribed for the Eighth Air Force.

5. General Plan and Forces Required

a. It would be highly desirable to initiate precision bombing attacks against German fighter assembly and engine factories immediately. However, our present force of day bombers is too small to make the deeper penetrations necessary to reach the majority of these factories. Considering the number of German fighters which can be concentrated laterally to meet our bombers on penetration, and again on withdrawal, it is felt that 300 heavy bombers is the minimum operating force necessary to make deep penetrations.

The general tactical plan of operations with this minimum force involves the following general conception. A holding attack intending to attract German fighters to a particular area and prevent their massing against the main attacking force. For this purpose, fifty (50) heavy bombers with fighter escort are required. Second, a main striking force to penetrate through the fighter defenses and carry out the destruction of targets in Germany and return. Two hundred (200) bombers is considered the minimum requirement to provide self-protection and at the same time carry out worthwhile destruction. Third, the covering force to attack still another area and attract fighters in order to divert them from the main force on withdrawal. Again, fifty (50) bombers with fighter escort is the minimum force to carry out such a function.

b. In order to establish a yardstick to be used in the determination of the number of bombers required to destroy the objectives desired, the following procedure was employed:

Twelve successful missions were conducted in January, February, and March. Approximately 100 bombers were dispatched on each. It was found that sufficient bombs fell within a circle of a 1,000-foot radius centered about the aiming point to cause the desired destruction. For each prospective target the number of 1,000-foot radius circles necessary to cover it has been calculated. The yardstick as determined by experience is therefore: the number of 1,000-foot radius circles of destruction, each requiring 100 bombers.

c. The plan of operations is divided into four phases. The depth of penetration, the number of targets available, and the capacity of the bombing forces increases successively with each phase. (See Chart E.)

Seventy-six precision targets have been selected for Eighth Air Force bombing operations. Having selected these seventy-six (76) targets, the questions arise: Can they be effectively destroyed, and if so how many bombers will be required? As to the first question, operational experience answers yes.

Effectiveness of Eighth Air Force

The operations of the U.S. Army Air Force in daylight bombing of defended objectives in German occupied Europe have been sufficient to establish a criterion of precision daylight bombing effectiveness; the operations of the RAF Bomber Command leave no room for doubt of the ability of that force to devastate industrial areas.

The daylight operations of the Eighth Air Force from January 3, 1943, to April 6, 1943, definitely establish the fact that it is possible to conduct precision pattern bombing operations against selected precision targets from altitudes of 20,000 feet to 30,000 feet in the face of anti-aircraft artillery and fighter defenses.

Of 20 missions dispatched by the U.S. Eighth Air Force in that period, 12 have been highly effective. These 12 daylight missions have been directed against a variety of targets, including:

Submarine Bases.
Locomotive shops.
Power houses.
Marshalling yards.

Shipbuilding yards.
Motor Vehicle and Armament works.
Airplane Engine Factory.

The average number of aircraft dispatched against these targets has been eighty-six.

The destructive effect has, in every case, been highly satisfactory. From this experience, it may be definitely accepted that 100 bombers dispatched on each successful mission will provide entirely satisfactory destructive effect of that part of the target area within 1,000 feet of the aiming point, and that two-thirds of the missions dispatched each month will be successful to this extent.

In computing the force required, a yardstick of 100 bombers dispatched per target area of 1,000 feet about each aiming point has been accepted as a reasonable product of actual experience to date. Each target has been evaluated in terms of these "Target Units," or the number of 1,000-foot radius circles in which this destructive effect must be produced.

Experience in the Theater to date indicates that at least 800 airplanes must be in the Theater to dispatch 300 bombers on operations. Hence, until the level of U.S. bomber strength in this Theater reaches approximately 800, it will not be feasible to sustain a precision bombing offensive against the German fighter factories. It is estimated that we will be able to accommodate and train a force of this capacity by July of this year. In the interim every effort should be made to reduce the German fighter force by attack of those fighter factories which *can* be reached, and by combat under favorable conditions. The repair depots and airdromes are included for the purpose of giving commanders the necessary tactical latitude. Concurrently, operations can be conducted against submarine installations within reach and against other targets contributing directly to the principal objectives which are within covering range of our own fighters, or which do not require deep penetration. Some operations will have to be conducted to provide the necessary training for the incoming forces; such operations must be conducted against objectives within the listed categories.

During the next phase, from July to October, in which it is estimated that we will be able to penetrate to a limit of 400 miles, a determined effort must be made to break down the German fighter strength by every means at our disposal, concentrating primarily upon fighter aircraft factories. During this time interim an additional increment of 248 bombers are required so that the strength in the Theater by October should be approximately 1,192. This would provide a striking force of 450 bombers at the end of this period. The average striking force during this period would be 400.

During the third phase the German fighter force must be kept depleted, and the other sources of German strength must also be undermined. During this phase, our bombing offensive forces must be adequate to perform all their major tasks.

From October to January an additional increment of 554 bombers are required, bringing the total to 1,746. This should provide an operational striking force of 655 bombers at the end of that time. The average striking force during this period will be 550 bombers.

During the last phase—early 1944—the entire force should be used to sustain the effect already produced and to pave the way for the Combined Operation on the Continent. This will require a force of 2,702 heavy bombers.

It will be observed that these charts of the actual location of the targets to be attacked in each phase show the joint bombing effort of each phase. (See Map First Phase.) It will be noted that in the first phase, operations are limited to relatively shallow penetration. They include submarine bases along the coast, submarine construction yards, and the Focke Wulf airplane factory at Bremen. Actually, of course, these operations have all been undertaken with the small forces available and in the case of the submarine yards, Vegesack and the Focke Wulf plant at Bremen, a long step has already been taken toward completion of the plan. There are two (2) other systems of operations calling for deep penetrations shown in this phase. One of them calls for an attack against oil installations in the Ruhr. This operation is entirely contingent upon an earlier attack from the Mediterranean area against the oil refineries at Ploesti in Rumania. Such an attack is under consideration now and if it is carried out we will be forced to operate against the Rhur refineries in order to exploit the advantage achievement in Rumania. The other attack calls for a very deep penetration at Schweinfurt. This operation might be undertaken as a surprise attack in view of the tremendous advantage accrued from a successful destruction of these plants; however, it would be most unwise to attempt it until we are perfectly sure we have enough force to destroy the objective in a single operation. Any attempt to repeat such an attack will meet with very bitter opposition. (See Map Second Phase.) In the second phase, the plan calls for a concentration of effort against the German fighter assembly and fighter aircraft factories as well as attacks against airdromes and repair facilities. It is anticipated that approximately 75% of the striking force will be applied to this end during this phase. The other 25% is directed against submarine construction yards. (See Map Third Phase.) In the third phase an all-out attack against all the principal objectives is provided as well as repeat operations to continue neutralization of installations which have been destroyed and which can be repaired. (See Map Fourth Phase.) During the fourth phase these operations are continued and allowances made for concentration of attacks against military installations more directly associated with a cross-channel operation such as rail transportation, arsenals, military installations, etc.

The determination of the number of aircraft required in each phase has been based strictly upon past experience. As to rate of operations, we have averaged six (6) per month over the past six (6) months' experience. In the past three (3) months we have actually carried out twelve (12) highly successful operations out of a total of twenty (20). This plan is based on a total of twelve (12) successful operations in each three (3) month phase and recognizes the probability that the other six (6) will for one reason or another be less satisfactory. Experience has shown that about 3/8 of the total number of airplanes in the Theater can be dispatched on operational missions at any one time. This makes allowances for the airplanes in depot reserve, those in depot repair, and those being ferried and modified. There is every reason to believe that our forces will be more effective in the future than these figures would indicate. We will have the benefit of experience gained up to date; however, in order to be as realistic as possible the plan has been based in each case upon actual past experience.

(See Map Fourth Phase.) This chart tabulates all the targets for contemplated destruction by the U.S. and British bomber forces to carry out the mission. The precision targets for attacks by the U.S. Bomber Command are shown as small symbols. The cities and towns in or near those precision targets and which constitute the complementary targets of the RAF are shown as red circles. The German fighters are at present deployed in four (4) main concentrations positioned well forward toward the coast. In general, the day fighters are in four (4) lots of approximately 100 each in the general areas of northwest coastal Germany, Holland and Belgium, the channel coast of France and Western France in the vicinity of the submarine pens. These fighters are capable of concentrating laterally from bases at least 200 miles away so that forces of 300 fighters might be employed against our main efforts if we penetrated directly toward the Ruhr without distracting or diverting part of them.

(See Chart D.) This chart is illustrative of the effect of this plan of operations upon the intermediate objective, German fighter strength. This chart must be considered as pictorial rather than precise. The top line shows the increase in German fighter strength. That is a German capability if they choose to follow it. If German production is not interrupted and if German wastage is not increased it is possible for Germany to have in operation 3,000 fighters by next April. The broken line shows the effect of our operations upon that German fighter strength. In the first phase we do not expect to accomplish a great deal because our forces will have not have been built up to decisive proportions. In the second phase, our attacks against German fighter factory and engine factories and the increased attrition should cause the levelling off of the German fighter strength. In the third phase the full effect of the attacks against German fighter production should make themselves felt so that German fighter strength should fall off rapidly in this phase. In the fourth phase that German fighter strength should decline at a precipitant rate. This second line has been computed in the following manner. The decrease in German fighter strength is the result of two factors. One is the attacks against German fighter factories, the other the accelerated rate of combat wastage caused by our increased bomber forces. This wastage rate has been computed in an extremely conservative manner. It is realized that past claims evaluated of enemy aircraft shot down may seem high, although our evaluation of them is very careful and is, I believe, quite sound; nevertheless, in order to avoid any charge of unwarranted optimism, we have arbitrarily divided our combat claims by four (4), the resulting decrease in German fighter strength dependent upon expected combat wastage is at a rate only one quarter as great as our present combat claims. Even under these very conservative assumptions, it is apparent that the German fighter strength will have passed its limit by the end of the second phase, and its powers of resistance should decline very rapidly thereafter.

d. Medium Bombers: It will be noted that no U.S. medium bombardment aircraft have been specifically included in the computation of force required above. That does not mean that medium bombardment is not necessary to implement this plan. Supplementary attacks against all strategic targets within range of medium bombers are anticipated as necessary adjuncts to the heavy bomber attacks. In addition, medium bombardment is required in order to conduct repeated attacks against German fighter airdromes, to aid the passage of heavy bombers until the attacks against the German aircraft industry make themselves felt. Medium bombardment will be necessary to support combined operations in early 1944. The crews must be operationally trained in this Theater by that date.

RECAPITULATION OF U.S. BOMBER FORCES REQUIRED

	Heavy	*Medium*	
1st Phase	944	200	Bombers required by June 30, 1943
2nd Phase	1,192	400	Bombers required by September 30, 1943
3rd Phase	1,746	600	Bombers required by December 31, 1943
4th Phase	2,702	800	Bombers required by March 31, 1944

e. At all times there is a need for an extensive U.S. fighter force both to protect the bombers and to assist in the reduction of the German fighter strength. Prior to the initiation of operations on the Continent, this fighter strength must be at a maximum, and must be fully trained for operations in this Theater.

f. This plan deals entirely with the requirements for the strategic bombing force, except for its use in the 4th Phase on missions which will render most effective support to surface operations on the Continent, which may begin in early 1944. In order to supplement this force in providing the close support required for the surface operations, steps must be taken early to create and train a Tactical force in this Theater. This force must include light bomber, reconnaissance, fighter, and troop carrier elements.

Conclusions

a. If the forces required as set forth above are made available on the dates indicated, it will be possible to carry out the Mission prescribed in the Casablanca Conference. If those forces are not made available, then that mission is not attainable by mid-1944.

b. Depletion of the German fighter strength must be accomplished first. Failure to neutralize that force will jeopardize the prosecution of the war toward a favorable decision in this Theater.

c. The following list of bombing objectives should be destroyed under the provisions of the general directive issued at the Casablanca Conference:

    Intermediate Objectives:
        German fighter strength.

    Primary Objectives:
        German submarine yards and bases.
        The remainder of the German aircraft industry.
        Ball Bearings.*
        Oil.* (Contingent upon attacks against Ploesti from the
            Mediterranean.)

    Secondary Objectives in Order of Priority:
        Synthetic rubber and tires.
        Military motor transport vehicles.

d. The following statement of principle is concurred in: As expressed by the Operations Analysts:

> In view of the ability of adequate and properly utilized air power to impair the industrial source of the enemy's military strength, only the most vital considerations should be permitted to delay or divert the application of an adequate air striking force to this task.

Discussion Following the Presentation

GENERAL MARSHALL asked what strength would be required in air troops to carry out the proposed plan.

GENERAL EAKER replied that there would be 367,000 air troops required. This includes all of the ground echelons as well as civilian employees. It does not include any troops of the Army Service Forces. He said that there are now in England 44,000 air troops, approximately 39,000 ground troops, and 41,000 Army Service Troops. General Eaker was not prepared to state how many additional Army Service troops the buildup of the 367,000 Air Corps troops would entail.

GENERAL McNARNEY asked, "How far back does the maintenance extend in the proposed force of 367,000?"

---

*A successful initial attack on the key element of either of those systems would demand the immediate concentration of effort on the remaining elements of that system to exploit the initial success.

GENERAL EAKER replied that it extended to 4th echelon maintenance.

GENERAL MARSHALL recalled that in his presentation General Eaker had said that the plan was based on making 6 missions per month; he had also indicated that if the force reached a certain level, 10 missions a month could be accomplished.

GENERAL MARSHALL asked what the effect on the plan would be if the figure of 10 missions per plane per month were used as a basis.

GENERAL EAKER said that he felt confident that if the force had been built up to 500 heavy bombers, 10 missions per month per plane could be carried out. However, he said he was not prepared to assure the successful accomplishment of the plan with less than the number of planes which it called for. If 10 missions a month do become possible, more destruction will be attained.

GENERAL MARSHALL asked what type of fighter aircraft was necessary and what the range should be.

GENERAL EAKER said that they should be of the P–47 type with a 400-mile range.

GENERAL MARSHALL asked whether the limiting factors to the plan were fields or gasoline.

GENERAL EAKER said that the airdromes were not a limiting factor, there being 95 available at the present time. He added that the materiel people figured that the plan could be accomplished insofar as the availability of gasoline is concerned.

GENERAL MARSHALL asked what difference there was in the number of missions per month between the months of June and July and the months of December and January.

GENERAL EAKER said that from October to March there are at least 5 days per month that are suitable for bombing operations, whereas from March to September there are 8 days per month. He pointed out that it has often been said that weather was the handicap to bombing operations from the United Kingdom. He felt that in the future the weather would actually be an aid rather than a hindrance in view of new devices which have been developed for bomber aircraft which act as leaders. At the present time he has 2 such aircraft fitted up in England and in the near future he expects to have 8. Experiments have been conducted using aircraft as leaders which have been fitted with these special devices and in one run 6 bombers hit an airdrome 81 miles distant from their base when the weather was completely overcast and visibility nonexistent.

GENERAL MARSHALL then asked what had been the percentage of losses, eliminating the first 10 raids.

GENERAL EAKER replied that in 54 missions the loss rate had been 4.6% but that eliminating the first 10 raids it probably would have amounted to about 5%. He cited March as a particularly good month in which the loss rates had only been 2.2%. He said the Bremen raid has been the most disastrous but at the same time very remunerative. This was largely because the route to the objective had been taken over the North Sea, and German reconnaissance had located the U.S. bombers shortly after they had taken off from their airdromes. This gave an opportunity for the German defenses to be alerted, both as to their fighter aircraft and their flak.

GENERAL EAKER said he felt that the U.S. bombing methods were too much "in a groove" at the present time. All bombing missions have been at high altitude, and the Germans have come to know that this will be the case. He indicated that new methods of low altitude bombing would be adopted in order to introduce flexibility and surprise. He added that the crews, of course, all favored the high altitude bombing as it placed them above hostile anti-aircraft.

ADMIRAL KING said that he had heard statements that doubling or trebling the number of aircraft in a mission could be accomplished with an almost negligible increase in the percentage of losses.

GENERAL EAKER said that this was true. He cited the Bremen raid as an example. This raid was made in two waves of one wing each. The first wing had suffered considerable loss while the second wing was almost unmolested, although the second one followed the first by only 3 minutes. He said he thought that during the raid it would have been possible to attack other targets in entirely different directions with negligible loss, this because the Germans had been informed of the Bremen raid and had concentrated their forces against it.

ADMIRAL KING said that he could see that successive waves in a single objective could be expected to have fewer losses than the leading wave. He favored the idea of attacking other objectives at times when the German defenses were concentrated on one of our attacks.

ADMIRAL KING then asked what General Eaker had meant by causing attrition to the German fighter strength through their attacks on our bomber forces.

GENERAL EAKER replied that the Germans had suffered a 25% loss of planes used in their fighter attack against our bombing missions. The British had thought this figure to be too high and therefore on General Eaker's request had had several of their outstanding pilots accompany American flights. When they returned, each said that the Americans were not claiming enough losses.

GENERAL EAKER said that in preparing this plan, the German losses in fighter aircraft have been estimated to be 25% of the number claimed in the past.

GENERAL MARSHALL asked what the U.S. operational losses in heavy bombers had been.

GENERAL EAKER replied that 17 airplanes had been lost other than in combat, and these were due largely to inexperienced crews and partly to bad weather.

GENERAL MARSHALL then asked what was the percentage of planes lost in transit to the theater.

GENERAL EAKER replied that of the last 120 planes delivered only 3 had been lost. He thought that this established a fair percentage rate for planning in the future.

ADMIRAL KING asked if air facilities now exist or if it would be necessary to build them in order to carry out the proposed plan.

GENERAL EAKER replied that there are now 95 airdromes available and that 17 more will be needed to carry out the plan. These are now under construction.

ADMIRAL KING stated that he was interested in this in order to determine what effect the necessity for new facilities would have on the shipping problem.

GENERAL McNARNEY asked if the airdromes available included those necessary for all types of aircraft, to which GENERAL EAKER replied in the affirmative.

GENERAL McNARNEY then asked how many sorties there would be per month with the 2,700 airplanes available in the fourth phase of the plan.

GENERAL EAKER said that a practical operational yardstick based on the experience of the 8th Air Force during the past 8 months is: 10 missions per month with 1/3 of all the heavy bombers plus a maximum effort once a week of 75 to 80% of the force assigned to the tactical units.

ADMIRAL KING asked if the objective assigned under the proposed plan gave full consideration to the necessity of combating the submarine, such as the installations on the Bay of Biscay.

GENERAL EAKER said U.S. officers think they can effectively strike at submarine bases. The British are not in full agreement. He pointed to the recent attack on Lorient and said that that city is devastated. The Germans are publishing warnings to the workers who have not returned to the city that they will lose their pensions if they fail to do so.

ADMIRAL KING said he was pleased to note in General Eaker's presentation that it was proposed to bomb the same objectives intermittently in order to give the Germans an opportunity to utilize materials and labor in starting reconstruction before striking at them again.

GENERAL McNARNEY asked what replacements per month would be necessary when the goal of 2,700 heavy bombers had been reached.

GENERAL EAKER said he figured the replacement would be about 33 ⅓ % per month.

GENERAL EAKER said that the figures used by the Army Air Forces for attrition were 20% per month but that he and the officers of the Eighth Air Force felt that they were too low and should be at least 30% per month.

GENERAL ARNOLD pointed out that the immediate concern is the number of aircraft needed to be allocated in 1943 which amounts to about 1,750 by December 31st. When that figure was reached, the monthly replacement rate would be about 340 per month.

GENERAL EAKER said that while initially the loss rates would be high they would decline rapidly once the offensive against the German fighters had begun to take effect.

The Joint Chiefs of Staff:

a. Directed that the Joint Staff Planners study the plan presented in JCS 277, as amplified by General Eaker in his presentation, in order to determine if the aircraft necessary to carry out this plan could be made available and, at the same time, fulfill the present and future commitments of aircraft to all other theaters of operations.

b. Directed the Joint Staff Planners to submit the report referred to in **a.** above, to the Joint Chiefs of Staff prior to their meeting on Tuesday, May 4th.

c. Directed the Secretary to arrange to have General Eaker make a presentation of the proposed plan to the representatives of the British Chiefs of Staff on Friday morning, April 30th.

(Note by Secretary: Arrangements have been made for such a presentation at noon, Friday, April 30th.)

SELECTED BIBLIOGRAPHY

Sources included in this bibliography generally met at least one of two criteria. Either they were judged to bear directly on the central arguments developed in this study, or else they were cited often enough that a reader might have difficulty locating the full citation in the chapter notes.

Air War Plans Division, Air Staff (Harold L. George; Haywood S. Hansell, Jr.; Laurence S. Kuter; and Kenneth N. Walker)

Graphic Presentation and a Brief: A-WPD/1, Munitions Requirements of the Army Air Forces to Defeat Our Potential Enemies, Part 1, August 1941, file 145.82, Albert F. Simpson Historical Research Center (AFSHRC), Maxwell AFB, Alabama. This document consists of two oversized (14 by 17 inch) sheets. One is a colored version of the map in Figure 1 (page 20); the other is a condensation of AWPD-1. The complete munitions plan can be found in AFSHRC file 145.82-1.

Allison, Graham T.

Essence of Decision: Explaining the Cuban Missile Crisis. Boston: Little, Brown and Company, 1971. This book is the natural result of organizational and political theorists following the same intellectual path taken by Kuhn in *The Structure of Scientific Revolutions.*

Baucom, Donald R.

"Technological War: Reality and the American Myth." *Air University Review,* September–October 1981.

Beck, Ludwig

Truppenfuehrung (Troop Leading): German Field Service Regulations. Part I, trans. US Army, Report No. 14,507, 18 March 1936. General Beck chaired the committee of officers that produced this document in 1931 and 1932 (Larry H. Addington, *The Blitzkrieg Era and the German General Staff, 1865–1941* (New Brunswick, New Jersey: Rutgers University Press, 1971), p. 36).

Bendiner, Elmer

The Fall of Fortresses. New York: G.P. Putnam's Sons, 1980. Bendiner was a B-17 navigator with the 379th Bomb Group, US Eighth Air Force, from May through November 1943. As a survivor of both Schweinfurt missions, Bendiner's personal account squarely faces the question of whether these costly raids vindicated Billy Mitchell and the American idea of high altitude, precision bombardment.

Boyd, John R.

"Destruction and Creation" (unpublished paper, 3 September 1976). Boyd's abstract begins by pointing out that to "comprehend and cope with our environment, we develop mental patterns or concepts of meaning." The paper's purpose is then described as being "to sketch out how we destroy and create these patterns to permit us to both shape and be shaped by a changing environment."

Patterns of Conflict. Briefing, April 1982. Boyd's *Patterns of Conflict* has been growing and evolving since 1976. As of September 1982, the paper copy of the slides for this briefing ran 177 pages.

Organic Design for Command and Control. Briefing, 11 March 1982.

Brodie, Bernard
Strategy in the Missile Age. Princeton, New Jersey: Princeton University Press, 1959.

The Atomic Bomb and American Security. New Haven, Connecticut: Yale Institute of International Studies, Memorandum Number 18, 1 November 1945.

Frederick S. Dunn et al., Bernard Brodie ed., *The Absolute Weapon: Atomic Power and World Order.* Freeport, New York: Books for Libraries Press, 1972, reprint of 1946 Yale Institute of International Studies ed.

"The Development of Nuclear Strategy." *International Security,* Spring 1978.

Bronowski, Jacob
The Ascent of Man. Boston and Toronto: Little, Brown and Company, 1973. Chapter 11 of this book, "Knowledge or Certainty," is a poetic and powerful indictment of the view that human knowledge can aspire to absolute certainty.

Clausewitz, Carl von
On War, ed. and trans. Michael Howard and Peter Paret. Princeton, New Jersey: Princeton University Press, 1976. Paret and Howard's 1976 translation has made Clausewitz's masterpiece far more accessible to English-speaking readers than ever before. However, while their translation is accurate on a literal, sentence-by-sentence basis, the more metaphorical connotations implicit in the original German (and intuitively appreciated by native Germans) tend to be lost. For this reason, I would urge those who can to read *On War* in the original.

Vom Kriege. Bonn: Ferd. Dummlers, 1980.

Craven, Wesley F., and James L. Cate, ed.
The Army Air Forces in World War II. 7 vols. Chicago: University of Chicago, 1948–55. The detailed descriptions of the European air war in Volumes 2 and 3, which appeared in 1949 and 1951 respectively, have stood the test of time surprisingly well.

Creveld, Martin van
Fighting Power: German Military Performance, 1914–1945. Potomac, Maryland: Canby and Luttwak Associates, December 1980. This study, which was done for the Director of Net Assessment, Office of the Secretary of Defense, was published by Greenwood Press in 1982.

DeLong, Howard
A Profile of Mathematical Logic. Menlo Park, California: Addison-Wesley, 1970. If you are going to read one book on mathematical logic in your life, consider DeLong's *A Profile of Mathematical Logic.*

d'Olier, Franklin et al.
The United States Strategic Bombing Survey: Over-All Report (European War). Washington, DC: US Government Printing Office, 30 September 1945. The Strategic Bombing Survey prepared 212 reports on the European air war alone, all but three of which were published in one form or another (MacIsaac, *Strategic Bombing in World War Two: The Story of the United States*

Strategic Bombing Survey, p. 144). This particular report has been as widely cited to attack the Combined Bomber Offensive as to defend it.

Doolittle, James H. (with Beirne Lay, Jr.)
"Daylight Precision Bombing." *IMPACT: The Army Air Force's Confidential Picture History of World War II*, Book 6.

Douhet, Giulio
The Command of the Air, trans. Dino Ferrari. New York: Coward-McCann, 1941.

Dupuy, Trevor N.
A Genius for War: The German Army and General Staff, 1807–1945. Englewood Cliffs, New Jersey: Prentice-Hall, 1977.

Eaker, Ira C.
Minutes of Meeting: Presentation of Combined Bomber Offensive Plan to the JCS, National Archives Record Group 218, CSS 334, 71st–86th Meetings, 29 April 1943. I consider this document, which is reproduced in full in the Appendix, persuasive evidence of the mechanistic mindset that has dominated mainstream US air doctrine.

Einstein, Albert
"On the Electrodynamics of Moving Bodies," trans. W. Perret and G.B. Jeffrey in H. A. Lorentz et al. *The Principle of Relativity: A Collection of Original Memoirs on the Special and General Theory of Relativity*. New York: Dover, 1923. While the body of this paper makes difficult reading for those unfamiliar with mathematical physics, the opening paragraphs, in which Einstein explains the motivation for the special theory, provide a clear example of metaphysical qualities like simplicity being used to justify a scientific revolution.

"Autobiographical Notes." *Albert Einstein: Philosopher-Scientist*, ed. Paul A. Schilpp. La Salle, Illinois: Open Court, 1949.

Ethell, Jeffrey, and Alfred Price
Target Berlin, Mission 250: 6 March 1944. London: Jane's, 1981. An exhaustive reconstruction of a rather bloody mission as seen through the eyes of more than 160 American and German participants, in the air and on the ground.

Fabyanic, Thomas A.
The Development of Airpower Between the Wars. Author's transcript of the video tape of a lecture to the Air Command and Staff College, Maxwell AFB, Alabama, 3 February 1983. Based on Fabyanic's doctrinal dissertation, "A Critique of US Air War Planning, 1941–1944" (unpublished PhD dissertation, St Louis University, 1973), this lecture represents one of the very few attempts that have been made to judge Air Corps Tactical School precision bombardment doctrine on the basis of its performance in combat during World War II.

"Strategic Analysis and MX Deployment," *Strategic Review*, Fall 1982.

Flugel, Raymond R.
United States Air Force Doctrine: A Study of the Influence of William Mitchell and Giulio Douhet at the Air Corps Tactical School, 1921–1935. University of Oklahoma, Norman, Oklahoma: PhD dissertation, 1965.

Freeman, Roger A.
The Mighty Eighth: Units, Men, and Machines (A History of the US 8th Army Air Force). Garden City, New York: Doubleday, 1970.

Mighty Eighth War Diary, with Alan Crouchman and Vic Maslen. London: Jane's, 1981. A mission-by-mission compendium of the US Eighth Air Force packed with statistical details that are not found even in the official histories.

Friedberg, Aaron L.
"A History of the US Strategic 'Doctrine'—1945 to 1980." *Journal of Strategic Studies,* December 1980.

Futrell, Robert F.
Ideas, Concepts, Doctrine, A History of Basic Thinking in the United States Air Force 1907–1964. Maxwell AFB, Alabama: Air University, 1971.

The United States Air Force in Korea 1950–1953. New York: Duell, Sloan and Pearce, 1961. The official US Air Force history of the Korean War.

Galbraith, J. Kenneth et al.
The Effects of Strategic Bombing on the German War Economy. Washington, DC: US Government Printing Office, 31 October 1945.

Goedel, Kurt
"On Formally Undecidable Propositions." *From Frege to Goedel: A Source Book in Mathematical Logic, 1879–1931,* ed. Jean van Heijenoort. Cambridge, Massachusetts: Harvard University Press, 1967. DeLong considers this "the most important single paper in metatheory" and van Heijenoort's translation the best available (DeLong, p. 268).

Guilmartin, John F., Jr.
"Military Experience, the Military Historian, and the Reality of Battle." Address at the Shelby C. Davis Center for Historical Studies, Princeton University, 8 October 1982.

Hansell, Haywood S., Jr.
The Air Plan that Defeated Hitler. Atlanta, Georgia: Higgins-McArthur/Longino and Porter, 1972. Hansell's account of the thinking behind Air Corps Tactical School precision bombardment doctrine is that of the insider; his defense of Eaker's conduct of the CBO from the United Kingdom, however, is that of the advocate.

"The Plan that Defeated Hitler." *Air Force Magazine,* July 1980.

Harré, R.
"Pierre Simon de Laplace." *The Encyclopedia of Philosophy,* ed. Paul Edwards. New York: Macmillan and the Free Press, 1967, Vol. 4.

Hastings, Max
Bomber Command. New York: Dial Press/James Wade, 1979.

Holton, Gerald
Thematic Origins of Scientific Thought: Kepler to Einstein. Cambridge, Massachusetts: Harvard University Press, 1973.

Hurley, Alfred P.
Billy Mitchell: Crusader for Air Power. Bloomington and London: Indiana University Press, 1975.

The Aeronautical Ideas of General William Mitchell. Princeton University: PhD dissertation, May 1961.

Jeffrey, Richard C.
Formal Logic: Its Scope and Limits. New York: McGraw-Hill, 1967. The beauty of Jeffrey's tree method is that it readily enables even novices to the field of mathematical logic to develop a concrete appreciation of decidability in propositional and predicate logics.

Kennedy, Robert F.
Thirteen Days: A Memoir of the Cuban Missile Crisis. New York: Norton, 1969.

Kepner, William E.
Eighth Air Force Tactical Development: August 1942–May 1945. England: Eighth Air Force and Army Air Forces Evaluation Board, European Theater of Operations, July 1945. This account of Eighth's combat activities during the air war against Hitler's Germany was initiated by General Doolittle in November 1944.

The Long Reach: Deep Fighter Escort Tactics. England: Eighth Fighter Command, 29 May 1944.

Kuhn, Thomas S.
The Structure of Scientific Revolutions. Chicago: University of Chicago Press, rev. ed., 1970.

"Reflections on My Critics." *Criticism and the Growth of Knowledge,* ed. Imre Lakatos and Alan Musgrave. London: Cambridge University Press, 1970. Also of interest in this collection is Margaret Masterman's essay "The Nature of a Paradigm." Among other things, her cataloguing of 21 different senses of 'paradigm' in the original 1962 version of *The Structure of Scientific Revolutions* led Kuhn to add a postscript to the 1970 edition.

Lambeth, Benjamin S.
Selective Nuclear Options in American and Soviet Strategic Policy. Santa Monica: Rand Report R-2034-DDRE, December 1976.

"Uncertainties for the Soviet War Planner." *International Security,* Winter 1982/1983.

Leader, C. A.
"The Kriegsakadamie: Synthesizer of Clausewitzian Theory and Practice." Unpublished paper, 30 July 1982.

Lupfer, Timothy T.
The Dynamics of Doctrine: The Changes in German Tactical Doctrine During the First World War. Fort Leavenworth, Kansas: US Army Command and General Staff College, July 1981.

MacIsaac, David
The Air Force and Strategic Air Power 1945–1951. Washington, DC: Woodrow Wilson International Center, working paper number 8, 21 June 1979.

Strategic Bombing in World War Two: The Story of the United States Strategic Bombing Survey. New York and London: Garland, 1976.

"Voices from the Central Blue: Theories of Air Warfare (continued)." April 1980 draft of work in progress.

Manstein, Erich von
Lost Victories, trans. Anthony G. Powell. Chicago: Henry Regnery, 1958. Von Manstein is regarded by his peers as having been "Germany's greatest strategist during World War II" (see, for example, F. W. von Mellenthin, *Panzer Battles: A Study of the Employment of Armor in the*

Second World War, trans. H. Betzler, Norman, Oklahoma: University of Oklahoma Press, 1956, pp. 251–52).

Marshall, Samuel Lyman Attwood
Men Against Fire: The Problem of Battle Command in Future War. New York: Morrow, 1947.

Mitchell, William M.
Notes on the Multi-Motored Bombardment Group Day and Night. Mitchell papers, container number 35, Library of Congress, Washington, DC.

Skyways. Philadelphia and London: J. B. Lippincott, 1930.

Winged Defense. New York and London: G. P. Putman's Sons, 1925.

Momyer, William W.
Airpower in Three Wars (WW II, Korea, Vietnam). A. J. C. Lavalle and James C. Gaston eds. Washington, DC: US Government Printing Office, 1978.

Montross, Lynn
War Through the Ages. New York: Harper and Brothers, 3d ed. 1960.

Murray, Williamson
Strategy for Defeat: The Luftwaffe, 1933–1945. Maxwell AFB, Alabama: Air University Press: 1983.

Newton, Isaac
Mathematical Principles of Natural Philosophy, trans. Andrew Motte in *The Great Books of the Western World*, ed. Robert M. Hutchins. Chicago: Encyclopedia Britannica, 1952. No scientific theory was ever as well established as Newton's, and it is unlikely that there will ever be one so well established again (see Karl R. Popper, *Objective Knowledge: An Evolutionary Approach* (Oxford: Oxford University Press, 1972), p. 9).

Norris, Joe L.
The Combined Bomber Offensive: 1 January to 6 June 1944 (Short Title: AAFRH–22). Washington, DC: Headquarters Army Air Forces, April 1947. Captain Norris prepared this "AAF Reference History" during the winter and spring of 1946 (p. iii). General H. H. Arnold's frontispiece memorandum states that because such reference histories incorporated "Top Secret" materials and contained "controversial issues which might prejudice at some future time either national or international relations," they were to be classified as "SECRET and REGISTERED" documents, and restricted to military personnel (p. i). This particular reference history was not declassified until January 1961.

Shannon, Claude E. and Warren Weaver
The Mathematical Theory of Communication. Urbana, Illinois: University of Illinois Press, 1980. Originally published in 1949, this volume contains the paper in which Shannon first linked uncertainty in the information with entropy.

Shapere, Dudley
"Isaac Newton." *The Encyclopedia of Philosophy,* ed. Paul Edwards. New York: MacMillan and the Free Press, 1967, Vol. 5.

Smith, Perry McCoy
The Air Force Plans for Peace: 1943–1945. Baltimore and London: Johns Hopkins, 1970.

"Douhet and Mitchell: Some Reappraisals." *Air University Review*, September–October 1967.

Sprey, Pierre
Translation of Taped Conversation with General Hermann Balck, 12 January 1979, and Brief Biographical Sketch. Columbus, Ohio: Battelle, 1979.

Summers, Harry G., Jr.
On Strategy: The Vietnam War in Context. Carlisle Barracks, Pennsylvania: US Army War College, 1981.

Vigor, Peter H.
Soviet Blitzkrieg Theory. New York: St Martin's Press, 1983.

Withrow, G. J.
"Entropy." *The Encyclopedia of Philosophy*, ed. Paul Edwards. New York: MacMillan and the Free Press, 1967, Vol. 2.

Wohlstetter, Albert
"The Delicate Balance of Terror." *Foreign Affairs*, January 1959.

INDEX

The Absolute Weapon: 88, 89.

Adaptation (relative to the enemy): 1, Douhet's rejection of 5, 47, by the German army during World War I 57 n20, by *Luftwaffe Jagdgeschwaders* 71 and 97 n31, by the *Reich* war industry to Allied bombing 75, of the Chinese Communists to interdiction 87, 121.

Aerial strategy: as choosing targets 6, in AWPD-1 22, in Brodie 33, 44, in the CBO plan 135–6.

Air Corps Tactical School (ACTS): xv, history of 14 n17, doctrine of 18, achievement of 21, mindset of 23, 24 n2, Douhet's influence on 24 n3, 24 n4, 28, 36, views on army and naval forces 40 n11, basic beliefs of 43–4, 53, 59–60, 81, 85, 106.

Aircrew attrition in World War II: 15 n32, Eighth Air Force's in October 1943 63, US on second Schweinfurt raid 67, effects on *Luftwaffe* 80, US due to strafing 81, German fighter units (in early 1944) 99 n50, and strafing 100 n58, 100 n59, Eighth Air Force's (late February to 30 April 1944) 101 n70.

Aircrew training: *see* training.

Airfield attack: *see* bombardment of *Luftwaffe* airfields in the CBO.

The Air Plan That Defeated Hitler: 53, defense of the CBO plan in 56 n13, 59, 60, 61, 81, 154.

Air power: traditional American theories of 1 and 18, and the long-range bomber 27, in World War II 34, potential decisiveness of 40 n11, fundamental American tenets of 44, conditions for decisive application of 46, attitudes of American airmen towards 60 and 95 n7.

Air Service Tactical School: 14 n17, 25 n3.

Air supremacy: Douhet's denigration of 6, in Mitchell 10–11, Trenchard's views on 14 n23, in the fall of 1943 15 n30, in AWPD-1 44, Mitchell's views on 44–5.

Air War Plans Division: 17.

Allison, Graham: xv, 104 n108, on the escalatory potential of the Cuban missile crisis 104 n110.

Army Air Corps: 5, 17, bomber enthusiasts 45, 50, messianic view of air power in 60, 146.

Army Air Forces: 47, 51, 61, 63, 76, 95 n12, 120, 127 n49, 149.

Arnold, Henry H.: 18, 23, role in creation of Rand 39 n6, 56 n18, on the 14 October 1943 Schweinfurt mission 66, 27 December 1943 letter 96 n 14, 133, 149.

Aron, Raymond: 88, 102–3 n91.

Assumptions: role in channeling thinking xv, xvi, Walker's about bomber vulnerability 17, about probability in AWPD-1 26 n20 and 74, 27, Brodie's 29, of US air doctrine 43–4, of AWPD-1 and the CBO 53–4, 58 n34, 58 n35, 58 n37, of the CBO about Germany's "industrial fabric" 75, of Operation Strangle 87, in the "The Delicate Balance of Terror" 103 n98, of US air power theorists about friction 105, of US airmen regarding determinism 106–8, of Newton about space and time 124 n19; *also see* paradigm.

Atmosphere of war: xv, 2, 48, 53, 57 n26, 60, 93, 116; *also see* friction.

AWPD-1: 17, formulation of 18–19 and 22, graphic depiction of 20, image of war in 22–3, 26 n25, and air superiority 44, 46, failure of to consider collective risk 53–4, 60, 85, 86, mindset of 87, and electric power 101 n67, and pursuit fighters 101 n69, 108, 151.

AWPD-42: 25 n6, 56 n13, 101 n67.

Balck, Hermann: limits of technical solutions 1, military record of 3 n2, and friction 129–30 n68.

Baucom, Donald R.: 105, "where will our soldiers come from . . ." 128 n51.

Big Week (February 1944): 71, 72, effects on German fighter production 75 and 98 n40, USSTAF sorties and targets during 98 n35, US bomber losses during 98 n40.

Blumentritt, Guenther: on character 129 n67, on the *Kriegsakademie*'s use of Clausewitz 130 n70.

Boelcke, Oswald: 126 n33.

Bombardment doctrine: *see* industrial bombardment.

Bomber invincibility: Walker's formulation of 17 and 25 n2, 54, 58 n37, in the CBO 71, 76, 96 n15, 97 n29, 110, 120.

Bomber kill claims: *see* kill claim inflation.

159

Bomber losses: 6 March 1944 mission to Berlin 52, Eighth Air Force's in October 1943 63, on the second Schweinfurt raid 67, during Big Week 98 n40, Big Week through 30 April 1944 101 n70.

Bombing accuracy: in Douhet 6, 14 n22, in AWPD-1 26 n20, against Hitler's Germany 58 n35, in the CBO 107.

Bombardment of *Luftwaffe* airfields in the CBO: 62, 96 n15,101 n66, 143, 145.

Bombing effects: Mitchell's tests against ships 9, 13 n11, 14 n22, estimated against New York City 25 n9, Brodie on Douhet's overestimate of 27, time compression of caused by atomic bomb 29 and 41 n22, at Hiroshima 32 and 40 n14, against cities in World War II 39 n4, atomic weapons against cities 40 n12, "Mike" thermonuclear test at Elugelab 41 n15, "how could we predict . . ." 60, problems of assessing 72 and 75, 95 n12, during Operation Strangle (1951–52) 102 n83, assumed in the CBO plan 107 and 141.

Boyd, John R.: 58 n32, Observation-Orientation-Decision-Action cycles 115–16 and 127 n45, "Destruction and Creation" 123 n4, and air combat theory 127 n44, 151.

Brodie, Bernard: xvi, 5, on Douhet and a perfect defense 27, assumptions of 29, image of war in missile age 33–5, on the rub in deterrence 36, on the development of *Strategy in the Missile Age* 39–40 n7, bombardment as the dominant form of war 40 n10, 41 n21, on what makes deterrence credible 42 n47, on winning an all-out nuclear war 41 n49, on the utility of arms control 41 n55, basic beliefs of 44–5, 53, 54, 59, 60, on the Cuban missile crisis 88, 89, on the delicate balance of terror 90, on first strikes with impunity 91, 92, 93, on sheltering US bombers 103 n97, 103 n99 and n100, 105.

Bronowski, Jacob: xv, on the limits of scientific knowledge 109, on the method of art as the method of science 125 n23.

Canonical exchange calculations: 47, as a basis for the MX missile 56 n19, 108, 110, 124 n17.

Cartesian hypotheses: in Newton 109, examples of 124 n19.

Casablanca directive: 107, 146.

Chance: as a component of friction 2, role in war 43, 48 and 57 n25, 59, 95 n11, 106, 108, 116.

Character: 117, 119, identification of 129 n60, Blumentritt on 129 n67.

Chinese Communist Forces (CCF): 85.

Church, Alonzo: 109, theorem of stated 125 n24.

Claims: *see* kill claim inflation *and* fighter kill claims.

Clausewitz, Carl von: xvi, 1, 2, 3 n3, reactive enemy 5, simplest thing in war is difficult 17, on the unexpected in war 43, on war's dominant tendencies 48, atmosphere of war 53 and 54, on the idiocy of rules 55 n2, combat experience of 57 n21, 59, Liddell Hart's criticism of 58 n31, argument for subordinating war to politics 58 n33, pure concept of war versus actual practice 60–61, on the harmful effects of pat formulas 95 n10, on weather as a source of friction 95 n11, 108, factors affecting strategy 112 and 126 n34, on military genius 117, 118, on theory versus practice 119, 121, 130 n70, on overcoming friction 130 n72, 152.

Clausius, Rudolf: 121, 130 n77.

COHORT system: 129 n61.

Collective risk: characterized 54, 60, in the CBO 62, in Operation Strangle 87, 121; *also see* friction.

Combat experience: unimaginability of 57 n21, 60, erosion of in the *Luftwaffe*'s defeat 76 and 80, 108, Eighth Air Force's in early 1943 141–2.

Combined Bomber Offensive (CBO): 11, planning of 25 n6, Craven and Cate's description of 34, assumptions of 53–4, Hansell's assessment of 56 n13, friction in 59, 60, and the *Luftwaffe* 62, 72, 75, 76, 81, diversions from Eaker's plan 85, 87, planning for 95–6 n13 and n15, and Normandy invasion 96 n14, 97 n29, bomb tonnages during 101 n68, essential train of logic in 107–8, 110, 113, decisiveness of 116–17, frictions during 120, and mathematical certainty 124 n15, the Strategic Bombing Survey's assessment of 127 n49, and the Eastern Front 127–8 n50; *see* Combined Bomber Offensive plan.

Combined Bomber Offensive plan: mission and objectives 135–6, target systems 136–8, intermediate objective (German Air Force) 138–9, 1000 foot radius "circles of destruction" 141, Schweinfurt 143, medium bombers 145, forces required 145.

Command of the Air (Il Domino dell'Aria): as an exemplar of US air doctrine 5, 6, 9, 13 n2, 53.

Coup d'oeil: Clausewitz on 117, 118, and *Fingerspitzengefuehl* 128 n52; *also see* implicit knowledge.

Craven, Wesley F., and Cate, James L.: on the CBO 34, 63.

Creveld, Martin van: on FM 100-5 versus the *Truppenfuehrung* 115.
Cromwell, Oliver: xv, influence on US military xvii n2.
Cuban missile crisis: Brodie on 88, 92–3, 104 n 108, risk of nuclear war during 104 n109 and n110.

Danger in war: 2, 48, 57 n21, in *On War* 57 n22, 120, 130 n72.
Defense: impossibility of against bomber attack 7, Brodie on 27, near impossibility of in atomic era 29, meaningful 33, potentially perfect 36, in US air doctrine 44, against bombers 44–5.
"The Delicate Balance of Terror": 88–90.
DeLong, Howard: 109, on Geodel's first incompleteness theorem 125 n25.
Determination: and military genius 117, 128 n52.
Determinism: 106–8, failure of 109–10, 113.
Deterrence: xv, post-Hiroshima theories of 2, 5, 27, Brodie's framework for 34–35, paradox of 36–37, views at Rand on 39–40 n7, and the military man 42 n46, 44, Mitchell's influence on 55 n7, as a matter of collective risks 89.
"The Development of Nuclear Strategy": 60, thrust of 88, 89, 91, 92, 93.
Doolittle, James H.: most important decision of World War II 80 and 99 n53, 82, 85, 119.
Douhet, Guilio: on "An Independent Air Force" 5, image of war 6–7, 9, 11, on pursuit aviation 13 n6, 19, 25 n3, gravest error 27, 28, 33, 35, 36, 37, views on the ascendancy of strategic bombing 40 n10, basic beliefs of 44–5, 53, 59.
Drop tanks (for escort fighters): 76, 77, 98 n43, 99 n47.
Dupuy, Trevor N.: 40 n14, on the Eastern front 127–8 n50, 128 n53, on the fighting power of the World War II *Wehrmacht* 128 n54.

Eaker, Ira C.: 25 n6, CBO plan of 62, and bomber invincibility 71, 76, 81, 96 n15, 97 n29, 98 n33, 107, 108, 124 n14 and n15, 133, 134, 146–9.
Eastern Front in World War II: 127–8 n50.
Eighth Air Force: 34, launch rate in World War II 58 n34, effects of European weather on 61, October 1943 attempt to penetrate unescorted 62–3, 68, tactical defeat of 71 and 85, 76, 82, 96 n15, aircraft and crew strength data 100 n61, 100 n64, bomb tonnages 105 n65, 106, 107, 108, 120, 135, 140, effectiveness of in early 1943 141–2.
Eighth Army: in Korea 85.
Eighth Fighter Command: offensive employment of 80–81, 85.
Electric power (as a target): 19, 81, Hansell's views on 101 n67.
Engineering-science view of war: characterized 2, in Douhet 6–7, in Mitchell 9, 13 n11, in AWPD-1 22–3, in Brodie 35, 43, 44, 47, 61, 106, in the CBO plan 107–8, 113, 114, 119, 121, 123 n7, of McNamara 126 n39; *also see* mechanistic image of war.
Einstein, Albert: rejection of absolute space and time 109, on scientific theories and experience 124 n21.
Entropy: 120, 121, and the second law of thermodynamics 130–31 n77, as information 131 n78, 156.
Escort fighter: 62, US development of during the CBO 76, 84, Eaker's views regarding (April 1943) 96 n15, 100–01 n66, in AWPD-1 101 n69.
Exertion in war: 2, 48, in *On War* 57 n23, 120, 130 n72.
Ethell, Jeffrey: 52, 84, 98–9 n46, 100 n59.
Experience of war: *see* combat experience.

Fabyanic, Thomas A.: xiii, on Hansell 25 n4, 26 n20, 53, notion of collective risk 54, 59, on the essence of war 60, on MX basing 106, 153.
Fairchild, Muir S.: 18, "Air Power and the City" 25 n9.
The Fall of Fortresses: 68, 97 n31, 151.
Far East Air Forces: 87.
Ferguson, Alfred B.: on German aircrew training as the "bottleneck within the bottleneck" 76 and 80.
Fifth Air Force: 86, 87.
Fighter kill claims: air-to-ground credits in Eighth Air Force 81 and 99 n55, 96–7 n21, use of gun-camera film to verify 97 n23.
Fighter versus fighter combat: Douhet's rejection of 6, Michell's views on 7, 100 n59, 112, 115, 125–6 n32, 126 n33.

Fingerspitzengefuehl: 128 n52.
Flak: 52, 70, around German airfields 81 and 99 n55.
FM 100-5: 115, 1941 version compared with *Truppenfuehrung* 126–7 n43.
Form of war: impact of bomber on 6, 27, impact of nuclear weapons on 28, as a series of marvelously swift sorties or shots 33, in Brodie and Douhet 40 n10, unprecedented concentration of atomic bomb damage in time 41 n21, impact of technology on 44.
Formulas: Rupprecht and S. L. A. Marshall on 43, in AWPD-1 46, 47, 53, Clausewitz on the idiocy of 55 n2, 61, Clausewitz on 95 n10, 112, and military genius 117.
Friction *(Friktion):* xv, xvi, as the difference between real war and war on paper 1, components of 2, treatment in *On War* 3 n3, 27, in Clausewitz 47–8 and 53, components of 48, in the CBO 49–52, as danger 57 n22, as exertion 57 n23, as uncertainty 57 n24, as chance and unpredictability 57 n25, general concept of 57 n27, between war and politics 57–8 n29, Clausewitz's metaphorical use of 58 n40, in the CBO 59–60, and weather 61, in October 1943 71, during Big Week 75, as a weapon 76 and 80–81, in the CBO 85, in Strangle 87, emergence in Brodie's thought 91–2, in the Cuban missile crisis 92–3, neglect of by American air power theorists 105, and the human costs of war 110–11, in the *Truppenfuehrung* 115, as the atmosphere of war 116, and entropy 119–21, as an impediment and as a weapon 121, and quantum physics 124 n22, and strategy 126 n34, ways of overcoming 129–30 n68 and 130 n72.
Fry, Gary L.: 52, 84, 100 N59.
FW-190: 76, 84, versus P-51B/C 98–9 n46.

Galland, Adolph: on the *Luftwaffe*'s decline 80.
George, Harold L.: 17, role in AWPD-1 18, 19, 22, 23, at the ACTS 25 n4, 26 n25, 46.
Genius (in war): nuturing 117–19, and the *Kriegsakademie* 128 n53.
German Air Force: *see Luftwaffe.*
German General Staff Academy: *see Kriegsakademie.*
German war production: 72 and 75, 98 n39, of fighters 98 n40 n42; *also see* industrial web concept *and* industrial bombardment.
Goodbye, Mickey Mouse: 99 n55.
Goedel, Kurt: 109, 121, 123 n4, first incompleteness theorem 125 n25.
Guderian, Heinz: 3 n2.
Guilmartin, John F.: 57 n21, on war 105, on the drivers of combat outcomes that change least over time 112.

Hamburg: 1943 bombing of 39 n4.
Hansell, Haywood S., Jr.: xiii, xvi, 17, 18, 19, 21, 22, guiding conceptual thinker at ACTS 25 n4, 27, 35, basic beliefs of 44–5, 46, 53, assessment of the CBO 56 n13, 59, 60, 61, views on attacking electric power 101 n67, 107, 108, assessment of the CBO's decisiveness 127–8 n50, 154.
Harris, Arthur: 107.
Heisenberg, Werner: uncertainty principle of 109 and 124–5 n22, 121, and Boyd 123 n4, Bronowski's metaphor for indeterminacy principle of 125 n23.
Hiroshima: and Nagasaki 28, pre-strike photo of 30, atomic burst at 31, bomb damage at 32, 33, and Nagasaki 36, casualties at 40 n14, 43, and Nagasaki 85.
History: use of xvi, importance in critical judgment and awareness of friction 59, learning from 116–17.
Holton, Gerald: on Newton's Cartesian hypotheses 109.

Immelmann, Max: 126 n33.
IMPACT magazine: 51.
Implicit knowledge: 119, and *coup d'oeil* 128 n52, and critical combat situations 129–30 n68, at the *Kriegsakademie* 130 n69.
Incompleteness theorems: Goedel's first 109 and 125 n25, and Boyd 123 n4.
Industrial (or strategic) bombardment: xv, 2, in Douhet 6–7, in Mitchell 9, ACTS theory of 18, of the enemy's means and will to resist 40 n11, basic doctrine of 44, of North Korea 46, of Nazi Germany 56 n13, of German war production 72 and 75, assessment of as a theory of war 85, 96 n15, and Laplacian determinism 106–8.

Industrial web concept: 18, in AWPD-1 19, and vital targets 54, tautness of in CBO planning 75, 85.
Information: uncertainty in 2, open to doubt in war 43, as a component of general friction 48 and 57 n24, 62–3, imperfections in during the CBO 75 and 97 n24, in war 106, carried by particles like the electron 109, and entropy 120, in Heisenberg's uncertainty principle 124–5 n22 and 125 n 23, in Shannon 102 n74.
Intelligence: 47, 57 n24, 130 n72; *also see* information *and* ULTRA.
Interdiction: of railways in North Korea 85–7, 102 n75, 102 n83.
Israeli Air Force: 118, aircrew screening in 129 n59.

Jeffrey, Richard C.: "tree method" of 125 n24.

Kahn, Herman: 27, 39 n7, on the "fog of war" 87 and 102 n86, 102–3 n91.
Kampfkraft (fighting power): 115, 118, of the World War II *Wehrmacht* 128 n54 and n55.
Keegan, John: 27.
Kennedy, John F.: 88, during the Cuban missile crisis 92–3.
Kepner, William E.: 80, 82, 83, 85, and Doolittle's decision to employ Eighth Fighter Command offensively 99 n53.
Kill claim inflation: by Eighth Air Force bomber crews 62–3, frictional effect of 71, USSTAF statistics on 96–7 n21, bomber claims from the second Schweinfurt mission 97 n24, allowance for in the CBO 144.
Knowledge: *see* implicit knowledge, scientific knowledge, *and* paradigm.
Korb, Lawrence J.: on case for the MX 56 n19.
Korean war: strategic bombing during 46, railway interdiction 1951–52 85–7; *also see* Operation Strangle.
Kriegsakademie: 117, treatment of *On War* at 119, history of 128 n53, role of in synthesizing Clausewitzian theory and practice 130 n69, 130 n70, influence of Clausewitz on 130 n72.
Kuhn, Thomas S.: on paradigm debates 111, two senses of paradigm 123 n7.
Kuter, Laurence S.: 17, 18, 22, at ACTS 25 n4, 46.

Lambeth, Benjamin S.: 88, 91, on a limited nuclear option 92, on Soviet planning uncertainties 124 n17.
Lanchester, Frederick W: 7, linear and square laws 13–14 n14.
Laplace, Simon Pierre: 107.
Laws of war: *see* principles of war.
Leader, C. A.: 119, 129 n68, on the role of the *Kriegsakademie* 130 n69.
LINEBACKER: 55–6 n12.
Liddell Hart, B. H.: failure to appreciate friction 58 n31.
"Little Boy" atomic bomb: 30.
Logistics: 112.
Luftwaffe (German Air Force): World War II pilot attrition 15 n32, as intermediate objective in AWPD-1 19, 44, 52, objective second to none 62, attrition during the fall of 1943 63 and 71, 72, 76, 77, loss of air superiority 80–1, 84, 85, in Eaker's CBO plan 95–6 n13, fighter crew losses (early 1944) 99 n50, relative contributions of US fighters and bombers to the defeat of 100–1 n66, in the CBO plan 108, standards of officership in 118, psychological bonds within during World War II 129 n63, 137.

MacIsaac, David: on *Strategy in the Missile Age* 39 n5, on assessing bombing effectiveness 72.
Manstein, Erich von: 3 n2, 1940 plan for invasion of France 26 n22, on uncertainty in war 43, 119, 129 n68, 155.
Marshall, Andrew W.: recollections on the writing of *Strategy in the Missile Age* 39–40 n7.
Marshall, George C.: 19, 133, 146–8.
Marshall, S. L. A.: on formulas in war 43, on the final problem of the battlefield 105, on the elementary psychology of World War II infantry soldiers 111, on the nature of victory 113, on firing by US infantrymen during World War II 125–6 n32, 126 n42.
Mathematical Principles of Natural Philosophy: 106, assumptions about space and time in 124 n19.
The Mathematical Theory of Communication: 130 n73 and n74, 156.
McNamara, Robert S.: and ROLLING THUNDER 55 n12, counterforce second-strike 103 n104, mindset of 126 n39.

Me-109: 76, versus P-51B/C 98-9 n46.
Mechanistic image of war: in Douhet 6–7, in AWDP-1 22–3, in Brodie 33–5, in AWPD-1 46, of American airmen 107–8, S. L. A. Marshall on 113, 115, and McNamara 126 n39; *also see* engineering-science view of war *and* organic image of war.
Mitchell, William M: image of war 7 and 9–10, 8, influence on ACTS 25 n3, 27, 28, 33, 36, basic beliefs of 44–5, 46, 47, 53, 59, 105, 106, 110.
Momyer, William W.: on decisive application of air power 46 and 56 n12.
Murray, Williamson: on World War I trench warfare 15 n33, on Eighth Air Force and *Luftwaffe* attrition in the fall of 1943 71, 97 n29, 99 n50, on German standards for officership in World War II 118, 156.

Nature of war: in Douhet 6, in Mitchell 10, according to the ACTS 18, in the missile age 33–4, in strategic analysis since 1945 47, in Clausewitz 48, *the* overriding dimension of 59, pure concept versus actual practice of 60–1, views on (S. L. A. Marshall, Baucom, and Guilmartin) 105, 110, and the psychology of combat 111–12, as a clash of independent wills dominated by friction 115, implications of 120–1.
Newton, Isaac: worldview of 106–7, 120, 123 n7, discovery of universal theory of gravitation 123–4 n8, assumptions of about space and time 124 n19, 156.
Nitze, Paul: 88, 91.
Nixon, Richard M.: and LINEBACKER 55–6 n12.
Normandy invasion: 46, 56 n13, 81, 96 n14, USSTAF bombing in support of 101 n68, 102 n71, 108.
Notes on the Multi-Motored Bombardment Group Day and Night: 14 n17, 45.

Observation-Orientation-Decision-Action cycles: 116, 127 n45.
O'Donnell, Emmett: hopes for strategic bombing of North Korea 46, 55 n11.
On Strategy: The Vietnam War in Context: 113.
On War (Vom Krieg): problem of friction in 3 n3, 48, *Schwerpunkt* of 53, the essential task of 106, treatment of at *Kriegsakademie* 119 and 130 n70, difficulties of translating 152; *also see* von Clausewitz.
Operation Strangle: 86–7, history of 102 n75, effects of 102 n83.
Organic image of war: in Balck and Clausewitz 1, in Clausewitz 4, arguments for 110 and 116, in the German *Truppenfuehrung* 114–15, characterized 116, 119, 121.
Ostriesland: sinking of 9, 46.

P-38: 76, 100 n66.
P-47: 76, 81, versus Me-109 or FW-190 at low altitude 99 n52, Kepner on role in defeating the *Luftwaffe* 100 n66, 147.
P-51: emergence as a true "deep escort" fighter 76 and 81, combat radius and "teething problems" of 77, "high cover" escort formation 78, versus Me-109G and FW-190A 98–9 n46, 99 n48, 100 n66.
Paradigm: of US airmen 43–4 and 45–7, of Newton's successors 106–7, of the CBO plan 107–8, basis for change in 110–11, deterministic versus organic 114–15, of war as a clash of independent wills dominated by friction 115 and 118, Clausewitzian 121, Kuhn's characterization of 125 n29, problems defining 155.
Planck, Max: on the triumph of new scientific truths 125 n29.
POINTBLANK: 72, 107: *see* combined bomber offensive.
Political ends: 35, and nuclear weapons 42 n47, meaningful 47, subordination of military instrument to 48, as a source of friction 57–8 n29, 58 n33, 59, 93, stability over time 112, of US in Vietnam 126 n38.
Precision bombardment: xv, 18, assumptions of 53–4; *see* industrial bombardment.
Predicate logic: 109, 125 n24.
Principles of war: traditional and Brodie's rejection of 34, Brodie's formulation of mass (or concentration) 41 n34.
Psychological screening: in the *Wehrmacht* 118 and 128 n57, in the Israeli Air Force 118 and 129 n59, difficulties of 129 n60.
Psychology of combat: 52, 81, 92–3, 99 n55, as context 111–16, 121, and *Finterspitzengefuehl* 128 n52, and *Luftwaffe* unit cohesion 129 n63.

Quantum physics: 109, Heisenberg's uncertainty principle 124–5 n22.

Rand: 28, origins of 39 n6, contributors to *Strategy in the Missile Age* 39–40 n7, 89.
Retaliation: Brodie on 27, 34, 36–7, 44.
Riefert, J. B.: 118.
ROLLING THUNDER: 55 n12.
Roosevelt, Franklin D.: role in AWPD-1 18, 26 n10.
Rupprecht, Crown Prince: 43.

Schema: 121, characterized 131 n79.
Schlesinger, James R.: 88, 91, 103 n104, rationale for developing limited nuclear options 103 n105.
Schewinfurt mission (14 October 1943): 63, penetration and withdrawal 64, first wave 65, third wave 66, heading home 67, post-strike 68, 71, bomber kill claims from 97 n24, bombers dispatched on 97 n30, German defensive tactics during 97 n31, 106, in the CBO plan 143.
Schwerpunkt: discussed 26 n22, of *On War* 53 and 58 n30.
Schratz, Paul: on Clausewitz 59.
Scientific knowledge: Bronowski on the nature of xv, as paradigm in AWPD-1 22, as a paradigm in American air doctrine 107–8, limits of 108–9, methods of attaining 125 n23, and Newton's physics 156.
Second law of thermodynamics: stated 120, 123 n4, 130–1 n77.
Selective nuclear options: 88, 92–2, Schlesinger's rationale for 103 n105, risks of 104 n107.
Selected Nuclear Options in American Strategic Policy: 92.
Shannon, Claude: 120, concept of information of 130 n74, 156.
Simonet, Max: 118.
SIOP (Single Integrated Operational Plan): 26 n25, 91, 92.
Skyways: 45, 55 n10.
Spaatz, Carl T.: 85, 98 n33.
Speer, Albert: 75, 98 n42.
Strangle: *see* Operation Strangle.
Stimson, Henry L.: 19.
Strafing: 80–1, 84, 85, 100 n58 and n59, utility after the Normandy invasion 102 n71.
Strategic Air Command: 45.
Strategic bombardment: pre-World War II theory of 18, absolute dominance of in nuclear era 35, as the dominant form of war 40 n10, fundamental tenets of 44, in Korea 46 and 55 n11, decisiveness of 55 n5 and 127 n49; *also see* industrial bombardment.
Strategic Bombing Survey: *see* US Strategic Bombing Survey.
Strategy: paradox of in missile age 36–7, Schratz on American 59, USSTAF's against the *Luftwaffe* prior to Normandy 80, as choice 93, elements of in Clausewitz 112 and 126 n34, US in Vietnam 113, framework for 116; *also see* targets (choice of as strategy).
Strategy in the Missile Age: 28, 29, 33, 34, 35, MacIsaac's assessment of 39 n5, development of 39–40 n7, 45, 53, 89, 90, 91, 105.
Summers, Harry G., Jr.: on US strategy in Vietnam 113, 126 n38.

Targets (choice of as strategy): in Douhet 6, in Mitchell 11, in AWPD-1 19, 23, in the SIOP 26 n25, 44, in the Korean War 86–7, in the CBO plan 107.
Technology: impact on war 6, in Mitchell 9–10, 27, impact after Hiroshima 28, 29, role in rescuing pre-Hiroshima bombardment doctrine 35, in US air doctrine 44, and force structure 47, Arnold's views on 56 n18, of P-51B/C's range 76 and 77, 89, and friction 93, Guilmartin on 112.
Terrain: 112.
Theory versus practice: 1, 2, 3 n3, 6, 34, 35, 43, and political aims 58 n33, 59, in Clausewitz 60–1, in the fall of 1943 71, in assessing bomb damage 72, in Brodie 91, 111, and combat psychology 112, and victory 113, synthesis of at the *Kriegsakademie* 119 and 130 n69, Einstein on 124 n21.
Thermodynamics: 120, laws of 130–1 n 77.
Training: role of in the *Luftwaffe*'s decline 76 and 80, in the Israeli Army 129 n66, 130 n72.
Trenchard, Hugh: 14 n23.

Truppenfuehrung: introduction from 114–15, 117, psychological premise of 126 n42, compared with FM 100–5 126–7 n43, 129 n66, and Balck 129–30 n68.
Twelve O'Clock High!: 95 n7.

Ultimate pursuit of the enemy: 80, in the air and on the ground 84.
ULTRA: 75, 98 n41.
Uncertainty: as an aspect of friction xv, in information 2, of the numbers of dead and missing at Hiroshima 40 n14, one unvarying factor in war 43, as a component of friction 48, a fog of 57 n24, Fabyanic on 59, of bombing effects 72, during the Cuban missile crisis 93, 108, in quantum physics 109, of war 116, 120, 121, in Soviet war planning 124 n17, Heisenberg's principle of 124–5 n22 and 125 n23, and entropy 156.
Undecidability: 109, 121, 123 n4, of first-order predicate logic 125 n24, of arithmetic 125 n25.
Unexpected (in war): 43, resulting from enemy's unpredictability 48 and 57 n25, in CBO 50–51, 71, 75, 106, and military genius 117, 120.
USSTAF (US Strategic Forces in Europe): 72, 81, 83, 97–8 n33, and Ultra 98 n41.
US Strategic Bombing Survey: on German economic output 75, 100 n65, on the decisiveness of the CBO 127 n49.

Victory: xv, in Douhet 6, uselessness of in the atomic age 35, Brodie's views on winning a nuclear war 42 n49, through air power alone 60, role of economic potential in 100 n63, basis of in war 113, 114, 117, 121, Vigor on 125 n28.
Vietnam war: 5, 46, ROLLING THUNDER and LINEBACKER 55–6 n12, US strategy during 113, 114.
Vigor, Peter: 100 n63, 125 n28.
Vital targets: 54, in 1951–52 railway interdiction campaign 86–7, in the CBO plan 107; *see* industrial web.

Walker, Kenneth N.: bombing effects calculations 13 n11, bomber will always get through 17, 18, 22, 25 n2, at ACTS 25 n4, 46.
War (nature of): *see* nature of war; *also* engineering-science view of war, mechanistic image of war *and* organic image of war.
Weather: 49, influence on the CBO 61, Clausewitz on 95 n11, as an aid rather than a hindrance 147.
Will of the enemy: to resist 40 n11, in mainstream US air doctrine 44.
Wilson, Donald: industrial web concept 18, 22, 25 n8, 35.
Wehrmacht (German Army): 115, World War II performance of 117–18, techniques for selecting officers 118, 119, superior fighting power of 128 n54, psychological screening techniques of 128 n57.
Weltanschauung (worldview): of Newton 106, of US airmen 111, 116.
Winged Defense: 9, 10, 11, at Mitchell's court-martial 14 n15, 45, 105.
Wohlstetter, Albert J.: 39–40 n7, 88, 89, 90, on a surprise Soviet nuclear attack 103 n98.
World War I: trench warfare 11, 15 n33, 27, trench warfare versus World War II city bombing 39 n4, and Clausewitz 58 n31, 110.

Zeiberg, Seymour L.: 124 n17.
Zemke, Hubert: 81.